Interviewing and Counseling
in Communicative Disorders

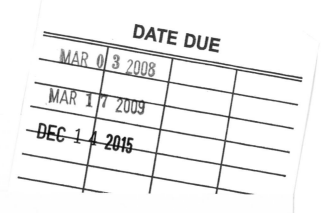

DATE DUE

MAR 0 3 2008			
MAR 1 7 2009			
DEC 1 4 2015			

Interviewing and Counseling in Communicative Disorders

PRINCIPLES AND PROCEDURES

Third Edition

Kenneth G. Shipley

Celeste Roseberry-McKibbin

pro·ed
An International Publisher

8700 Shoal Creek Boulevard
Austin, Texas 78757-6897
800/897-3202   Fax 800/397-7633
www.proedinc.com

An International Publisher

© 2006, 1997, 1992 by PRO-ED, Inc.
8700 Shoal Creek Boulevard
Austin, Texas 78757-6897
800/897-3202   Fax 800/397-7633
www.proedinc.com

Library of Congress Cataloging-in-Publication Data

Shipley, Kenneth G.
  Interviewing and counseling in communicative disorders : principles
and procedures / Kenneth G. Shipley, Celeste Roseberry-McKibbin.—
3rd ed.
      p. cm.
  Includes bibliographical references and index.
  ISBN 1-4164-0120-2 (pbk. : alk. paper)
  1. Communicative disorders—Patients—Counseling of 2. Interviewing in psychiatry. I. Roseberry-McKibbin, Celeste. II. Title.
RC428.8.S55 2005
616.85'506—dc22

                                                        2005004924

Art Director: Jason Crosier
Designer: Nancy McKinney-Point
This book is designed in Fairfield LH, Gill Sans, Triplex, and Jacoby ICG.

Printed in the United States of America

1 2 3 4 5 6 7 8 9 10   10 09 08 07 06 05

Contents

Preface to the Third Edition

The purpose of this book is to describe the fundamentals of effective interviewing and counseling in speech–language pathology and audiology. To accomplish this purpose, we have integrated sources in the professional literature on interviewing and counseling, along with our experiences providing clinical services, supervising clinical practica, and teaching a variety of courses in communicative disorders, including interviewing and counseling classes. The basic principles and procedures of interviewing and counseling and the specific techniques and suggestions in this book are applicable to children and adults, to clients and caregivers, and to all settings in which clinicians provide service.

Professionals working with communication disorders have long recognized the importance of effective interviewing and counseling skills in clinical activities. Yet, as many authorities and clinicians have lamented for years, interviewing and counseling are neglected areas within most professional education programs. Many graduates go into clinical and educational services workplaces with neither coursework nor effective practicum experiences in interviewing and counseling. Too often, clinicians must learn how to interview and counsel on their own, in a "hit-and-miss" fashion, while on the job. Learning such essential skills this way is difficult for clinicians and is a disservice to many clients. Also, such a method of learning does not necessarily mean that the most effective methods of interviewing and counseling are discovered along the way.

This book is designed for use by students or professionals working with communication disorders. The first and second editions have been used as both primary and secondary texts in many communication disorders courses. They have been used in undergraduate- and graduate-level courses dealing with interviewing and counseling, in assessment and diagnostics courses, and in clinical methods coursework. The book also has been used with clinical practica, in internships, and in student teaching. Professionals, particularly those who never had specific coursework or practica in interviewing and counseling, found that the book addressed a wide range of pertinent, practical topics. This third edition should be useful in these same ways; it treats a variety of situations clinicians face and describes methods and techniques applicable to students as well as professionals.

In this third edition, more than 100 new references have been added; over 90% of these were published between 2000 and 2004. We have also added practical case studies and examples to help readers with clinical application of the information. One phenomenon we observed as we have taught counseling over the years is that students often say, "That idea sounds good on paper, but what exactly would you *say* to the client? What exact words would you use in that circumstance?" In this edition, we use many more concrete, real-life examples of both appropriate and inappropriate wording that can be used in counseling and interviewing situations. We have also provided brief, real-life scenarios and questions, with space for students to respond with ideas based on the materials they have just read. We encourage instructors who use this book to have students share their responses with the class. This can be done in the whole-class context or in small groups. The questions can also be used as take-home essay questions for tests or assignments. Again, we have found that the mere description of general principles is not enough; students, as beginners, need concrete, "real-world" examples, especially if they have no clinical experience. We have used these real-life scenarios to help students apply and integrate information during the course of the class, and also to help them realize that counseling is a truly important area of our profession.

A short anecdote illustrates this point. Several years ago, the second author had dinner with Dawn H., who had been a student in the first author's counseling class at the university and who was doing her clinical fellowship year in a hospital. Dawn commented, "When I took Dr. Shipley's counseling class, I sorta half-listened and didn't think it was that important. You know, I thought it was one of those 'fluff classes.' But when I started working in the hospital setting, I *constantly* referred to Dr. Shipley's notes and textbook. I had no idea how important this information was to my work in the hospital. I mean, I counsel people every single day. Dr. Shipley's textbook is now so dog-eared I may have to buy a new copy!"

Students, especially if they are young and have had no clinical experience, frequently do not realize the importance of counseling clients and their families. If students and instructors discuss actual cases to which the information in the text is applicable, students will realize, even in their undergraduate work, that counseling is indeed an indispensable and foundational component of our profession.

Both of us have taught at the university level for a number of years. On our student evaluations, particularly in our counseling courses, students frequently make positive comments about the stories we tell—stories about actual clients and how the textbook information applies in the real world. Years later, students tell us that out of all they learned in our classes, what they recall most is the stories we told. Thus, we hope that the inclusion of more real-life cases in this third edition will help students who are learning how to deal effectively with people: the clients and their families who make our profession so rewarding.

Chapter 1 of this edition provides an overview of interviewing and counseling and their uses. Chapters 2, 3, and 4 address the prerequisites for effective interviewing and counseling, the factors that influence communication in interviewing and counseling situations, and the skills and techniques clinicians need to develop to become effective interviewers and counselors. Chapter 5 deals with specific techniques clinicians can use in obtaining information, and Chapter 6 deals with providing information. Chapter 7 addresses areas of counseling, and more information is included about the application of such therapeutic schools of thought as rational-emotive-behavioral therapy and cognitive therapy to situations in communicative disorders. Numerous examples are provided to help students apply these theories and methods to real life. Chapter 8 deals with working with linguistically and culturally diverse clients and their families. This edition also contains more multicultural references and illustrations in each chapter of the book.

In Chapter 9 we discuss difficult situations such as working with patients who are in the midst of grief or crises, or who are contemplating suicide. Chapter 10, in which we address issues pertaining to working with families of children with disabilities, is new in this third edition. Readers are given very specific information about dealing with issues such as contentious meetings with challenging parents, working with low-income families who have few resources, helping parents come to terms with having a child with disabilities, and more. Chapter 11, another new addition, was contributed by Dr. Larry Boles, an internationally recognized expert on aphasia. Dr. Boles discusses issues in working with older, neurologically impaired clients and their families, and he describes group therapy methods in detail. We are most pleased to have this new chapter contributed by a well-known scholar and clinician.

Chapter 12 deals with a number of ethical, procedural, and professional matters that affect interviewing and counseling activities. Many of these topics are discussed in relation to the Code of Ethics of the American Speech-Language-Hearing

Association. Chapter 13 contains a few final thoughts, particularly about learning to interview and counsel and about increasing one's skills in these areas. Checklists for learning and self-evaluating particular skills are found in several chapters.

The literature on interviewing and counseling in communication disorders is rather sparse, but a large body of information is available from disciplines such as counseling, psychology, social work, education, and even medicine. Thus, many of the fundamental principles and techniques addressed here are drawn from those fields as they apply to our disciplines.

One thing that readers will not find in *Interviewing and Counseling in Communicative Disorders* is a focus on particular communication disorders. Different disorders are mentioned in various places, but readers will not find specific sections on how to interview or counsel the client who is stuttering, who has a laryngectomy, or who is experiencing a hearing loss. Rather, this work focuses on how to interview and counsel effectively across disorders because interviewing fundamentals cut across disorders, age levels, and settings of practice. The precise content areas for interviewing and counseling with different disorders are easily adaptable to these basic skills. For example, students and professionals can draw on information from their coursework and experience with different types of articulation, fluency, hearing, language, and voice problems and directly apply this information to their interviewing and counseling activities.

It is our hope that readers, whether students or practicing clinicians, will come away with a wealth of practical ideas and information to support them as they work with persons with communication disorders and their families. Speech–language pathologists and audiologists frequently play a key role during the most vulnerable times of people's lives. The lives that clinicians touch may be forever altered by the supportive, healing interaction that takes place during interviewing and counseling sessions.

Acknowledgments

We are very grateful to many people for their contributions to the first, second, and third editions of this book. Peggy Kipping of PRO-ED merits special appreciation for her support and advice as we wrote the third edition. We also thank Dr. Larry Boles, a nationally recognized expert on aphasia, for contributing a valuable chapter on working with older, neurogenically impaired clients and their families. His work makes a valuable addition to the third edition of this book.

I wish to acknowledge Dr. Kenneth W. Burk, Professor of Communicative Disorders and Sciences at Wichita State University, for spawning my interest in interviewing and counseling. I also thank Jeanne Hagen Stoddard, a very special student and now an exceptional speech–language pathologist, who was immensely helpful in my original research for this book. My wife and daughter, Peggy and Jennifer, have been unfailingly supportive and I cannot thank them enough. I love you both!

—Kenneth Shipley

I could not have completed this without the love and support of my husband Mike and my son Mark. Thank you both. I love you so much. And I thank my students at California State University, Sacramento, for their insightful questions, comments, and stories which have helped shape this third edition into a text that is even more "real world" than the previous one. Thanks, guys! And most of all, I am deeply indebted to the many children and their families who have taught me that working with clients is about so much more than just assessment and treatment of the communication disorder—it is about serving the *person* as a fellow human being who is journeying along the path of life with me. I am grateful for each day that I am able to continue to learn this lesson.

—Celeste Roseberry-McKibbin

ONE

Interviewing and Counseling in the Clinical Process

CHAPTER OUTLINE

- Methods of Obtaining Information
- Interviews
- Concluding Comments

nterviewing and counseling are extremely important activities for clinicians working with people experiencing speech, language, or hearing disorders (English, 2002; Flasher & Fogle, 2004; Haynes & Pindzola, 1998; Luterman, 2001; Shames, 2000). For example, consider the following quotes:

> *Overall, every aspect of our work as diagnosticians and clinicians includes counseling as an integral part of interaction with clients, patients, and their families. The people we try to help may not remember our therapy techniques that helped them improve their abilities to communicate as much as they remember how we listened to them and talked with them about the sensitive issues surrounding their hearing, speech, language, cognitive, or swallowing problems.* (Flasher & Fogle, 2004, p. 19)

> *[In audiology,] as far as we have come or will go in the future with technology, we will probably never be released from the task of counseling as a part of the process toward successful hearing aid fittings. We can do a good job with the mechanical process of hearing aid fitting, but the interface between the user and the device is dependent on effective counseling.* (Van Vliet, 2002, p. 84)

These are just two examples from many that could have been included here, because it is well recognized that interviewing and counseling activities are vitally important for delivery of services in speech–language pathology and audiology. The need for effective interviewing and counseling cuts across types of disorders, severity of disorders, settings, age groups, and cultural backgrounds.

Despite the general acceptance of interviewing and counseling as necessary and important for effective practice, preprofessional coursework and practice in these areas is woefully inadequate (Clark, 1994a; Johnson, 1994; Luterman, 2001; Rollin, 2000; Shames, 2000). Many professionals have little or no coursework in the areas of interviewing and counseling, and only minimal preprofessional clinical practica dealing specifically in these areas (Weindling, 2000). Thus, many practitioners begin their careers with some fear of interviewing and counseling because they learn these skills by trial and error. This type of learning may occur at the expense of patients along the way. This circumstance is, indeed, unfortunate and certainly not in the best interests of either clinicians or those they serve.

The following section addresses some of the basic information-gathering techniques used in diagnostic and assessment activities. Then the three basic types of interviews—information-getting interviews; information-giving interviews; and persuasive, influencing, or counseling interviews—are introduced along with discussion of the basic principles of learning or improving interviewing and counseling skills and abilities.

Methods of Obtaining Information

All clinical treatment services—from providing one-to-one intervention, to group treatment, to implementing home or classroom activities, to dispensing amplification devices—are based on the clinician's understanding of the client's communicative abilities and needs. This understanding develops as the clinician gains information from the client or from others who are familiar with the client (parents, significant others, caregivers, adult children, teachers, physicians). Clinicians typically gain most of their initial information from case history questionnaires, interviews, and, when available, written reports from other professionals who have worked with the client (Shipley & McAfee, 2004). Clinicians gain further information from direct observation and direct evaluation of communicative skills.

A clinician's evaluation of a patient typically culminates in identifying the presence or absence of a problem. If a problem exists, a diagnosis, an estimate of prognosis, and a plan of action or treatment are developed, and are subsequently shared with clients or their caregivers in an information-giving interview. This entire process of collecting the case history; observing and evaluating the client's communicative abilities and needs; determining a diagnosis, prognosis, and plan of action; and sharing these determinations may occur in one appointment in some settings and some cases. In other settings or with more complex cases, this process may take several days or weeks.

Case History Questionnaires

A questionnaire is a written form of a case history. Clients, or their parents or other caregivers, are asked to identify and describe various factors that may relate to a communicative disorder. Common areas of inquiry on case history forms include speech, language, and motor skills and family, social, medical, educational, or other appropriate histories.

Written case histories should be viewed as starting points for further investigation and inquiry. By their very nature, case histories have some inherent limitations. According to Shipley and McAfee (2004), the following are several of these limitations:

- Respondents may not understand some of the terminology used on the form, and incomplete or inaccurate information is the result.

- There may be insufficient time to complete the entire form or think about answers.
- Respondents may not know, or only have a vague recall of, some information requested.
- Significant amounts of time may have gone by between the onset of problems and the current assessment.
- Other events or circumstances, either at present or in the past, may hinder the recall of information.
- Cultural differences, or difficulties with the language, may interfere with providing information.

In many settings, respondents complete the written case history form and return it before the first visit with the clinician, or bring the form with them to the first visit. Other service providers supply the written case history form to clients at the first visit; it is then completed before an assessment session or during an initial interview. These variations are based on policies and the needs of the professionals.

One advantage of having a written history completed before the first visit is that the client or other informant may be able to supply more reliable information regarding the speech, language, hearing, medical, academic, social, or other appropriate histories. The client or informant has a chance to think about the questions in private and determine what information is being requested (Martin, 1994). The individual completing the form can also talk with family members, teachers, or other persons who can provide additional information regarding the specifics sought.

Another advantage of having a case history form completed beforehand is that time can be saved during the initial visit. Having already collected and reviewed the basic case history information, clinicians have a starting point and some sense of the most important areas that need to be discussed. Preliminary information about the problem and its progression can then be further explored, expanded, and validated during the initial interview. When a diagnostic session is scheduled on the same day, having the case history completed and returned in advance allows clinicians to prepare for the assessment session. Knowing such details as the client's age and gender and having someone's perceptions of the problem can help clinicians select appropriate materials, including formal or informal test procedures, or prepare in other ways for the diagnostic session (Peña-Brooks & Hegde, 2000).

There are, however, several potential disadvantages to having the case history completed and returned before the first visit. Haynes and Pindzola (2004) note that some settings use generic or universal questionnaires—that is, the same form is used for many disorder types. Generic forms cannot address all the information needed for specific types of disabilities (for fluency, voice, articulation, etc.). Most settings do have separate forms for children and adults, but these forms may not adequately distinguish differences between age levels of children. There are, for example, important differences between infants and toddlers, and between preschool-, elementary school-, junior high-, and high school-age children. One way to overcome part of the problem of generic forms is to use a generic case history for basic information and a second, more specific history form that focuses on particular communicative disorders (fluency, hearing impairment, early childhood language, aphasia, etc.).

Another potential disadvantage of having the case history completed beforehand is that questionnaire items that deal with prenatal and birth experiences, medical history, and communicative development may cause informants to feel threatened or guilty. Sometimes, such reactions are discovered during an initial interview; at other times, such reactions are not shared with clinicians.

Supplying a case history before a first visit can cause other problems. Informants may not understand questions or may misinterpret them. As a result, inaccurate or incomplete information is provided. Clients or respondents with poor reading and writing skills may be unable to complete the form, may accidentally supply inaccurate or incomplete information, or may become embarrassed or intimidated by their inabilities. Completing case history forms can be very difficult and frustrating for some clients who do not have adequate skills in the language used on the form or are unsure why certain questions need to be answered. In such cases, it is wise for the service provider to complete the form with the client (Roseberry-McKibbin, 2002). Having the case history form available in different languages is useful in some settings.

Completing a case history form with clients is time consuming, and it can prevent the participants from interacting freely and naturally with each other. The scope of discussions may be restricted to those topics covered by the case history form. Further, an informant may not be sufficiently prepared to give complete and accurate answers to the questions asked on the form.

In summary, there is no perfect answer to the question of whether case history forms should be completed beforehand or with the clinician. Rather, circumstances surrounding the case and the setting may dictate which approach works best. In general, our suggestion is to provide respondents with the case history form before the first visit with the request that they fill in the information that is known. Respondents' questions will be discussed during the first meeting. This gives the client or informant an opportunity to think about the questions and find any information that is not readily available. Answers that are incomplete or need further clarification and discussion can then be reviewed with the client during the first visit.

Points to Ponder #1

Discuss two advantages and two disadvantages of obtaining information through case history questionnaires before the first session.

Observation

Observing behavior is an important technique for obtaining information and insight. Observation plays an important role in assessment as well as treatment activities. Darley (1978) outlines two basic types of observational approaches: spectator observation and participant observation. *Spectator observation* occurs when an observer is physically removed or at a distance from the client and the situation. The clinician may be in sight of the client or out of the room; if the clinician is out of sight, the observation may take place through a one-way mirror, by video monitor, in a classroom, or on a playground. Presumably, such observations produce objective, firsthand information because the communicative behavior is observed unobtrusively. However, the range of behaviors and the types of communicative interactions available for observation can be limited in many settings. For example, clients are most frequently observed in clinical or educational settings where their behavior can differ, sometimes considerably, from what might be seen in other environments. Thus, the communicative behaviors or interactions observed may not be representative of an individual's normal functions.

The second type of observation is participant observation, which is used frequently in speech–language pathology and

Spectator observation
Observation during which the observer is physically removed or at a distance from the client and the situation.

audiology. *Participant observations* allow clinicians to structure situations to elicit specific responses or behaviors. Standardized testing is one form of participant observation. Another form is a speech–language sample in which clinicians observe and record samples of an individual's actual communicative skills.

A disadvantage of participant observation is the potential influence that clinicians themselves and their presentation of tasks can have on a client's behavior. In effect, what is presented by the clinician may dictate what is actually observed. Or, the very structure of the situation, like the setting for the spectator observation, may not be conducive to eliciting representative samples of the client's communicative behavior. Despite these potential variables, however, participant observations typically provide valuable information about clients, their families or other caregivers, basic patterns of interacting, and actual communicative skills and needs.

A clinician's observations are typically focused on how well the client speaks, hears, comprehends, and uses language. The clinician may also try to judge a client's level of comfort in the setting, as well as the client's general attitudes toward the communicative problems. When a client's family members or caregivers are present, the interactive relationship between the client and those persons is frequently observed. Both what is said and how it is said may be important. For example, is a parent's speech and language use appropriate for the child? Does the spouse seem to dominate the interaction? Do the individuals appear to get along? These are only three examples of the kinds of dynamics the clinician can observe to gain information and insight.

Good observational skills increase with concentration and practice. Skilled observers are able to see, hear, and sense specific details in a client's behavior or interactive style that an untrained observer is likely to miss. Skilled observers are also able to distinguish relevant from irrelevant details in order to develop an understanding of the individual and the communicative problem.

> **Participant observation**
> *Observation during which the clinician structures situations to elicit specific client responses or behaviors.*

Interviews

The case history questionnaire and a clinician's preliminary observations can provide information that sets the stage for the interactions that follow. The questionnaire may or may not be completed before the first interview, but either way, the clinician will have an opportunity to address and clarify areas of concern revealed on the case history form, or by observation, during an initial interview. During the interview, new information can emerge about the origin, course, and present state of the problem as well as the client's or informant's feelings and attitudes about problems experienced. The information gathered during the initial interview, together with the information from an assessment session, will become the foundation for determining the diagnosis, prognosis, and treatment recommendations.

Definition of Interviews

An *interview* is a serious conversation conducted for one or more important purposes. It is a communicative event between someone with specific knowledge or expertise in an area and someone who presumably will benefit from that expertise. Dillard and Reilly (1988b) note that there are three significant dimensions to an interview: a purpose, a plan of action, and good communication. Inadequacy in any of these dimensions precludes optimal effectiveness in an interview.

Interviewing is a process of "dyadic communication" with a predetermined and serious purpose (Shipley & Wood, 1996; Stewart & Cash, 2003). A *dyad* is a form of interpersonal communication involving person-to-person interactions in which pervasive feedback occurs between two parties. There may be more than two people involved in a dyad, but there are never more than two parties involved—an interviewer party and an interviewee party. For example, when an entire family interacts with one interviewer, the two parties of the dyad are the family and the interviewer.

A predetermined purpose distinguishes the interview from other types of conversations. Communication in a communication disorders interview is designed to focus on specific matters, which are typically the client's communication development, abilities, disabilities, and needs.

Interview

A serious conversation that is conducted for one or more purposes and involves someone with specific knowledge or expertise and a second person who presumably will benefit from that expertise.

Dyad

A form of interpersonal communication involving person-to-person interactions in which pervasive feedback occurs between two parties.

Unique Aspects of Interviewing and Counseling Activities

Stewart and Cash's (2003) excellent book, *Interviewing: Principles and Practices,* contains considerable information on the unique aspects and usefulness of interviews. Some of the information in this section is based on Stewart and Cash's work.

Besides being useful for obtaining basic facts, interviews provide information about people's feelings, thoughts, attitudes, and beliefs. Interviews tend to focus on personal needs or problems, whereas other communicative events (e.g., a cordial conversation, a speech, a lecture) operate in less sensitive and less personal areas. Interviews encourage the use of various types of questions. Interviews are also unique in that, for a variety of reasons, digressions occur and should be expected. In fact, digressions into subjects previously discussed are often both necessary and planned. But in contrast to such communicative events as a speech or a lecture, in which a speaker can plan exactly what to say, the give-and-take nature of an interview does not afford the luxury of knowing the exact topics of discussion that may arise.

There is an element of personal risk for both parties during interviewing and counseling activities. Clients, for example, may risk being judged as doing the wrong thing; appearing to be poor parents, spouses, or caregivers; revealing something that might later be regretted; or appearing to be weak or uninformed. Clinicians, meanwhile, risk not knowing the answers to questions, responding inappropriately, or appearing novice-like or inadequate. These risks are some of the reasons beginning clinicians are fearful of interviewing and, to an even greater extent, of counseling (Luterman, 2001). These perceived risks also help explain why even experienced clinicians may enter into interviewing and counseling activities with varying degrees of anxiety or uncertainty.

Types of Interviews

An interview regarding a communicative disorder is typically held for one of three reasons: (a) to secure information, (b) to provide information, or (c) to influence or alter someone else's feelings, attitudes, or behaviors. Thus, depending on its purpose, an interview may be an information-getting interview, an information-giving interview, or an influencing, persuading, or counseling interview (Shipley & Wood, 1996). For example, if a clinician needs to determine what factors are contributing to a speech or hearing problem, an *information-getting interview* is in order. If the clinician is describing assessment results, sharing suggested treatment options, or providing ongoing feedback on treatment progress, an *information-giving interview* is conducted. If the clinician is trying to assuage, modify, or alter someone's activities or feelings, a *counseling interview* is used (English, 2002).

Interviews often involve a combination of these functions. For example, a clinician may have completed a diagnostic session and be involved primarily with providing information about the findings (information-giving) but, during the same session, continues to seek additional information deemed necessary (information-getting). Similarly, some information-getting interviews conducted primarily to obtain information also may involve helping people vent frustrations, or to persuade or counsel.

The following sections contain an overview of the three major types of interviewing and counseling activities. Chapters 5 and 6 contain more complete discussions of these three basic types of interactions.

Information-Getting Interviews

Information-getting interviews are important because the basic information obtained from clients, their caregivers, or other professionals can be a key to diagnosis and remedial planning (Haynes & Pindzola, 1998; Peterson & Marquardt, 1994; Shipley & McAfee, 2004). Thus, information-getting interviews are, or should be, a routine part of the assessment or diagnostic process in all settings. During this type of interview, the clinician may seek objective information such as dates, specific conditions, and events that preceded a communicative difficulty, and may seek subjective information such as the interviewee's interpretations, attitudes, and feelings about the communicative problem.

An information-getting interview is often the first interaction between a clinician and the client, the client's family, or caregivers. This type of interview is also conducted with clients who are enrolled for ongoing services to determine, for example, whether newly learned behavior has been generalized to other situations or other people, or to learn the results of medical, educational, or psychological testing done elsewhere. As the initial contact, an information-getting interview is the foundation on which the client–clinician relationship begins to develop. Thus, appropriate approaches and techniques for gathering information are important.

Information-Giving Interviews

Clinicians frequently are involved in providing information to others. Test results, diagnostic impressions, suggestions, and recommendations may need to be conveyed to clients, their families or caregivers, or other professionals. Following diagnostic sessions, clinicians typically provide information concerning the nature of the communicative difficulty, any prognostic implications, and a proposed plan for case management. Information-giving interviews also occur in the course of treatment. For example, conscientious clinicians use this type of interview, even if it is somewhat informal, to provide feedback to clients and their families regarding treatment progress.

Providing information to others is an important function, and the clinician must choose what information to provide and how to accurately convey it. When accurate information is not provided, clients or caregivers are likely to be confused and misinformed.

Counseling Interviews

Counseling is a general term that embraces a number of clinical activities. Interviews that are used to influence behaviors or attitudes can be called helping, influencing, persuading, or counseling interviews (Ivey, 1994; Okun, 2002; Shipley & Wood, 1996; Stewart & Cash, 2003). In this book, these types of interactions are referred to as counseling interviews. In addition to altering behaviors or attitudes, counseling interviews provide release, support, and encouragement for interviewees.

Audiologists and speech–language pathologists often see clients with devastating communication disorders that profoundly affect the lives of both the clients and their families. This impact creates a substantial need for counseling as an integral part of the assessment and treatment of clients with a wide range of communication disorders. Counseling has been used as part of the treatment of clients who have disorders of voice, fluency, articulation, and other functions. Patients who have undergone laryngectomies and their families frequently need substantial counseling to adjust to the profound life changes that are experienced after the laryngectomy. Adults who have traumatic brain injury, strokes, and other neurological insults and their families need ongoing counseling support. Adults with communication disorders secondary to acquired degenerative diseases such as Parkinson's and Alzheimer's are living longer and requiring a great deal of care, and the caretakers of these patients may need just as much counseling and support as the patients themselves (Weindling, 2000). Parents who have children with disabilities or conditions such as profound hearing loss, cerebral palsy, autism, and cleft palate need a great deal of emotional support in the form of ongoing counseling. Adults with acquired sensorineural hearing losses also need counseling as part of their habilitation.

Many clinicians are uncomfortable when they have to deal with feelings. Clinicians may think thoughts such as, "My job is just to test this person's hearing and fit her for hearing aids. That's it" or "All I need to do is teach this client esophageal speech. It's not my job to help his wife through her sorrow about his laryngectomy." Many of us may wish that we did not have to deal with emotions at all. But emotions are part and parcel of assessment and treatment of clients with communication disorders and their families. The ideas and techniques in this book are designed to help clinicians feel more comfortable, knowledgeable, and competent in dealing with the emotional aspect of communication disorders. As Shames (2000) states,

> *Many of us see ourselves as being limited to only our primary functions of helping the communicatively disabled change the way they communicate … we have a natural tendency to focus on our functions as source of information, diagnostician…. However, such an exclusive focus may be too narrow because it does not take into account the emotional sequelae associated with communication problems…. Counseling around such issues is directly related to the specific communication problem involved. Counseling focuses on the emotional and feeling components of communication problems, and their impact on the person's behavior.* (pp. 4–6, 15)

Through counseling, the clinician provides support and direction and encourages the client and family members or caregivers to express important feelings and attitudes about the difficulties encountered. The client's family members or caregivers also may be helped to modify their methods of interaction, assist in treatment activities, or understand and correct ways they may be hindering the client's progress. Other similar types of support are also possible for a wide range of ages and disorders.

Points to Ponder #2

You are a clinician who has practiced for 5 years, and you have been given a student intern for a semester. She has the choice of taking an elective course titled "Interviewing and Counseling in Communicative Disorders." She tells you that she doesn't really see the relevance of this class and says, "All I really need is to be knowledgeable and technically sharp. Why take this class?" What would you say to her?

▷ Concluding Comments

The interview plays a significant role in the clinical process. Interviews are the means by which clinicians obtain information, provide information or teach, help people ventilate feelings and frustrations, and modify behavior and attitudes (Okun, 2002). The foundation for the clinician's work is the understanding of the client that develops from various sources of information: case history questionnaires, the initial information-getting interview, and direct observation during assessment sessions or observations. The clinician's understanding is represented by a diagnosis, a prognosis, and plans for remediation, which are usually shared in information-giving interviews. Although we have distinguished three different kinds of interviews—information-getting, information-giving, and counseling interviews—an interview at any time during the clinical process can involve any combination of the three functions.

TWO

Prerequisites for Effective Interviewing and Counseling

CHAPTER OUTLINE

- Interviewer Characteristics
- Conditions That Facilitate Good Communication
- Concluding Comments

Effective interviewers and counselors possess an interest in others, know the field of communicative disorders, are able to provide appropriate counsel, and use a variety of techniques to facilitate communication. Successful clinicians also possess certain basic personal characteristics that facilitate effective communication with others.

Interviewer Characteristics

Some personal attributes, attitudes, and beliefs are characteristic of clinicians who perform interviewing and counseling functions well. The following list describes some basic prerequisite characteristics that contribute to working successfully with others. These fundamental attributes are identified in interviewing and counseling sources such as Biggs and Blocher (1987), DeBlassie (1976), Dillard and Reilly (1988c), Hackney and Cormier (1994), Kennedy and Charles (2001), Moursund (1993), Okun (2002), Shertzer and Stone (1980), Shipley and Wood (1996), and Stewart and Cash (2003), and from experience conducting interviews and counseling in communicative disorders and teaching interviewing and counseling coursework.

> **Spontaneity.** Clinicians need to be able to respond immediately and appropriately to situations and discussions that arise.
>
> **Flexibility.** Clinicians need to be secure within themselves, and they need knowledge of the field and of people and the ability to be spontaneous. There is no single right or fixed method for all clinicians to interview or counsel; clinicians must vary their approaches when dealing with different clients, their families or caregivers, or others who often are involved (Moore-Brown & Montgomery, 2001).
>
> One practical technique for implementing flexibility is to find out as much about the clients and families as possible before meeting with them. This technique helps clinicians to be more personal and flexible in their approaches.
>
> **Concentration.** Clinicians must be able to concentrate as completely as possible on what is occurring during interactions (Shafir, 2000).
>
> **Openness.** Clinicians must be able to hear, understand, and accept the values and feelings of other people without distorting their own feelings or what they need to convey. Clinicians also must be careful not to impose their values inappropriately on others.
>
> **Honesty.** Honesty is a key factor in developing trust and effective relationships. As Okun (2002) commented,

honesty is more than just being truthful; it is also being open to exploration and fair in evaluation.

Emotional stability. Emotional stability involves, in part, security with self and the abilities to adapt to and flow with the experiences of life. Working in a helping profession is not always easy, so clinicians need to be emotionally stable and secure within themselves. To facilitate these qualities, it is important for clinicians to take care of themselves (Flasher & Fogle, 2004). Clinicians need to get adequate rest, nutrition, exercise, and leisure time to avoid burnout. Clinicians who work in extremely emotionally demanding jobs such as those in neonatal intensive care units may need additional emotional support for themselves. Clinicians should never be afraid or embarrassed to seek professional counseling, if necessary.

Trustworthiness. Clinicians have little opportunity for success unless they are able to engender the trust of their clients, peers, and other professionals.

Self-awareness. True self-awareness enables clinicians to understand their personal and professional strengths and weaknesses, the range and limitations of their abilities, and how others respond to them. Clinicians must also be aware of their own biases and stereotypes regarding members of different linguistic, cultural, or religious backgrounds. It is important to be aware of any such biases or feelings and not let these inappropriately influence clinical judgments.

Belief in people's abilities to change. Effective clinicians believe in change and in people's abilities to learn, grow, and change as a result of the clinical process.

Commitment to people. Deep commitments to people, human values, and the fulfillment of human potential are important characteristics of effective clinicians.

Cultural competence. As the United States becomes increasingly culturally and linguistically diverse, it is imperative that clinicians be culturally competent (Sue & Sue, 2003). As more fully described in Chapter 8, cultural competence involves self-awareness as well as knowledge about the cultural and linguistic characteristics of clients and their families that affect communication (Brice, 2002; Roseberry-McKibbin, 2002).

Knowledge and wisdom. Clinicians need to be wise, knowledgeable, intellectually active, and inquisitive. They need to develop wisdom in their understanding of themselves, others, the world, and the various conditions, experiences, skills, and techniques that promote optimal growth and self-actualization.

Good communicative skills. For interviewing and counseling, clinicians need good comprehension, listening, and expressive skills. Good verbal and nonverbal communication skills are imperative; poor or tentative verbal skills significantly hamper clinical interactions. Similarly, using too few, too many, or incongruent nonverbal behaviors detracts from clinical effectiveness.

Academic and clinical competence in speech–language pathology or audiology. Competence in the clinician's field of expertise is essential for interviewing and counseling to be effective. Without a solid understanding of the field, there is simply no basis for effective work with clients.

Today, many clients and families access the Internet for information about the nature, assessment, and treatment of communication disorders and related conditions. It is not uncommon, for example, for parents to come to Individualized Education Program (IEP) meetings armed with information they have downloaded and printed from Web sites. Now more than ever, clinicians in all settings need to remain current in order to be knowledgeable and keep up with the proliferation of information that is available to the general public at the touch of a computer key.

These are some of the characteristics of effective interviewers and counselors. Personality traits, feelings toward life, and individual attitudes are personal qualities, and clinicians do need to be aware of the characteristics and attitudes they project. In some cases, clinicians should modify counterproductive behavioral or attitudinal characteristics before they can provide effective services.

Points to Ponder #3

Describe two interviewer characteristics (e.g., flexibility) that you may need to improve to become a more effective clinician. What steps will you take toward improvement?

Conditions That Facilitate Good Communication

Effective communication in interviewing and counseling depends on the presence of certain conditions in the clinician–client relationship. These conditions include sensitivity, respect, empathy, objectivity, listening skills, and motivation. When these elements are shared by the participants, rapport can be established and maintained.

Sensitivity

Sensitivity is an important professional characteristic. Clinicians must realize that clients' feelings influence their thinking about and receptivity toward the topic under discussion, and that this thinking may or may not be in accordance with the clinicians' thoughts. Clinicians and clients may think differently about the severity of problems. A client who is deeply embarrassed about having a mild lisp, for example, may be irritated by being told that the problem is "relatively minor." Conversely, parents who do not think that their child's problem is severe often have difficulty understanding or agreeing with suggestions to the contrary. In both cases, a sensitive clinician will realize that client perceptions and feelings will affect reactions toward the specialist's observations.

Clinicians need to be sensitive to their clients' interests in and levels of concern about their problems. Some clients or caregivers may be extremely concerned about a problem; others may not be. At times, it can be difficult not to become annoyed with some clients' seemingly apathetic attitudes or statements. However, the clinicians' responsibility is to provide information and interpretations in straightforward communication. When clinicians encounter a lack of interest or concern, they may need to objectively, yet sensitively, demonstrate why greater concern is warranted and share the ramifications of their findings.

Sensitivity toward an interviewee's level of knowledge is also important. It is wise to remember that other people have

Sensitivity to the Client's Cultural Background

There are certainly many factors related to sensitivity when interviewing or counseling across cultures (Sue & Sue, 2003). For example, clinicians raised in traditional, middle-class families may become irritated when working with culturally or linguistically different individuals or families who appear apathetic toward a communicative disorder. Among some cultural groups, such as some Native Americans, a child with a disability is accepted as a gift from the Great Spirit. Other Native Americans believe that a child is born with a disability because the child chose the disability, prenatally (Harris, 1993). Some Asians believe that disabilities and birth defects result from sins committed by parents or ancestors; others believe that disabling conditions are fated and that nothing should be done to interfere with this fate. Certainly, the clinician who does not recognize such cultural beliefs will have difficulty with these sensitive issues when dealing with clients holding such views. Chapter 8 addresses a number of other factors related to cross-cultural sensitivity.

not had the years of training and clinical experience of a professional. Unless clinicians are sensitive in their use of language and to the amount of knowledge other people have about communicative disorders, patients and caregivers can become misinformed or confused. Inappropriate assumptions about other people's knowledge of communicative difficulties and technical terminology (e.g., terms like *sibilant, impedance, prognosis, diadochokinesis, sensorineural*) typically result in a failure to communicate. The client may have no idea what the clinician is talking about or may develop a mental picture that differs considerably from what the clinician intended to convey.

The use of technical jargon can also make the clinician appear insensitive, uncaring, or even arrogant, so its use should be avoided whenever possible. Clinicians need to use simple, nontechnical language in their explanations and discussions. This is not to imply that they should avoid saying what needs to be said or that they should provide false assurances. Rather, clinicians should balance their communication so that it is supportive as well as truthful. Sensitivity to clients' levels of concern and knowledge, as well as their emotional or psychological states, helps clinicians communicate effectively and promotes the changes deemed necessary.

Respect

Respect involves having regard for and showing appropriate courtesy. The words, actions, and behaviors that clinicians use convey respect or disrespect.

As a matter of respect and sensitivity, clinicians should keep in mind the possibility that some interviewees and counselees will pose questions or concerns that, in a strict clinical sense, do not seem particularly important or even appropriate. However, it is a good guideline to assume that any question or concern posed by an interviewee is important to that person. Even seemingly irrelevant, "dumb," or repetitious questions should be handled forthrightly, courteously, and respectfully (Shipley & Wood, 1996).

Empathy

Empathy is the quality of being able to identify with and share the feelings of others. In other words, the clinician truly feels and understands what the other person feels. Empathy is built on caring attitudes, sensitivity, knowledge, and understanding of an individual's circumstances and feelings. During an interview, the clinician simultaneously learns about and attempts to understand the individual.

Empathy
Identification with and sharing of the feelings of others.

The verbal and nonverbal exchanges that occur in interviews are reflections of the participants' conscious intentions to communicate certain information, as well as the unconscious processes that may be going on in their minds. These unconscious processes influence people's feelings and attitudes about an interaction. Again, interviewers need to be aware that their own attitudes create impressions and engender feelings and reactions. Skill in using techniques is certainly no substitute for having appropriate attitudes toward interviewing and empathy toward people in general. Techniques can be adopted to address a problem at hand, but to use techniques properly, clinicians must be able to empathetically evaluate an interviewee's attitudes and personality. This requires considerable skill in human relations and caring attitudes.

Objectivity

Speech–language pathologists and audiologists involved with interviewing and counseling must remain objective in their clinical roles. However, objectivity does not mean being impersonal, unfriendly, or insensitive. It simply means that a clinician does not allow personal emotions to influence the situation inappropriately. A realistic and practical point of view can be maintained when interviewers remain objective. A lack of objectivity is one indication that clinicians are concentrating on their own feelings rather than on the feelings of their clients.

Successful interviewing requires the use of the somewhat conflicting attitudes of empathy and objectivity. It is important for clinicians to understand the difference between subjective and objective information and reactions, and it is important to understand how clients can affect clinicians' behavior.

A clinician's role is not to judge others in a negative sense but to understand potential causes and sources of behavior and feelings. The clinician must understand the distinction between being a friend and being friendly. The delicate balance requires careful judgment, particularly when working across cultures. For example, in the traditional Filipino value system, professionals are expected to be personable, subject to reciprocal influence and affiliation, and sensitive to the family's desire for emotional closeness (Chan, 1998b). Other cultures, such as the general, White U.S. culture, expect friendliness but less of an emotionally close role.

Interviewers and interviewees should strive to become cooperative coworkers or partners, with clinicians maintaining the roles of directors and guides in the relationship. In these roles, clinicians need to appreciate their own degree of ego involvement in the interviewing and counseling activities. Everyone has the need to look and feel good, but clinicians' needs should not be tended at the expense of clients. Clinicians must hold interviewees' welfare in the highest regard; their own personal needs and issues are secondary.

Listening Skills

Listening is an essential ingredient in interviewing and counseling. It is a purposeful activity that requires considerable concentration and skill (Cappannelli & Cappannelli, 2002). Careful listening enables clinicians to obtain or provide the information needed for effective service delivery. Listening also allows clinicians to gain valuable insights into how patients think and feel about themselves and others, and how they perceive the information being discussed (Hansen, 2001). Careful listening helps clinicians begin to understand an interviewee's goals, ambitions, aspirations, values, and basic philosophies, as well as the types of coping strategies or defense mechanisms that may be present. Careful and effective listening can also provide a therapeutic function, in that a clinician may be the first person to understand the magnitude, effects, and various implications of the client's particular problem (English, 2002).

Effective listening is a skill. However, Mowrer (1988) suggests that speech–language pathologists, in particular, tend to be verbal people whose training has emphasized direct diagnosis and treatment. He notes that skillful listening in interviewing and counseling is not an automatic response for all clinicians. As Ivey (1994) comments, "You can't learn about the client if you are doing the talking!" (p. 24). Part of this problem is related to the lack of formal interviewing and counseling preparation in preprofessional programs. Audiologists and speech–language pathologists often have a considerable amount of training and experience in hearing how speech is produced, but they typically have far less training in other aspects of listening and understanding.

There are at least four critical factors in effective listening: concentration, active participation, comprehension, and objectivity (Barbara, 1958). *Concentration* requires hearing what is said, having patience, and removing any distractions from the interaction. The clinician should concentrate on the matters at hand—not other unrelated thoughts and concerns. *Active participation* requires that the clinician's mind remain ready, alert, open, flexible, and free from distraction. *Comprehension* involves hearing the surface messages as well as the underlying meanings. As noted earlier, *objectivity* requires the clinician to avoid inadvertently or inappropriately imposing personal feelings and attitudes on interviewees and what they may be expressing. All of these aspects of artful listening are relatively easy to acknowledge, but they require skill and discipline to implement.

Good Listening Skills in Action

The mother of a boy in a university clinic called the clinic supervisor and said that the assessment of her son was "a waste of time," her son was "being used as a human guinea pig," they were being "taken advantage of," and they wanted their money back. For a minute or two, the supervisor longed to tell the mother that there was a waiting list of 60 clients, that she was ungrateful and ignorant, and that this was *fine*—they could go elsewhere. However, good judgment and knowledge of appropriate listening skills prevailed, and the supervisor was able to see that underneath these accusations, the mother was fearful because the family only had money for one semester of therapy, and she was afraid assessment was taking up too much treatment time. A satisfactory (and calmly stated) arrangement was eventually reached.

Approaches to Listening

Stewart and Cash (2003) describe four basic types of listening approaches that interviewers and counselors can use: (a) listening for comprehension, (b) listening with empathy, (c) listening for evaluation, and (d) listening for resolution (dialogic listening). *Listening for comprehension* is a method of receiving content that requires little feedback from the listener. The listener remains objective and perhaps even somewhat detached rather than critically analyzing or responding to the other person's comments. *Listening with empathy* goes beyond simply receiving messages and actually conveys understanding of what the client may be experiencing emotionally. Listening empathetically often involves providing comfort, warmth, and reassurance. Clinicians who listen with empathy try to put themselves "in the other person's shoes," understand the other party, or express their understanding of the other's situation. *Listening for evaluation* means trying to use the information received for an evaluative conclusion. *Listening for resolution* means that the goal of the interaction is the resolution of a task together—not one person trying to solve the problem for the other one.

To illustrate these fundamental types of listening approaches, imagine that someone promised to complete a task but then ran out of time. During the explanation that followed, the individual who is listening for comprehension might be listening to obtain additional information about what happened, in order to understand more fully. The listening-with-empathy listener might be listening or even responding with empathy or sympathy (e.g., "You must have been overwhelmed"). Empathic listening is always centered on the other person, and the goal of empathic listening is to make the other person feel uniquely understood (Ciaramicoli & Ketcham, 2000). The listening-for-evaluation listener might be awaiting additional information that would confirm or rule out the possibility of time-management problems, inadequate abilities to complete the task, and so forth. The listening-for-resolution listener might ask, "How can we work together to avoid this situation in the future?" Clinicians need to recognize that these different types of listening exist and that, depending on the particular circumstances at hand, each of the four types of listening can be used when needed.

Listening for comprehension

Listener receives information but is not required to provide much feedback.

Listening with empathy

Listener conveys understanding of what the speaker may be experiencing emotionally.

Listening for evaluation

Listener uses the information to form an evaluative conclusion.

Listening for resolution

Listener interprets information with the goal of resolving an issue with the speaker.

Concentration

Listening well requires good attending skills (Shafir, 2000). The clinician can convey an impression of good listening and attending with appropriate eye contact, a slightly forward body posture to indicate interest, hand gestures and body postures, and appropriate verbal feedback to indicate that information is being heard and understood. However, there is more to good listening than simply appearing to hear what is being said.

Concentration on what other people are saying can be a difficult skill to learn. It does not come naturally to everyone. Many people's difficulties in truly listening and attending are well documented (Cappannelli & Cappannelli, 2002; Ellis, 2001; Glass, 2002; Luterman, 2001; Shafir, 2000). One reason that it is so hard for many of us to truly concentrate while another person is talking is that we live in an age in which we are constantly bombarded with information. Glass (2002) speaks of the "mental noise" that Americans experience in the 21st century. Information bombards us from various media, including the television, radio, Internet, fax, e-mail, voice mail, and regular mail. All these variables in modern life make it quite challenging to be relaxed and focused enough to listen and truly concentrate. If concentration is difficult, the following practical suggestions can help substantially:

1. Breathe deeply. This aids in relaxation, which promotes better concentration.
2. Do not interrupt the other person (unless necessary).
3. Keep good eye contact with the person who is speaking.
4. Rephrase and restate to make sure that you have understood the other person correctly.
5. Do not daydream. If other thoughts enter your mind, let them go.
6. Take occasional notes. When not overdone, this practice is helpful for many people.
7. Visualize what the speaker is saying. Actively paint a mental picture in your mind. For example, if the mother of a child with autism talks about how hectic her life is with four children, a job, a commute, and two dogs, try to vividly picture this situation. It probably won't be hard!
8. Plan in advance to have enough time for the meeting. Almost nothing destroys a clinician's concentration more than being rushed.

All topics introduced, all information presented, and all questions posed by clients are potentially important. It is helpful if a clinician is ready to provide the rationale behind any area of inquiry in case the respondent questions its importance. People will be less likely to be offended by questions if they know why these questions are being asked. This can be very important with multicultural clients for whom an interviewer's question appears too personal or embarrassing (Lian & Abdullah, 2001).

Clinicians should avoid becoming overstimulated by or emotionally involved with what an interviewee says. Emotionally loaded words, attitudes expressed, or particular positions taken should not be allowed to interfere with listening and understanding. Clinicians need to identify and recognize the types of words and attitudes that affect them emotionally so that their impact will be reduced when they are encountered in sessions. With emotions under control, clinicians should be able to attend carefully to what is being said, particularly with information that is difficult or hard to deal with (Moore-Brown & Montgomery, 2001).

The clinician should listen to more than just the "basic facts" being expressed and realize that the feelings or reasons behind the facts are sometimes as important as, if not more important than, any information conveyed. Effective interviewers and counselors concentrate on an interaction and avoid being distracted. The clinician should ask for a clarification if something is missed or not understood; this is a considerably better option than becoming confused or not fully understanding. The clinician also needs to make sure she or he understands any point the other party makes before commenting on it. These tenets are important in all interviewing and counseling situations. They are, of course, particularly salient in the presence of language barriers or when an interpreter is involved.

Points to Ponder #4

You are working in a hospital with adults who have acquired neurological disabilities (e.g., traumatic brain injury) and their families. You realize that your listening skills need improvement. Describe three aspects of good listening that you might need to work on in order to be a more effective clinician.

Listening and Activity Levels

A different way to view the act of listening is to compare listening versus nonlistening levels in relation to the levels of activity or passivity of the listener. In his book, *Communicating with Parents of Exceptional Children: Improving Parent–Teacher Relationships,* Kroth (1985) presents a model for looking at these factors and how they influence an interview (see Figure 2.1). The information in the figure applies to both clinicians and clients, and it complements the other information on listening presented in this chapter. Kroth's model is one way of interpreting the degree of listening and activity that occurs during interviewing and counseling sessions. It should also be noted that the degree of listening and activity can change at times during an interview. Participants' roles and actions in an interview may vary between being passive and active, between listening and not listening. Their activity levels and appearance while listening are also culturally relative, so care is needed when applying this model across cultures.

The participant who operates in Quadrant A of Figure 2.1 is a generally passive person who is listening and is, therefore, very much part of the interaction. This person may exhibit a variety of nonverbal signals (e.g., forward leaning of the body, smiling approval or understanding, positive head nodding) that suggest that the material under discussion is being received and understood. For clinicians, assuming the passive-listening role depicted in Quadrant A can sometimes be difficult if they usually take a more active role when interacting with clients.

The participant who operates in Quadrant B is also listening attentively and shows this in more active ways, both verbally and nonverbally. The Quadrant B clinician or client is very involved in active discussion. Clinicians may want to purposefully assume this active-listening role when they provide

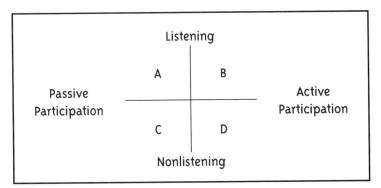

FIGURE 2.1. A listening paradigm. *Note.* From *Communicating with Parents of Exceptional Children: Improving Parent–Teacher Relationships* (p. 38), by R. L. Kroth, 1985, Denver, CO: Love. Copyright 1985 by Love Publishing Company. Reprinted with permission.

information to clients, or when they attempt to modify behavior or attitudes.

The participant in Quadrant C is a passive nonlistener. This person is neither listening nor active and is, therefore, rather difficult to work with. Little true communication occurs in interactions with this person. The person in Quadrant C may hear what is said while being caught up in inner thoughts or resisting the information provided.

Kroth (1985) described and gave an example of passive nonlistening:

> *The passive nonlistener often seems to "hear" what is being said but is not involved in listening to the feeling content of the messages. This posture can be frustrating to the one who is trying to communicate with another person.*

WIFE: I'm so tired. I've been to four stores today trying to find material for a new dress. You're not listening.

HUSBAND: (*folding the newspaper*) You said you've been to four stores looking for material for a new dress.

> *Although the content was accurate, the husband missed his wife's feelings of fatigue and frustration. She really could not argue that he was not listening because he was able to parrot back most of her words accurately; however, no real communication took place. These are two people physically in the same room, one who is trying to send messages to alleviate some of her feelings and the other who is submerged in his own thoughts.* (p. 39)

When we use this example in our classes, some married students share their feelings that their spouses operate in Quadrant C. Dealing with Quadrant C clients can be very frustrating for clinicians because these people seem to hear the information while actually remaining distant from what is being conveyed.

Finally, the participant in Quadrant D—the active nonlistener—is quite active in the encounter, but this person is not really listening to what is being conveyed. Effective communication does not occur. Kroth (1985) presented the following example:

> *Almost everyone has had the experience of being at a social gathering where a great deal of talk was going on,*

with virtually no listening. In this type of conversation, people talk to each other but seldom with each other.

MRS. SMITH: We're so glad you could come. I heard you were out of town.

MRS. JONES: We just got back. We were attending my aunt's funeral in California.

MRS. SMITH: California is so pretty this time of year. We were at Disneyland last spring. I enjoyed it so much.

MRS. JONES: We were in Albuquerque last spring. Oh, there's Ruby; I must tell her about the squash-blossom necklace I found. (p. 40)

This example is a little overstated from the point of view of most social interactions, but it does illustrate the case of two people who are not listening to each other. When neither party in an interaction listens, it is unlikely that either party will notice what happens. In the case that one of the parties listens but the other does not, communication will be one-sided, at best. Kroth (1985) gave this example of one-sided, active, nonlistening at a parent–teacher conference:

PARENT: Billy had the neatest thing happen to him on his way home from school.

TEACHER: How does he go home from school?

PARENT: Down Center Street and—

TEACHER: Isn't that past the fire station?

PARENT: Yes, and—

TEACHER: Last year five of our boys said they wanted to be firemen when they grow up. What does Billy want to be?

PARENT: A nuclear physicist.

TEACHER: Isn't that cute? And to think he can't even spell it. What happened to him on the way home?

PARENT: Well, he ran into this man who—

TEACHER: I hope he said "excuse me." We stress good manners in our room. We have a unit on the magic words—please and thank you. I hope you notice the improvement at home. (p. 42)

Again, this is an extreme example, but it does illustrate the idea of being verbally active but not listening.

It is important to remember that a participant's apparent activity during an interview can belie the actual levels of listening and receptivity. Clinicians must judge the other party's actual levels of listening and understanding.

For example, many Asian clients may be listening quite closely, but they may appear impassive or expressionless. This is often culturally related. As Fung and Roseberry-McKibbin (1999) noted, "Cantonese speakers are generally taught to suppress their emotions in public and remain expressionless ... Among many speakers of Cantonese, the open expression of anger is particularly unacceptable" (p. 311). On the other hand, clients from the former Union of Soviet Socialist Republics may listen and respond with a great deal of emotion (Roseberry-McKibbin & Domyancic, 2002). Again, listening is strongly influenced by cultural background (Sue & Sue, 2003).

It is also important for interviewers and counselors to understand their own attending and listening styles. Figure 2.1 provides one model for self-assessment, or for estimating the listening and activity levels of others during interviewing or counseling sessions.

Of course, no one fits definitively into a single quadrant. Individuals tend to operate within one of the quadrants more than others, but people may move into other quadrants depending on the situation, their comfort with various subject areas, and their responses to different people.

Specific conditions or situations also affect listening behavior. Physical factors like sitting in an uncomfortable chair, interacting in a room that is too hot or too cold, being in a noisy environment, or looking into bright light all affect listening. Listening is also negatively affected when listeners are uninterested in a speaker's views, disagree with what the speaker says, or have their minds made up and are therefore interested only in their own personal thoughts and ideas.

Shafir (2000) summarizes the helpfulness of skillful listening to clients and their families:

> *Listening can be a powerful tool of change. ... When a person is given a chance to tell his views without the threat of judgment or advice, even if his listener does not agree, that is the first step toward creating good feelings. A sense of openness on both sides allows for discussion and problem-solving ... an empathic listener provides helpful feedback that makes a speaker feel valued. This is a significant gift in a world where the human touch is a rare commodity.* (pp. 10–11)

Motivation

It is important to acknowledge that we may never fully understand the actions of others. Behavior is motivated, however, and the attainment of a client's goals depends in large part on the client's own motivation. In his book, *A Career in Speech Pathology*, Van Riper (1979) comments that "perhaps the most important of all the clinical skills required for effective therapy is the clinician's ability to motivate his [or her] clients" (p. 82). Van Riper shares several personal anecdotes from his career that illustrate the importance of motivation. One unusual but certainly illustrative story is retold here:

> One day a very determined young lady phoned and demanded an immediate appointment for herself and her husband. This is what she said: "We were married yesterday after a whirlwind courtship. I had never heard my husband stutter before but he's been stuttering horribly ever since the ceremony. I love him but I'm not going to bed with a monster until I'm sure that he can be helped. Can you cure him? We have separate rooms at the Burdick Hotel and must see you immediately. Can we come up right now?"
>
> Toujours l'amour, of course! The young man was indeed a very severe stutterer, gasping sequentially and compulsively until he blew himself up like a balloon, and only then could he utter the word he was trying to say. Pretty monosymptomatic, too. I told his wife, who did all the talking, that I didn't know if I could help him but I'd try. She turned to her man and laid it on the line. "OK, we'll see. I'll give you three weeks before I go after an annulment. Meanwhile, you'll sleep alone." A pretty hard-nosed gal. Well, I've never had any stutterer work harder than that man, day and night. Self-therapy at its best. All I had to do was make a suggestion, explain a procedure or point out a goal. He improved very quickly and soon eliminated all the gasping. Nevertheless, I was highly conscious of the calendar. Just before the three weeks were up, the man came in with a big cat-that-ate-the-canary grin on his face. "Well, Doc," he said, "I'm married at last, thanks to you!" (Van Riper, 1979, pp. 94–95)

Motivation is enhanced when clinicians and clients have the same goals. Both parties also benefit when everyone is aware of the purposes of an interaction, how any information shared will be used, and what is expected of the participants. Some basic principles that affect motivation include the following:

1. Motivation will be high if the goal to be achieved is important to the person and there is a good possibility of reaching that goal.

2. Motivation will be facilitated, even when the client's motives differ from those of the clinician, if the client can identify with and relate to the clinician.

3. Many goals or achievements have a primary value to one person (e.g., the clinician), but only incidental value to another person (e.g., the interviewee). In this case, one of the clinician's primary aims will be to link an accomplishment to something that is of greater concern or value to the client.

4. Motivation is often facilitated if one learns enough to generate at least a moderate level of anxiety about the issue. For example, one 24-year-old woman came to a university clinic because she was perpetually hoarse. She didn't think she needed to change her speaking habits until the clinician explained, in great detail, information about vocal nodules and polyps as well as possible surgery for these conditions. The woman hadn't realized that surgery might be imminent, and she willingly cooperated with an extensive vocal modification program. In another example, the second author has worked with parents who were not motivated to seek intervention for their unintelligible young children. When the second author explained that the children might be teased by their peers in elementary school, the parents were much more motivated to enroll their children in articulation therapy.

5. Motivation is enhanced if a clinician is concerned more about the ongoing implementation of the process than about the goals alone.

6. Motivation often increases with shared effort and responsibility. If the establishment of goals is desired, involving the client in the decision-making process will typically facilitate motivation. However, there are exceptions to this—some individuals from linguistically and culturally diverse backgrounds who come from authoritarian, rather than democratic, cultures will expect specific advice, suggestions, and directions to come from the interviewer or counselor.

7. If an exchange of information or the acquisition of a skill is desired, then in general the flow of influence between the parties should be reciprocal. Motivated learning is sustained best by a reciprocal flow of information and influence.

8. Motivation is affected by the frequency of contact between the parties, by tasks that are perceived as unfinished, by rewards that are acquired on an unpredictable schedule, and by information received in appropriate increments.

9. Success bequeaths success! Success in incremental
   small steps along the way facilitates long-range success
   toward larger, overall goals.

This list, although by no means all-inclusive, provides suggestions that relate to motivation in interviewing, counseling, and
other clinical activities.

Rapport

No interviewer or counselor gets very far without
establishing rapport with clients. Establishing
rapport is a process of creating and maintaining
trust, confidence, and goodwill between the parties throughout interviewing or counseling sessions. The development of rapport is a process,
not an isolated event. It should be of concern at
all times during clinical interactions.

Rapport
*Trust, confidence, and goodwill shared by
the parties through-
out interviewing and
counseling sessions.*

Acceptance and respect are key components in establishing rapport (Okun, 2002; Stewart & Cash, 2003). The
clinician demonstrates respect by accepting the client. This
respect, however, may not necessarily be reciprocated. During
the initial contact and, indeed, throughout the helping process,
clinicians earn the respect and confidence of their clients and
families. Specific procedures for establishing rapport cannot
be offered. Rather, rapport is an ongoing process initiated and
maintained by our abilities to develop trusting, caring, accepting, and understanding relationships.

There are three ways to achieve an understanding of another person (Benjamin, 1981; Kennedy & Charles, 2001):

1. The clinician can study information about the client,
   talk to others about the client, or listen as other people
   discuss the client. This basic level of understanding is
   clearly the most distanced method of learning about the
   client, and is often the most unreliable.
2. The clinician uses his or her internal frame of reference
   to view the client's background, experiences, feelings,
   and imagination.
3. The clinician tries to adopt the client's internal frame
   of reference in an attempt to see how the client thinks,
   feels, and views the world.

The development of rapport is ultimately influenced by
the personalities of the individuals involved and by the professionals' abilities and skills. Two clinicians using the same techniques to facilitate respect and acceptance may not achieve the

same results. However, being genuinely interested in people and giving clients direct, undivided attention are two excellent ways to start on the path to rapport.

When clinicians notice that a relationship with a client is developing negatively, it is time to evaluate whether they are contributing to the problem. There are actions that have detrimental effects on the establishment of rapport. Showing too much curiosity or getting too personal will hinder the development of rapport. Showing shock or surprise at something the client says or does can also seriously undermine a relationship. If there is no apparent cause of the negativity, one way for clinicians to gain or rebuild the interviewee's confidence and trust is to continue trying to understand the reasons for the difficulties. Clinicians can demonstrate consistent support and, if necessary, provide reassurance that they do not disapprove of their client's behavior. Thus, taking in stride what may be said or done can help maintain a close, harmonious working relationship.

In summary, rapport develops throughout the course of the relationship. It encompasses the clinician's attempts to achieve cooperation and harmony with the client in their interactions. An honest and frank approach, in which interest in and sincerity toward the patient are demonstrated, will help establish a positive working relationship.

Points to Ponder #5

You are working in a public school setting and have screened a kindergartener, Benny, whom you and the school team suspect may have autism. You have heard in the teachers' lounge that his parents are "difficult and very defensive—look out!" Describe how you might establish rapport with Benny's parents during the first meeting and also discuss how you might increase their motivation to agree to a comprehensive evaluation of Benny's speech, language, cognitive, and academic skills.

▷ Concluding Comments

There are a number of prerequisites for effective interviewing. These include interviewer characteristics such as spontaneity, flexibility, and concentration, and specific facilitating conditions such as sensitivity and objectivity, good listening practices by both parties, motivation, and the development and maintenance of rapport. Each of these factors is important in the effectiveness of interviewing and counseling activities. Effective interactions do not occur accidentally. They are the result of refined clinical skills, empathy and clinical insight, cultural awareness and sensitivity, appropriate helping attitudes, and hard work.

THREE

Physical and Emotional Factors That Affect Communication

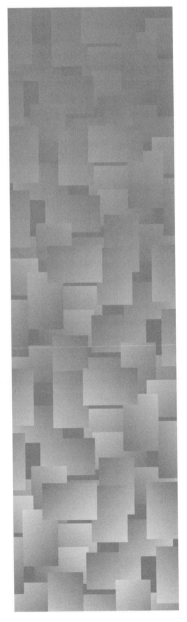

CHAPTER OUTLINE

Chapter 2 included discussion of prerequisite interviewer characteristics and other basic factors that facilitate rapport, understanding, and good communication. This chapter examines a number of other factors that affect communication between interviewing and counseling parties. These factors include conditions in the physical environment, the client's characteristics, psychological factors, and defense mechanisms. Effective clinicians are aware of these factors and are prepared to understand and deal appropriately with them in interviewing and counseling situations.

Physical Environment

The physical setting in which a clinician works influences the overall effectiveness of an interview (Kennedy & Charles, 2001). The environment should ensure privacy, appear professional, and be comfortable. Adequate time should be allowed for the interviewing or counseling session, and the environment should engender the feeling that an interviewer's time is devoted to clients or caregivers. Attention also should be paid to seating arrangements. The clinical environment in which such matters are neglected may affect clients in ways that hamper the clinician's effectiveness.

Privacy

Privacy and attention to those who are served are critical in interviewing and counseling. Disruptions should be avoided because they detract from privacy, take time, and divert focus from the client. Disruptions often engender uncomfortable and unproductive feelings of awkwardness for clinicians as well as for their clients. When a clinician interrupts a session to conduct other business—either in person or by telephone—clients may feel that they are in the way, and such feelings can influence their future participation. Meanwhile, the clinician may feel limited in what can be said to the other party in the presence of the client, and therefore, the quality of the clinician's service suffers all around. Many professionals instruct their fellow workers to prevent interruptions during patient contacts. Such procedures help ensure the concentration and continuity necessary for the clinician to accomplish what needs to be done and for clients to feel that the clinician's time is truly devoted to them.

Privacy is also affected by the physical structure and appearance of the interview environment. For ethical and practical reasons, it is important that clinicians working with communicative disorders have private offices or workplaces that have been specifically designed for comfort, confidentiality, and privacy. Deficiencies should be corrected, or at least improved. Clinicians need secure facilities where privacy can be ensured and confidentiality maintained. Public discussion of private matters is inappropriate and unethical. The need for confidentiality also applies to written materials—case files, test results, notes pertaining to clients—and the clinician's facilities should ensure the safe handling of these items.

Appearance of the Setting

Moursund (1985) comments that a client's real introduction to a clinician begins not through words but through the client's visual impressions of the setting. The location, the furniture, the color scheme, the pictures on the wall, activity levels, the sounds, and even the smells all influence a client's impressions of and feelings about a setting. First impressions affect how a client thinks not only about the facility but about the services rendered there and the capabilities of the clinician who works there. Thus, the client's first impression of the setting, whether or not it reflects accurately on the clinician, can influence how the clinician and client interact with and relate to each other.

The facilities in which professional services are provided should be clean, well lighted, as comfortable as possible, and free from distractions. The facilities should appear professional. Even in the worst possible setting, there is something that can be done to make the environment look like someone cares enough to try to provide a pleasant atmosphere. A few decorations like plants and pictures, as well as the use of soft colors, can brighten up almost any environment. These comments from McCroskey, Richmond, and Stewart (1986) are worth noting:

> *Research indicates that when placed in any ugly room, people become discontented, irritable, bored, fatigued, and generally want out of the environment. Conversely, people placed in attractive surroundings work harder, are less fatigued, communicate more, are less irritable, and do not mind remaining in the setting for a reasonable period of time.* (p. 135)

Time

The time that is available and the way that time is handled affect interviewing and counseling efforts. It is important not merely to have adequate time but also to appear to have adequate time. The appearance of adequate time is particularly important for some individuals from diverse ethnic groups (Sue & Sue, 2003). In the Hispanic culture, for example, at least a brief period of informal, friendly conversation sets the stage for subsequent discussions. "Getting down to business" immediately or appearing hurried may be considered rude to many Hispanics (Brice, 2002), and some Native Americans will not discuss issues of personal concern if they feel rushed or hurried (Roseberry-McKibbin, 2002).

The actual length of an interaction will vary according to the setting, the purposes of the meeting, and the individuals involved. Prior to any meeting, the interviewee should be provided with a general indication of the amount of time that will be involved. This general indication can be given when an appointment is made or at the beginning of the interview, or preferably on both occasions. A participant who is aware of time limits can make necessary arrangements and will come to an interview with clear expectations regarding the clinician's time.

Interviews that last longer than 45 to 60 minutes are exhausting and usually become nonproductive (Donaghy, 1990; Enelow & Swisher, 1986). If interviews are expected to last longer, it may be useful to take a break or continue the discussion on another occasion. If either party experiences fatigue, the session should be discontinued. Another meeting can be scheduled to complete any unfinished business.

The impression of having adequate time for the client is conveyed by the clinician's actions and words, as mentioned before, and even by the physical setting itself. A relatively clean work area conveys the impression that the clinician is organized and that time is to be devoted specifically to the client. Having test materials, files, or other needed items available expedites services, reduces impressions of disorganization, and minimizes the need for unnecessary delays or interruptions during the session.

One important aspect of time management is promptness (Dillard & Reilly, 1988c; Meier & Davis, 1993). Being prompt is particularly valued by people from Anglo-European backgrounds (Roseberry-McKibbin, 2002). In the Anglo-European perspective, when one party to an interview is late, the other party often develops negative feelings. Clinicians who are late for a meeting typically encounter clients who have developed some agitation. Of course, the later the clinician, the greater the agitation. Clinicians who consistently run late do themselves and their clients a disservice, and probably need to examine their ability to manage time. Because the value of time use and promptness varies across cultures, clinicians who work with individuals from cultural backgrounds where adherence to time is less important may need to clearly communicate the need for promptness and the reasons why promptness is considered important.

Seating Arrangements and Distance

Physical seating arrangements and distance between parties have received attention in the literature (Corey, 2001; Hays, 2001; Knapp & Hall, 1992; Stewart & Cash, 2003). These arrangements, as well as the more obvious physical considerations such as providing comfortable, appropriately sized chairs for the participants and minimizing any visual and auditory distractions, deserve the clinician's attention.

There is no absolute agreement among clinicians or researchers concerning which particular seating arrangement results in optimal communication. Years ago, Riley (1972) studied the effects of seating arrangements during counseling interviews and found that, although spatial arrangements did influence the clients' perceptions of the counseling relationship, no one specific arrangement emerged as being consistently superior. Rather, Riley found that clinicians' abilities, their actual behavior during interactions, and the relationships created between the parties were more important than the location of seats. This does not mean, however, that the physical arrangements of the interview should not be considered.

One of the most comfortable and productive seating arrangements occurs when the parties sit somewhat close together at 90-degree angles to each other with a small table between them (Benjamin, 1981; J. S. Taylor, 1992). This arrangement allows either participant to look directly at the other person, or to look straight ahead without appearing to avoid eye contact because it is simple and natural to look away to ponder information or determine what to say next. The use of a small table introduces an unobtrusive object that can mitigate any threat or discomfort that could result from an open space between the participants. Such arrangements have considerable merit but may not always be possible and are probably not the most critical factor in any interaction. It is, however, important for an interpreter, if one is needed, to be within view of all participants.

The distance that separates participants during interactions has been discussed by a number of authorities (e.g., Corey, 2001; Glass, 2002; Stewart & Cash, 2003). It is well accepted that smaller distances between people convey feelings of closer and more intimate communication. Greater distances are perceived as accompanying greater formality and less intimate communication (Mehrabian, 1972). Research regarding social distance shows that the *close phase* involves 4 to 7 feet of space between interlocutors; this is the distance of transacting impersonal business. The *far phase* of social distance involves 7 to 12 feet of space between interlocutors, and is considered appropriate for more formal business or social relations (Fast, 2002). Stewart and Cash (2003) state that for interviewing situations, a space of 2 to 4 feet is appropriate. Space that is closer than 2 feet or wider than 4 feet can inhibit effective communication. An ideal distance is often related to participants' genders, ages, and cultural backgrounds (see Roseberry-McKibbin, 2002; Stewart & Cash, 2003; Sue & Sue, 2003). Clinicians should choose the amount of space that is appropriate to the situation and the parties involved.

The following are some general observations concerning distance:

Close phase
Interaction in which interlocutors are 4 to 7 feet apart.

Far phase
Interaction in which interlocutors are 7 to 12 feet apart.

- Women tend to use closer distances than men.
- Between 4 and 8 years of age, children adopt adult space norms. Prior to that time, spatial requirements vary considerably among children.
- People who know each other utilize less space than people who are beginning a relationship.
- Less distance is typically seen when participants relate well to each other.
- Distances are related in general to culture. For example, people of Hispanic, Italian, Latin American, Jewish, Middle Eastern, and Puerto Rican heritages tend to employ shorter distances between parties when talking. Conversely, persons of European American, Chinese, German, and Japanese backgrounds tend to be more comfortable communicating from greater distances (Roseberry-McKibbin, 2002; Sharifzadeh, 1998).
- People with a high degree of status and authority tend to feel comfortable relating from less distance; people with less status and authority tend to desire greater distance.

Again, these are general observations only; there are many individual exceptions. Interviewers and counselors need to position themselves as close to their patients as is comfortable and otherwise appropriate. They also need to make judgments about seating arrangements, with a view toward promoting optimal communication while minimizing discomfort.

Points to Ponder #6

You are setting up your private practice to serve children, adults, and their families. You are designing your own office space. Discuss four considerations you will keep in mind to create a space that will be optimal for working with clients and families.

Clients' Characteristics: Attitudes and Background Factors

In addition to the physical environment factors that influence interviews, participants' attitudes also must be considered. An *attitude* may be thought of as a mental position, a feeling, or an emotion toward a fact, a state, a situation, another person, or a group of people. Attitudes are influenced by cultural background and heritage, educational background, and life experiences. They are expressed in behavior, manners, beliefs, and values. Attitudes influence perceptions and, thus, communication.

Attitude
A mental position, feeling, or emotion toward a fact, a state, a situation, another person, or a group of people.

Clinicians must accept the reality of never being able to comprehend all the factors that influence a client's attitudes. While acceptance involves a positive and active understanding of the client's feelings, it is important to recognize that some individuals have negative attitudes like prejudice, anger, and resentment. The clinician may need to accept the presence of these attitudes without developing negative feelings toward the other person. Interviewers, however, do not have to condone and should not reinforce unacceptable attitudes or behaviors (Garrett, 1982).

Communication in interviews is affected by a number of variables such as age, intelligence, cultural background, previous contacts and relationships with the clinician or the setting, the presence of specific difficulties (e.g., a language barrier or an emotional disturbance), and whether an interaction is the first meeting or part of a series of interactions between the participants (Corey, 2001; Kennedy & Charles, 2001). Other influential variables are educational background, family, friends, language abilities, religious background and beliefs, socioeconomic status, and living in a rural, urban, or suburban environment (Payne, 2001).

In the following sections, several of these factors are introduced. It is beyond the scope of this book, however, to describe these factors in great detail. The conscientious clinician will realize that careful analysis of these variables may be necessary on a case-by-case basis.

Support from Family and Friends

The support or lack of support that clients receive from their friends and families can affect the provision of services. Clinicians often seek the help of family members to complete case histories, to assist directly in remediative efforts, and to help promote the generalization of newly established communicative skills—that is, to encourage the use of new skills in a variety of situations. Among many cultures, special or rehabilitative services are a "family affair"; it is a mistake to treat the individual in isolation (Brice, 2002). For example, in the Carolinian and Chamorro cultures of Micronesia, major decisions are not finalized until older family members agree (Hammer, 1994).

In some settings, a client's friends or other acquaintances may be involved in clinical efforts by providing transportation to the clinic or educational setting, providing information about the client, or assisting with specific treatment activities. At other times, a client's coworker, employer, or teacher may be at least indirectly involved by helping to adjust the client's schedule so the individual can be seen for services. Support and encouragement for these efforts of others are important. Without such help, services for the individual may not be possible.

Clients receive moral support and encouragement, in varying degrees, from their families, friends, or caregivers. The presence and quality of this support can influence what happens in the clinical setting. For example, a child who is teased by peers about being enrolled for therapeutic help may be reluctant to cooperate fully with the clinician. In general, work with clients is positively affected when family and friends support the clinician's efforts. Conversely, the clinician's efforts are negatively affected when family or friends withhold support, for example, when they refuse to acknowledge that a problem exists or do not believe help is necessary. It is, therefore, important for clinicians to be aware of the type and level of support patients are receiving from family and friends. In some instances, this awareness will be the basis for understanding unproductive attitudes and for beginning a process of modifying feelings.

Cultural Heritage

Cultural heritage is an extremely powerful factor in people's lives, being of paramount importance for many individuals and having a deep influence on their thoughts, attitudes, and actions (Sue & Sue, 2003). The effects of cultural heritage operate at both conscious and unconscious levels for all individuals. Pederson and Ivey have written extensively on multicultural communication, interviewing, and counseling, and in 1993 they noted the following:

> *Culture controls our lives. We may attend to our culturally learned assumptions or we may ignore them, but in either case, these assumptions will continue to shape our decisions. Culture is not something outside ourselves, but, rather, an internalized perspective that combines the teaching of every significant person or group we have experienced, read about, or heard about and from whom we have learned something.* (p. 1)

No culture is inherently better or worse than another, but we tend to judge individuals from other cultures in light of our own cultural patterns and values. To work effectively with people from diverse cultures, clinicians need a strong grounding in cultural relativity. Clinicians work toward more effective understanding and interactions as they gain greater knowledge about their clients' cultures, and as they learn, for example, how the various mores of a culture are likely to influence attitudes and behavior. Even if professionals do not have a full understanding or appreciation of the cultures they encounter, they are still obligated to respect their clients and any cultural differences that may be present. Valuable resources for learning more about culture and working with different cultural groups include Battle (2002), Brice (2002), Coleman (2000), Lynch and Hanson (1998), Paniagua (1998), Pederson and Ivey (1993), Roseberry-McKibbin (2002), and Sue and Sue (2003).

Religious Beliefs

Clinical work is sometimes affected by a client's religious convictions. Some years ago, R. T. McDonald (1962) cited an example of a child with a severe communication impairment whose family refused to accept clinical services because the notion of therapeutic intervention violated their religious beliefs. Another example of religious beliefs that may affect acceptance of clinical services is Taoism. As Ima and Cheng (1989) note,

> *Taoism promotes passivity, and those that practice it may display a sense of fatalism about events surrounding them, resulting in resignation and inaction. This basic principle of nonintervention may have a deleterious effect when parents are asked to approve interventions for remediation of language or learning disorders.* (pp. 7–8)

Another example is that some Jamaican immigrants practice witchcraft and would rather consult with witch doctors than traditional Western health care professionals (McEachern & Kenny, 2002).

A different example of the influence of religious beliefs, and ill feelings that can occur, may be seen when a clinician fails to recognize distinctive holidays, celebrations, days of worship, or religious terminology. Is the clinician, for example, to speak of the church, the temple, the synagogue, or the mosque?

Another effect of religious belief is illustrated by the former patient of one of the first author's colleagues. This very religious young man enrolled for clinical treatment to remedy a /w/ for /r/, which was causing him considerable embarrassment. Through clinical treatment, the /r/ was developed; however, it was this patient's belief that the sound had developed because of his intensive prayer rather than because of the services rendered—God had made the difference, not the therapist. My colleague still feels, however, that her services also had something to do with this client's improvement.

Clinicians need to recognize the central importance of religious beliefs for many people, and that clients' attitudes may be influenced by their beliefs. In some cases, the support or lack of support of fellow church members can affect clients' attitudes toward services. Clinicians should be attuned to detect the presence of such influences and be prepared to deal with them, if necessary. One clinician works with older, neurologically impaired adults who tell her, "I don't need therapy. God will heal me." This clinician says, "Yes, He can. But I think that He might use therapy as one of His tools." This statement helps her clients to be more receptive.

Education and Language Use

Education is another factor that influences communication. A client's education may have come from formal schooling, real-world experience, or a combination of schooling and experience. Typically, interviewers and counselors have to adjust to wide ranges in knowledge possessed by clients.

It can be helpful for clinicians to remind themselves of their own educational experience. Most professionals working with communicative disorders have completed at least 18 or 19 years of formal education, the last several of which included intensive graduate-level academic coursework and clinical experience. Few interviewees have such an educational base. What is very familiar to the clinician frequently is new territory to others.

In general, clients' levels of knowledge are influenced by what they have experienced in life, not by the diplomas or degrees they may hold. The knowledge of a person with a doctoral degree in advanced physics may differ dramatically from the knowledge of a person with a doctoral degree in child development. A person with little formal schooling may know considerably more about children and the development of communication than someone who holds several college degrees. Clinicians need to look beyond the client's years of schooling to assess his or her knowledge about subjects under discussion.

The words clinicians use and the details of descriptions should correspond to the client's level of knowledge. In general, the longer clients have been exposed to treatment situations, the more familiarity they have with the type of information the clinician presents. Faulty communication not only causes confusion and misunderstanding in the present, but it can affect future interactions if clients develop negative feelings toward the clinician. Words can be a clinician's best allies, or they can make the clinician appear condescending, insensitive, uncommunicative, uncaring, pompous, or arrogant (Enelow & Swisher, 1986).

One problem in any professional field is the use of technical jargon. One dictionary defines *jargon* as noncoherent gibberish; the use of professional jargon can be just that to many people. McFarlane, Fujiki, and Brinton (1984) provided an excellent example of how clients erroneously interpret the use of jargon in communicative disorders. They commented that "to most people a *TACL* is a football maneuver, an *Arizona* is a state and a *PPVT* sounds like a childhood obscenity" (p. 9). Clinicians need to be careful in their use of acronyms, labels, and specialized terms. "Using direct, easily understood language may be the most basic step in maintaining an atmosphere that will allow all parties to make contributions, ask questions, and discuss the child's [or adult's] problem" (McFarlane et al., 1984, p. 10). Specialized terminology is useful for communicating with others working in the field or in related professions, but its use can be counterproductive for communicating with most nonprofessionals. Because there is a considerable amount of technical jargon in communicative disorders, clinicians should adjust the use of terminology according to the extent of the client's clinical experience. The patient involved in ongoing clinical treatment may understand terms like *articulation, final consonant deletion, conductive hearing loss,* or *impedance,* but it is unlikely that new patients will understand such terms.

It is also important to remember that in many countries of the world, children with disabilities fall into one of three categories: retarded, lazy, or crazy. Many multicultural families (and interpreters) have no awareness of terms such as *language disorder, phonological delay, dyslexia, attention deficit disorder,* and others. It is especially crucial to use clear, easy-to-understand terminology in these situations.

Age

Many young clinicians fear not being accepted or not being perceived as credible because of their age. A clinician's age can be a factor in interactions, particularly with members of linguistically and culturally diverse groups in which age is more respected or revered than in the general U.S. culture (Cheng, 2002; Westby & Vining, 2002). For example, Nellum-Davis, Gentry, and Hubbard-Wiley (2002) cautioned that when working with Muslims, clinicians should remember that "Elders are considered authorities. Older clients may not comply when younger clinicians, especially female clinicians, give instructions or use direct requests with imperatives. Indirect requests and suggestions are more desirable methods" (p. 468). It is also particularly important for younger clinicians to use family names or titles, rather than first names, with many older clients.

In general, working with older persons is different from working with younger people. In their book, *Interviewing and Patient Care,* Enelow and Swisher (1986) devoted an entire chapter to interviewing older adults. This chapter is highly recommended to students and professionals in all areas of health care. The following points are paraphrased from Enelow and Swisher, as well as from Haynes and Pindzola (1998):

• In our youth-oriented culture, many older clients feel discarded and useless. They resent the fact that their bodies are betraying them. Thus, it is helpful to listen to some of their memories of past achievements. If an older client has experienced a neurological insult such as a stroke, the family will often be quite anxious for the clinician to hear "what she was like before." Clinicians should patiently listen to and show appreciation for these stories and memories.

• Illness is much more common in the elderly. Although the elderly often have multiple chronic medical problems, this should not necessarily be accepted as the norm. Because these problems may be accompanied by denial, effective interviewing and the accurate taking of case histories play a crucial role in the care of the elderly.

- Remember that elderly clients grew up in a very different age. They have experienced world wars, depressions, the emergence of rapid communication and transportation systems, as well as the death of close friends and family members. They may be survivors who have been on their own for many years and are, thus, sometimes fiercely independent. This attitude can make their care difficult.

Although older persons grew up in a different era, they are also products of the here-and-now. They watch television, read advertisements, and may talk to friends about miracle cures, miracle hearing aids, and so forth. They are also subject to the myths of today's youth-oriented society, and to the notions, for example, that youth is beautiful and age unattractive. Their groundings in two different eras can make interviewing older patients especially interesting.

- The physical setting can be critical when interviewing or counseling older people. Adequate lighting is particularly important because many older patients have reduced aural and/or visual acuity. Light should clearly illuminate the interviewer's face to facilitate speechreading. Because many elderly persons have decreased aural acuity, it is especially important to speak distinctly and with sufficient loudness.

- It is important to begin sessions with older clients by first introducing yourself. Older people were raised in a time when propriety and decorum were held in great respect, and courtesy helps to set them at ease. Many older people prefer to be addressed by their surnames rather than their first names.

- Some older patients have difficulty responding to questions that pertain to their feelings or to psychological issues. They may have been raised in a social climate in which personal problems were not discussed openly—sometimes not even within one's own family. They may be hesitant to open up early in an interview; rather, they may wait until they trust the clinician.

- The time it takes to respond when asked a question or asked to perform tasks can increase with age. Many older patients are less likely to take risks and are less willing to make errors than younger patients. Hence, many older clients may think longer before answering questions.

- Many older people depend on other family members for support. The clinician should consider whether another family member should also be interviewed when seeing the older patient. If there are indications of memory problems, it is particularly important to corroborate the information presented by the patient. (Adapted from Enelow & Swisher, 1986, pp. 148–153; Haynes & Pindzola, 1998, p. 21)

Additionally, in marriages in which the husband has been the major decision maker, money manager, and head of the household, the husband's disability means that clinicians have to deal with many sensitive dynamics as the wife takes over these life responsibilities. We have worked with wives who did not drive or know how to write a check before the husband became disabled, a situation that is not uncommon among older Americans and older immigrants. Clinicians may need to refer the couple to a mental health professional if the role changes necessitated by the husband's disability seem insurmountable.

There are, thus, a number of factors for clinicians to consider when dealing with older clients. Cohen and Speken (1985) warn that, with many older adults, it is particularly important to watch for signs of fatigue. A series of several short interviews may be considerably more productive than one long interview, especially when an older adult has health concerns.

It is important to stress the fact that the preceding comments about people who are older are generalizations about tendencies and patterns that may be seen within the group, and do not necessarily apply to all individuals in that group. *Ageism,* or the imposing of one's beliefs and values on what older persons can or cannot do, or should or should not do, must be avoided. Clinicians also need to avoid discrimination on the basis of age. Discrimination can be reflected in avoidance of older people or in feelings that older people cannot be helped (Okun, 2002).

Ageism

Imposition of beliefs and values on what older persons can or cannot, or should or should not, do.

Age also can be a consideration in communication when the client is a younger person—especially an adolescent—and the clinician is considerably older (Bliss, 2002). Haynes and Pindzola (1998) suggest a number of considerations for minimizing potential age discrepancy problems with adolescents:

• Acquire an understanding of the many pressures and changes the teenager is experiencing: rapid physical growth, sexual maturation, conflicts between dependence and independence, a search for identity and life work, and intense group loyalty and identification. The empathy that flows from understanding these factors can be a powerful force in establishing a positive working relationship with adolescents.

• Understand that adolescents often have very intense desires to be like their peers. Thus, adolescents may find it extremely difficult to reveal a communicative problem, even if they want help, since the problem may suggest disability or difference. The adolescent may try to cover up the problem with a dense "it doesn't bother me" shell. Denial is often expressed, but clinicians cannot simply dismiss the client with a shrug. A straightforward approach is recommended: Acknowledge the forces that are influencing the adolescent, objectively point out the paths others have taken, and provide information about the economic and social penalties that can accrue from a communicative impairment. Try to demonstrate by demeanor and words that you care and can help.

  • Do not try to act like a teenager. Empathy is not the same as identification; do not abandon your professional role for that of a teenager. Attempting to do so will weaken your effectiveness, look ludicrous, and invite rejection.

  • Approach the adolescent with tolerance and good humor. Do not be shocked or annoyed by overstatements and superlatives. To maintain their protective armor, teenagers may resort to all sorts of strategies to confuse, defeat, or even anger the clinician. The ability to use humor in a gentle manner can be a real asset.

  • Demonstrate the competence to deal with the person and the problem at hand. At appropriate times, explain procedures, the use of specific tests and information, and what therapy will involve. Approach the adolescent as an adult, not as a child. (Adapted from Haynes & Pindzola, 1998, pp. 18–20)

Bliss (2002), Paul (2001), and English (2002) suggest additional considerations:

  • Remember to think about what specifically motivates the adolescent. For example, most adolescents desire effective discourse coherence for job interviews as well as social situations (Bliss, 2002).

  • Explain to adolescents why particular behaviors are being assessed (Paul, 2001).

  • When interviewing and counseling an adolescent, consider the ramifications of your suggestions on an adolescent's peer relationships (English, 2002). For example, when recommending the use of hearing aids, discuss possible peer reactions to the hearing aids.

Interviewing children can be a little difficult for some interviewers, particularly if they have not been around many youngsters. The following suggestions (Morrison & Anders, 2001; Shipley & Wood, 1996) are helpful to remember:

  • Most children are used to talking with adults: their caregivers, family members, babysitters, or teachers.

  • Children respond to being treated with courtesy and respect. Most youngsters like to be treated as "conversational equals."

  • Like adults, children need their "comfort zones" of space. Do not violate their space by getting too close, at least initially. Conversely, do not "put off" the child whose comfort zone is smaller than yours by reacting to the child's closeness.

  • Many children are uncomfortable being touched by strangers or those with whom they have had little previous contact.

  • Although children's vocabularies are still developing, they still know a lot about their language and world. Use vocabularies appropriate to their age and you will find that some 2- and 3-year-olds can carry on very "adult" conversations.

- Children will generally talk openly with adults who listen, suggest topics for discussion, let the children take the lead, and do not act in a judgmental manner. However, some children from linguistically or culturally diverse backgrounds (e.g., those from Asian and Native American groups) may have been trained to be silent and respectful in the presence of unfamiliar adults (Roseberry-McKibbin, 2002). These children will need to get to know the adult before really opening up.

- Children will talk rather openly if they trust the adult. Violate this trust and you may have a very nontalkative child.

- Young children often respond best to more direct, simple, and structured questions. The older the child, the more open-ended questions can be.

Age can be a factor that influences interactions. The effects of age differences are minimized, however, when clinicians are sensitive to others and to various needs at different age levels, are more concerned with matters at hand than age differences, are self-confident, and are focused on providing the most effective services possible. Chapter 8 contains additional comments about age as it applies to cross-cultural practice.

Gender

A factor in interviewees' responses may be the clinician's gender (Burgoon, 1994; Giles & Street, 1994; Hulit & Howard, 2002). It is important for clinicians to remember that there are differences in the ways males and females communicate in mainstream U.S. culture. Knowledge of these differences may help prevent misunderstandings, hurt feelings, and miscommunication that can disrupt the clinician's relationships with clients and their families. Many variables, including age, cultural background, sexual orientation, and other factors, affect the way a person communicates. Although there will frequently be exceptions, general male–female communication differences are summarized here (Burgoon, 1994; Glass, 2002; Hulit & Howard, 2002; McCroskey et al., 1986; Obler, 2001; Pachter & McGee, 2000; Tannen, 1994):

- In verbal communication, females tend to disclose more information about themselves, their families, and their friends.

- Females tend to be more outgoing, expressive, and open, whereas males are often more reserved and less verbal.

- Women are often more indirect than men, and use more "softeners" such as "I could be wrong, but …."

- Females tend to make more eye contact, smile, and nod.

- Males are less likely to cry during interviews, but are more likely to show their anger through facial expressions.

- As a rule, males tend to interrupt females much more than females interrupt males.

- Women tend to feel that they need to give the gift of listening, whereas men feel that they need to give the gift of information. As Hulit and Howard (2002) note, "Many men who feel a strong need to be self-reliant are comfortable in giving information or advice to others but are not at all comfortable about accepting advice or information" (p. 352).

- Tannen (1994, pp. 27–28) also observes that men may be very willing to give information but are reluctant to seek it. They may believe that asking for information puts them in a one-down position with the person from whom the information is sought. Women, however, tend to be quite willing to seek information and are not nearly as concerned about how others perceive them when they ask for information.

- Women tend to apologize more than men. To some men, this makes women look weak.

- Some men enjoy confrontation, but many women do not. Many men enjoy situations in which there are winners and losers, whereas women tend to want to work things out and have all parties save face and remain friends.

- In general, men use language more for competition and to inform, persuade, and impress. They use logic and reason. Women use language to establish rapport and connect with others, and tend to emphasize feelings and attitudes.

- Men tend to use more powerful language than women, and thus they are perceived as more credible (Timmerman, 2002).

If clinicians understand these gender-related communication tendencies, they will be more effective in relating to clients and family members of the opposite gender and in establishing and maintaining credibility and rapport. When a clinician meets with both the mother and father, knowledge of styles of communication can help the clinician understand the potential differences between the mother's and father's reactions.

Although the two genders exhibit different types and frequencies of communication behaviors, this does not mean that either is particularly more effective in delivering services. Shertzer and Stone (1980) reviewed a series of studies regarding the role of gender in counselor effectiveness and concluded that overall counselor effectiveness was unrelated to a clinician's gender.

As discussed in greater detail in Chapter 8, there are differences across cultures with regard to gender. For example, some Middle Eastern males might not want to be questioned by a female interviewer; they also might not allow their wives to speak alone with an interviewer. Some Middle Eastern men, particularly those from traditional Muslim families, may view themselves as the sole agents of communication between the family and the clinician (Sharifzadeh, 1998).

Points to Ponder #7

You are a 32-year-old female clinician working in a hospital setting. You have been given a new patient: an 80-year-old Laotian man who had a severe stroke and has both expressive and receptive problems. He immigrated to the United States 20 years ago, and you find out that he and his family practice Taoism. You also learn that his English is quite limited and that in Laos he only had 6 years of formal education. His daughter, born and raised in the United States, tells you somewhat apologetically that her father "would rather work with an older man." Describe how you will handle this situation.

Personality, Appearance, Attraction, and Prestige

Several other factors that can influence interviewing or counseling sessions include the participants' personalities and appearance, their attraction to each other, and their prestige (Glass, 2002; Meier, 1989; Moursund, 1993). The participants' personalities affect their ability and willingness to participate openly in interviews, particularly during initial sessions. One participant who is attracted to the other participant typically is more willing to communicate freely in an interview.

The clinician's appearance can influence a client's feelings and, subsequently, the course of an interview. Most authorities recommend that interviewers and counselors dress conservatively to convey a professional manner. Meier and Davis (1993) suggest that a counselor's attire becomes a problem when it calls attention to itself. Nose rings, tongue studs, multiple earrings, eyebrow rings, or combinations of these are not inherently wrong, but older clients and conservative, multicultural families may feel alienated if, for example, they are considering advice from a clinician who is sporting a nose ring and seven earrings. Clinicians may want to consider temporarily removing some of this jewelry when serving older or more conservative clients.

Kleinke (1986) notes that people prefer professionals to dress formally enough to maintain an image of expertise but not so formally as to appear stuffy or inapproachable. Kleinke also notes that interviewers come across as more competent when their clothing is in style rather than out of date.

An interview can be influenced by the perception of prestige of the interviewer or the interviewee. Interviewees often approach an interaction with confidence and high expectations when the interviewer is a respected authority. Such pre-interview confidence may be lacking in the absence of such prestige. Likewise, a client's prestige within a community can influence some clinicians' delivery of services. The professional may approach—consciously or unconsciously—an encounter differently when clients or their families are well known or highly respected members of the community (i.e., public officials, prominent business people, sports figures, entertainers, physicians, colleagues).

These observations are not meant to imply that clinicians should ever vary the quality of their service according to the prestige of their clients. It is important to recognize, however, that variables like socioeconomic status, ethnicity, gender, appearance and attraction, and prestige are factors that can affect a clinician's behavior and attitudes.

Psychological Factors: Emotions

Feelings and emotional states affect clinicians and clients. Experts such as Hershorn (2002) and Meier and Davis (1993) write that counselors look for the "big four" feelings: anger, sadness, fear, and joy. It is helpful to remember that clients or their loved ones are experiencing disabilities with respect to one of the most important human skills—the ability to communicate. It is natural, therefore, to expect that a considerable amount of emotion will surround these impaired abilities.

The clinician should also recognize that many individuals react first to stimuli on an emotional basis and then to actual content. The clinician may notice emotional responses in the client's verbal and nonverbal reactions to certain questions, statements, or comments. Such reactions may be obvious or quite subtle, and can include relief, joy, surprise, shock, anger, or resentment. Positive emotional reactions are typically pleasurable for everyone involved, but ambivalent or negative reactions may be much more difficult to understand and handle.

Many clinicians feel real anxiety when clients express negative emotions, so it is important to have the tools for dealing constructively with these situations (see Luterman, 2001; Roseberry-McKibbin & Hegde, 2006; Shames, 2000). Besides fear of the immediate situation and for the future, some of the more common emotions seen in interviewing and counseling situations are disappointment, guilt, anger, and anxiety.

Disappointment

Disappointment is a natural reaction when the reality of a situation does not correspond with hopes or anticipations. Clinicians can experience disappointment when information is not accepted in the way that they think it should be. Interviewees can experience disappointment, for example, when the presence of a disorder is confirmed or when a poor prognosis is presented. The disappointment may be general in nature or a specific reaction to events. From whatever source, feelings of disappointment are natural human reactions. Clinicians need to be prepared to accept that disappointment occurs and to help disappointed clients appreciate the reality and any positive aspects of their situations.

Guilt

The emotion of guilt is often closely related to the emotions of anxiety and shame (Kübler-Ross & Kessler, 2000). Feelings of guilt may be expressed during initial interviews or they may not emerge until later in a relationship. Sometimes clinicians recognize these guilty feelings only as time passes and after repeated interactions with clients.

Guilt often occurs when clients feel they have "sinned," or that they created a problem because of something they did or something they failed to do, or because they did something that now appears to have been wrong (Rossetti, 2001). Sometimes speech–language pathologists and audiologists engender these feelings in clients. Consider, for example, how parents might react to these commonly asked questions: "Where else has your child been seen? Has your child seen a physician recently? What have you done to try to help? When did you first notice the problem?" Other questions that may be necessary can also engender guilt: "Did you use any alcohol or drugs during the pregnancy? Why did you discontinue therapy? Why did you...?"

Feelings of guilt or feelings of negligence can sometimes be intensified when clinicians suggest that early treatment would have been useful, that the problem could have been detected earlier, or that what was done for the client may not have been the most effective thing to do. The second author's son, an intelligent and verbal 6-year-old in the fall semester of his kindergarten year, was diagnosed by an occupational therapist as being in the first percentile for fine motor skills. He had a great deal of difficulty with writing, and would cry about it in the evenings. The second author struggled with feelings of guilt for not having "done something" sooner so that this situation could have been avoided. She had noticed that her son's fine motor skills were not as developed as those of his peers when he was 4 years old. She sought the opinions of experts such as occupational therapists and resource specialists. She was told that because her son was left handed, she needed to relax and not worry; he would catch up in time. One lesson the second author learned from this is that parents, especially mothers, feel a great deal of guilt and blame themselves when their children have problems.

In cases such as these and others, clinicians may need to provide reassurance to counter feelings of guilt. Clinicians should remain objective, listen to the feelings of the client or family members, correct any misperceptions or inaccurate information they may have received, and generally help these persons work through their guilty feelings. Guilt needs to be processed (Kübler-Ross & Kessler, 2000). Guilt does not typically disappear after the first reassurance that "it is not your fault" or "it's okay." Rather, the reduction of guilty feelings takes time and sometimes requires a more complete understanding of the situation. One of the major tasks of clinicians who encounter clients with guilt is to help these individuals gain better perspectives on their situations so they can move forward with the tasks at hand (Moore-Brown & Montgomery, 2001).

It is inappropriate to provide false assurances in an attempt to modify feelings of guilt. There are times when clinicians cannot say, "It's okay." The task in such instances is to help people move from counterproductive guilt to constructive feelings and activities—that is, feelings and activities that will assist patients in the here-and-now and with the future. Involving people with guilt in treatment activities can be helpful because the concern becomes focused on the present (Zebrowsi & Schum, 1993). Individuals experiencing guilt often benefit when they are made to feel part of the solution rather than part of the problem (Dodge, 2000).

Guilt also can be related to cultural beliefs. For example, within some groups in the Filipino culture, there is the belief that a child with a disability is due to the parents' or ancestors' sins (Chan, 1998b). Among some Middle Easterners, the mother may be held responsible and feel guilty if a child is born with a disability, whereas the father feels shame and a sense of personal defeat. Such feelings can be associated with denial, isolation, overprotection, or even abandonment of the child (Sharifzadeh, 1998). Among some Samoans, children are viewed as gifts from God; thus, a child with a disability can be interpreted as God's displeasure with the family (Mokuau & Tauili'ili, 1998).

Anger

Anger can have a number of sources. Hackney and Cormier (1994) write that

> *different kinds of stimuli often elicit anger. One such stimulus is **frustration.** Others are **threat** and **fear.** Conditions such as competition, jealousy, and thwarted aspirations can become threats that elicit angry responses. Anger often represents negative feelings about oneself and/or others. Many times, fear is concealed by an outburst of anger. In such cases the anger becomes a defensive reaction because the person does not feel safe enough to express fear. Anger is also a cover-up for hurt. Beneath strong aggressive outbursts are often deep feelings of vulnerability and pain. ... Remember that anger covers a broad group of feelings and can be expressed in many ways.* (p. 96)

Thus, the emotion of anger is often a mechanism employed, consciously or unconsciously, for self-protection (Hershorn, 2002). Hartbauer (1978) feels that expressions of anger may occur for several reasons: The client may not understand the situation, the alternatives, or the need for treatment, or may be unhappy about being unable to resolve the problems.

When a client's anger is directed at clinicians, they need to consider what aspects of their own behaviors may be creating or engendering the problem. Lateness, using language that is too technical, appearing insensitive, failing to truly understand what the client is saying—all these are among possible sources or contributors to a client's anger. At other times, of course, anger that is directed toward clinicians actually has little to do with them. Rather, the clinicians may simply be the most available people on whom to vent feelings.

Finally, be aware that anger may not be demonstrated by individuals from certain cultural groups, even when those individuals are quite angry. For example, many Asians will not express their anger out of respect for the other person (Chan,

1998a; Roseberry-McKibbin, 1997). The second author remembers a Filipino father who left an IEP meeting, angry at her suggestion that his daughter would not benefit from continued speech therapy unless she underwent additional surgery to address her velopharyngeal incompetence. The father did not allow his daughter to come to therapy again after that meeting even though he left smiling and thanking the second author for her time.

Individuals from the Chamorro and Carolinian cultures tend to avoid conflict and refrain from expressing anger, particularly when interacting with persons who have more perceived authority (Hammer, 1994). Clinicians need to exercise care in assuming that, just because someone does not express anger, such a feeling is not present.

Anxiety

There are many sources of anxiety that can accompany a communicative difficulty. A client may feel anxious because of uncertainties about the present and future course of the difficulty and about the social, vocational, or educational consequences. For example, Carmen and Uram (2002) state that hearing loss promotes anxiety because the hearing loss never goes away, and almost always gets worse.

Other sources of anxiety may be the clinician's personality, the methods or attitudes conveyed by the clinician, questions about the outcome of the clinician's efforts, or doubts whether the clinician will be able to handle the client's problems (Hartbauer, 1978). Feelings of anxiety are often present during initial encounters because people are unsure exactly what to expect. As the discussion of orientation sessions in Chapter 4 indicates, feelings of anxiety during initial encounters can be reduced by the provision of appropriate presession information.

Clinicians should be able to detect many instances of anxiety. These feelings may be seen in clients' direct verbalizations or in their hesitancy, passivity, anger, or verbally aggressive behavior. Often, the open expression of anxiety should be encouraged because it allows clinicians to deal with areas of concern, which in turn helps provide clients with more objective, accurate information or with appropriate assurances.

Clients from linguistically or culturally diverse backgrounds may have considerable anxiety coming into interview situations, particularly if there is a language barrier or if a large group of professionals is present. It is often wise to keep groups of professionals rather small and to provide an interpreter, if necessary (Langdon & Cheng, 2002; Roseberry-McKibbin, 2002).

Defensive Reactions and Defense Mechanisms

We all need to defend ourselves, to maintain a sense of self-esteem while securing time to begin resolving problems that would otherwise be too overwhelming; therefore, some degree of defensive behavior is often merited and useful (Shipley & Wood, 1996). However, defensive behavior can have a negative effect if it is used excessively, or when it conceals problems that truly need attention and resolution. Defensive behavior also can preclude successful communication, understanding, and cooperation. People exhibit various degrees of defensive behavior, and interactions are affected differently by mild defensiveness versus very adamant defensive reactions.

Defensive feelings can be engendered when clients feel misunderstood, or if they become frustrated when conflicting opinions arise about whether someone has a problem or about the frequency or type of treatment needed. Defensiveness can result in aggressive behavior, extreme passivity, chronic disagreement with others, self-perceptions of omniscience or omnipotence, or the tendency to intellectualize.

Sigmund Freud's work with ego protection led to the description of a number of defense mechanisms: denial, intellectualization, reaction formation, suppression, repression, rationalization, displacement, and projection. Clinicians are apt to encounter these defense mechanisms (Hutchinson, 1979; Rollin, 2000), and it should be noted that they are frequently, although not always, employed unconsciously. The following sections describe reaction formation, suppression, repression, rationalization, displacement, and projection. Chapter 9 addresses denial and intellectualization. For additional information on defense mechanisms, refer to Anna Freud (1967) or any of a number of textbooks in psychology.

Reaction Formation

Reaction formation
A defense mechanism in which individuals develop attitudes or behaviors that are opposed to their real feelings.

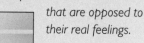

A reaction formation may occur when the emotions people experience are so shocking or contrary to their previous thoughts that the new feelings are considered unacceptable and inappropriate. In reaction formation, individuals develop positive attitudes that are opposed to their new, shocking, real feelings about a subject. They then adhere only to these more positive and "acceptable" thoughts. External reactions and activities then do not directly reflect or express the person's true feelings. For example, the mother who has a very deep resentment toward her child with disabilities may actually immerse herself in exuberant involvement with her child, with charity organizations dealing with the child's disorder, and so forth. Reaction formation is also exhibited by some individuals who fight against all odds in the hope that their loved one will be the one-in-a-million who overcomes a difficulty.

These examples illustrate how the activities subsequent to a reaction formation can be positive while the real questions about how the individual truly feels remain unresolved. The positive appearance of the reaction formation masks the real problem that still exists. As Clark (1994b) notes,

> *Although reaction formation can affect management negatively, it can also have a positive influence. In avoiding the initial urge to deny the diagnosis, some parents may become strong advocates for services to the hearing impaired or may become hearing providers themselves (Mitchell, 1988). However, it is certainly within the [speech–language pathologist's] purview to help direct parents appropriately so that during this period other family responsibilities do not fall along the wayside.* (p. 34)

The severity of reaction formations vary and, although some positive activities may occur subsequent to a reaction formation, there is still an underlying problem that needs resolution: how the individual really feels about the "unacceptable" subject. Hutchinson (1979) points out that reaction formation is difficult for untrained persons to deal with, and that referral for professional counseling is often indicated for people exhibiting this defense mechanism.

Suppression

Suppression is somewhat similar to self-control. It is a reaction in which individuals keep their impulses, wishes, and desires under control and out of view of others. Their true feelings may be held inside and even denied publicly. In some instances, this can be counterproductive for the person as well as for the clinician's treatment efforts.

Clinicians need to understand that, in accordance with the customs of some cultures, individuals tend not to express personal or negative feelings as it is considered rude or otherwise inappropriate to share their real feelings with someone "in authority." Thus, particularly with individuals from linguistically and culturally diverse backgrounds, care is necessary before presuming that true suppression is being exhibited.

Suppression
A defense mechanism in which individuals keep their impulses, wishes, and desires under control and hidden from others.

Repression

Repression has been described as being one step beyond suppression (Clarke, 1968). Rather than controlling or suppressing feelings, the person actually represses feelings and henceforth is unable to recognize them. For this reason, a problem does not exist at a conscious level and there is, therefore, little or no reason for concern or action.

Repression presents exasperating treatment difficulties for clinicians who work, for example, with the severe stutterer who has repressed any recognition of the stuttering, or the parent who has repressed awareness (and thereby any possible acceptance) of a nonverbal 5-year-old's communication problem, or a hearing-impaired person who insists that his hearing is "clear as a bell." After all, for the person who represses, the problem does not exist.

Repression

A defense mechanism in which individuals suppress their impulses, wishes, and desires to such an extent that they no longer consciously recognize their true feelings.

Rationalization

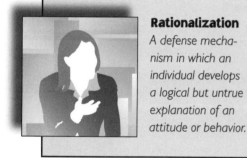

Rationalization

A defense mechanism in which an individual develops a logical but untrue explanation of an attitude or behavior.

Rationalization involves a logical but untrue explanation of an attitude or behavior that allows an individual to explain why an expectation has not occurred (Shipley & Wood, 1996). Rationalization helps an individual maintain a positive opinion of self while attempting to justify certain actions or failures. From time to time, most people have used rationalizations to explain away shortcomings or failures. A problem emerges, however, with the frequent, excessive, or counterproductive use of rationalization.

A clinician may encounter rationalization as a form of resistance to treatment. The patient may have been "too busy" to see the physician for the medical clearance that would have allowed the clinician to dispense the hearing aid or to begin voice therapy. There also may be a general tendency to rationalize the history of a problem. Rather than getting caught up in rationalizations about what did not get done, clinicians should focus on the positive actions that need to be accomplished from this point.

Displacement

Displacement occurs when an individual transfers hostile feelings from the person or problem that caused the hostile feelings onto a "safe" per-

Displacement

A defense mechanism in which an individual transfers hostile feelings from the person or problem that caused the hostile feelings onto another person or object.

son or object. When doors get slammed, when someone acts aggressively toward innocent family pets, when children throw blocks or books off the table, when adults pick fights with their spouses—these actions frequently are examples of displaced emotion. The persons or events that triggered the anger or hostility lie elsewhere.

Displacement satisfies an immediate need to vent anger in a safer manner than would be possible by confronting the actual source of irritation. Displacement allows the individual to avoid addressing the real source of hostile feelings, but displacement can cause new problems because it creates scapegoats.

Points to Ponder #8

You are working in a clinic that specializes in serving hearing-impaired children. An 18-year-old mother brings her 3-year-old daughter, Brianna, to you. Brianna has a severe bilateral sensorineural hearing loss, and her mother is afraid that Brianna will "not fit in" in kindergarten in 2 years. The mother repeatedly says that if she had taken better care of herself during her pregnancy, Brianna might have been normal. The mother is very angry that her friends are partying, attending college, and enjoying life while she struggles with a low-paying job and a daughter with a disability. Most of the time, Brianna's mother is controlled, but occasionally she erupts in anger and is quite unpleasant. Discuss four pointers that you will implement in order to work effectively in this situation.

Projection

Projection involves a distortion of reality that goes beyond displacement. The individual who employs this defense mechanism shifts responsibility to someone else. Feelings or motives that belong to the individual are attributed to another person

Projection
A defense mechanism in which an individual attributes his or her feelings or motives to another person.

(Ellis, 2001). Projections can be used to transfer blame, to excuse failures, or to minimize personality problems or weaknesses.

A person does not need to do anything to become the target of a projection. A physician can be blamed for failing to prevent or identify a problem, when in reality the patient should have had a checkup earlier. A teacher can be faulted for being a "bad teacher who doesn't like me," when in reality the student did not study for the test. A speech–language pathologist can be condemned for "not knowing what she's doing," when in reality the patient resisted therapy. The audiologist can be blamed because the hearing aid does not restore normal hearing. The spouse or family member can be faulted, for whatever reason. Although there may be truth in some of these complaints on occasion, clients who employ projection are distorting reality in attempting to relocate the blame for their own failures or frustrations.

Clinicians must realize that they may be targets of such projections (Hutchinson, 1979; Schum, 1986; Shipley & Wood, 1996). If good service has been rendered, a patient's complaints may relate more to the need for ego protection than to something the clinician may or may not have done.

Emerick's Advice for Clinicians

Lon Emerick has contributed to a number of fine resources dealing with interviewing, diagnosis, stuttering, and the clinical process for students and professionals working with communicative disorders. A considerable portion of the information in this chapter has been adapted from materials found in several of Emerick's works (Emerick, 1969; Emerick & Hatten, 1979; Haynes & Pindzola, 1998).

Throughout this text, the point has been emphasized that both parties in the interview affect an interaction. Emerick (1969) indicates that a clinician, particularly a beginning clinician, may bring certain feelings or attitudes to an encounter that influence the behavior of both parties. He describes several hang-ups sometimes found with beginning clinicians. One is a fear of not being accepted as a professional because of age. Another is the fear of encountering a defensive parent who will not accept what the beginning clinician is conveying. The clinician also may fear being questioned by parents. Needless to say, these fears apply to more than just working with parents.

Emerick (1969) also reminds us that many clinicians can be too judgmental when viewing behaviors. Based on his thoughts regarding working with parents, it is useful to consider the following points:

- Every person has his or her unique needs and concerns. Parents, caregivers, spouses, and other concerned persons are more than just vehicles for gaining information or help with clinical treatment.
- Family members—whether children, significant others, parents, or other relatives—can be difficult to cope with, and the presence of a communicative disorder can accentuate any problems that may already exist.
- All observations must be carefully interpreted. Clinicians should avoid overinterpreting or prematurely interpreting their observations or impressions.
- People typically want what is best for their children, parents, relatives, and friends. They take whatever actions make sense to them personally, even if these actions do not make sense to the clinician. The clinician should assess behavior not only in terms of what was done but also in terms of why.
- Actions speak louder than words. When clinicians can demonstrate that their efforts produce changes in their clients' communicative abilities, their credibility is enhanced and other people will be more willing to cooperate with them. Nothing beats effectiveness for engendering greater cooperation.

Concluding Comments

This chapter describes a number of factors that influence the quality of communication in interview situations. Some of these factors, such as the immediate physical environment, are controlled directly by the interviewer. Other factors have to do more with what clients bring to the interview. Any of these factors can influence a clinician's overall effectiveness in delivering services. It is important for the clinician to monitor the effects of these factors—to determine, for example, when clients' or caregivers' attitudes or feelings are counterproductive to communicative improvement—and to make appropriate adjustments or suggestions for change.

Clinicians will need to work directly with some emotion-related difficulties, particularly as they affect a communicative disorder and its treatment. With some of the defense mechanisms described in this chapter, and some other concerns discussed in Chapter 8, there will be times when clinicians need to make referrals to other professionals. The competent clinician is willing and able to make such referrals, when necessary. Guidelines and suggestions for making referrals are in Chapter 12.

FOUR

Skills and Techniques for Interviewing and Counseling

CHAPTER OUTLINE

Effective interviewers and counselors have many skills and techniques in their repertoire that affect communication. Among these tools are several distinct kinds of questions, specific verbal and nonverbal behaviors, and a number of other clinical techniques that facilitate communication. Skilled clinicians are conscious of these tools and have learned to employ them purposefully. This chapter describes a number of these tools. But, before that discussion, general suggestions for promoting appropriate interactions are presented.

General Suggestions

There are a number of widely recognized guidelines for use in interviewing and counseling. The following suggestions are based on Bingham, Moore, and Gustad (1959), Dodge (2000), English (2002), Okun (2002), Roseberry-McKibbin (2002), and Sue and Sue (2003):

- Decide before the initial interview what needs to be accomplished. Clinicians should have a good idea of what needs to be done and what types of information need to be obtained or shared. Beginning interviewers should make a brief list of the major areas to be discussed.
- Learn as much as possible about the interviewee, both before and during the interview. If the client is from a linguistically or culturally diverse background, learn about that culture. It can be helpful to interview members of that cultural community.
- Make sure the client understands in advance when the appointment involves an interview. Give the client a "thumbnail sketch" of the interview discussion topics.
- Make clear the approximate amount of time allotted for the interviewing or counseling session. If a client comes from a culture with a more relaxed view of time, the length of the interview may need to be addressed beforehand.
- Allow sufficient time for interactions, including presession preparation, the interview itself (especially if an interpreter is part of the interaction), and the collection of thoughts and any necessary paperwork afterward. Interviewing and counseling sessions are less effective when conducted on tight, counting-the-minutes schedules, or when clinicians are running behind schedule.
- Provide a private setting that maintains confidentiality.
- Learn to understand the other person's point of view. It is helpful to consider how you would react to the questions asked or the information presented.
- Develop understanding and empathy. Establish a relationship in which confidence and trust can develop.

- Understand your own personality, beliefs, and prejudices so they do not inappropriately affect interactions with others.

- Establish an atmosphere that is as pleasant and relaxed as possible. It is difficult for people to communicate effectively in unpleasant or tense situations. Clinicians are responsible for helping clients and families feel at ease and for engendering their willingness to share information and concerns.

- Help interviewees feel free to talk, and interfere as little as possible. Remember: the more you talk, the less the interviewee talks.

- Listen carefully. Good attending skills are critical to true understanding.

- Be aware of the effects of fatigue on both interviewers or interviewees. Fatigue considerably reduces communication. When fatigue occurs, participants should take a break or schedule another conference. Either of these options is better than trying to plod through an interview or cutting an interaction short at the risk of miscommunicating, failing to learn information, or failing to provide information.

- Avoid wasting time on unimportant matters, and avoid working at too slow a pace. Many interviewees react negatively to these problems. However, remember that individuals from linguistically and culturally diverse backgrounds may expect a brief period of informal chitchat before "getting down to business."

- Maintain control of the interview. Cover the points that must be addressed. Conversation should not be allowed to wander to irrelevant topics because this consumes time and, in some instances, causes interviewees to question whether clinicians really know what they are doing.

Students sometimes ask, "Yes, but what exactly do you *say* to get someone back on topic?" The clinician can start off with "Along those lines..." or "Speaking of that..." or "That brings up a good point" or "That makes me think of something you said earlier about [topic of interest]." Some of these may sound a bit phony, but they are courteous and the person is usually unaware of the shift back to the main topic.

- Use interviews discriminately. There is no need for an interview if the information can be effectively obtained or provided by other means, saving everyone's time and trouble. If the client and clinician use electronic mail (e-mail), this can be a tremendous convenience and time-saver. If clinicians find themselves getting "spammed" or inundated with e-mail from a client, however, an excellent way to stop this behavior is to simply not answer for a few days. The more prompt the clinician's answer, the more likely the person is to send another e-mail right back.

- Make sure the topics addressed in an interview are truly important and that the issues are understood by interviewees. Resentment can be a real problem when interviewees question why certain information is needed. Information may be perceived as highly personal, and the reasons this information requires discussion may need to be addressed. For example, if the interviewer asks about a child's birth history, the interviewer can explain that this information will help in the assessment and intervention process.

• Use interviews to confirm as well as gain information. Information that has been provided in a case history or by someone else may need to be confirmed by observation or discussion. It is helpful to say something like "I understand from the case history that Matthew has a history of middle ear infections. Can you tell me more about that?"

• Use interviews to gain subjective as well as objective information. Interviewees' opinions, attitudes, and beliefs are likely to have important influences on areas of discussion and overall interaction patterns.

• Know your field. Clients seek the clinician's help and expect the clinician to know the answers to concerns and questions. However, if there is something the clinician does not know, it is far better to say "I don't know" than to provide inaccurate information. It is even better to say, "I don't know, but I will find out and get back to you." Be sure to honor this commitment.

Clients may bring in information they have obtained from the Internet. It is impossible for any clinician to keep updated on all Web sites. In these cases, it is fine to say "I haven't accessed that particular Web site. Would you give me the exact address so that I can check it out?"

• Ask clear questions. Questions that are difficult to understand rarely elicit the desired information. Use terms that interviewees have a reasonable chance of understanding. For example, if you ask parents for their impressions of a child's oral mobility or use of interrogatives, they may respond, "Huh?"

• Ask one question at a time. A question with several parts often causes confusion that results in important points going unaddressed. Multiple-part questions also are very difficult for interpreters.

• Give respondents adequate opportunities to answer your questions. Some clients need more time than others to respond. When planning an interview, allow ample time for each topic to be addressed.

• Let interviewees tell their stories. Clients and caregivers often have feelings about the causes and effects of the problems. They often come prepared to share their frustrations about coping with the communication difficulties, fears about what lies ahead, hopes for securing adequate diagnosis or treatment, disappointment when problems have not been outgrown or remediated, or other fears and frustrations. It is vital that interviewees have the opportunity to share feelings. Interviewees' stories also can provide clinicians with valuable insight into attitudes that may affect treatment. Interviewers who do not provide these opportunities can be viewed, justifiably, as being insensitive and incomplete in their work.

However, sometimes the clinician runs out of time in a meeting. If this happens, especially when someone is sharing an emotional story, the clinician can say, "I am so sorry. I have another meeting in 5 minutes. I wish we had more time, because I want to hear more. Can we set up another appointment?" or "I just hate to cut this short, because I want to hear more, but there is another client in the waiting room. May I give you my card? Please call or e-mail me so that we can talk further." In this way, the clinician stays on schedule and clients do not (usually) feel rejected.

• Avoid a lecturing role. Interviewees should view clinicians as knowledgeable people who are capable of helping. They should not be made to feel that they are in an inferior or subservient role.

• Be straightforward and honest. Cleverness and deceit are rarely, if ever, effective in interviews. One characteristic of European-American culture is to be somewhat "up-front" or "blunt." However, certain individuals from other cultures (e.g., Filipino and Japanese) are accustomed to less directness. Some care is needed in this area, as described in Chapter 8.

• Look for the full meaning of each answer. Skilled practitioners carefully consider the actual words interviewees use, possible meanings behind those words, and any accompanying nonverbal behaviors exhibited.

• Be alert for inconsistencies in interviewee responses and, when they occur, double-check the information in question. This double-checking must be handled skillfully and in a neutral manner, not in an obtrusive or accusatory manner. Avoid wording like, "Earlier you said ABC and now you are saying XYZ. Which is it?" Better phrasing may be "I'm confused. Earlier you said ABC, but now you are saying XYZ. Can you help me understand which of these is correct?"

• Realize that there is a difference between a fact and someone's interpretation of the fact. There are differences between observable facts, alleged facts, inferences drawn from facts, and even inferences that masquerade as facts. It is important to distinguish between these representations and to view each in its proper perspective.

• Check representations of fact against your own observations. For example, parents might state that their child does not seem concerned about a speech problem, but the clinician's direct observation of the child suggests otherwise.

• Do not assume that agreement means validity. The client, the client's family, or another group may agree, but that does not necessarily mean it is correct.

• Assume the honesty of statements, but always be hesitant to conclude that everything is actually the way it is represented. For example, clients may say things they think a clinician wants to hear out of respect for the clinician's authority. There is certainly no need to distrust people in general, but professional judgments must be made carefully and tentatively.

These are useful guidelines for interviewing and counseling efforts. Many of the points are described in greater detail in this chapter and elsewhere in the book.

Questions in an Interview

Asking questions is the primary method used to obtain information from interviewees, particularly in interviews aimed at obtaining information. The use of questions helps clinicians secure information needed, clarify patients' statements, explore various thoughts that have been expressed, motivate people to communicate freely, and direct the focus of conversations (Shipley & Wood, 1996). The wording and the sequencing of questions guide interviewees into specific areas for further discussion or greater understanding. There are a number of good reasons for asking questions; however, the appeasement of curiosity is not a valid reason. It is, therefore, important for interviewers to understand their motives and reasons for asking questions. If an interviewer does not know why a particular question should be asked, the question should be omitted. It is also important to know the limitations of questions. As Pederson and Ivey (1993) comment,

> Questions are the most frequently used—and overused— tool of interviewers and counselors. Questions can be used to encourage or discourage talking. Usually the questions are asked by the interviewer and answered by the interviewee, putting the interviewer in control of the situation. Questions have a great deal to do with power. When counselors lose control in an interview, they sometimes ask a new question as the means of recapturing control. Question-asking skills increase a counselor's ability to collect specific information, redirect the interview, or encourage the interviewee to disclose general information. (p. 131)

There is more to the art of information gathering and posing questions than might appear at first glance. There are three major types of questions: open or closed, primary or secondary, and neutral or leading questions (Stewart & Cash, 2003). Questions are

1. open or closed, depending on how they are asked and the level of response specificity required
2. primary or secondary, depending on the order in which they are presented and the level of response specificity required

3. neutral or leading, depending on whether they are framed in a way that potentially biases or influences an interviewee's response

In addition to these three ways of distinguishing between questions, interviewers also distinguish types of questions as do reporters; they may employ *who, what, when, where, how,* and *why* questions to elicit distinct kinds of information. Questions such as *is* or *was,* or *could* or *would* may also be used.

Open and Closed Questions

Open Questions

Open questions allow patients or caregivers to respond in a number of possible ways. These kinds of questions allow maximum latitude to respondents (Morrison & Anders, 2001). A response with specific types or increments of information is not required. "What brought you here today?" or "What are some of your concerns?" are examples of open questions. This type of question encourages interviewees to respond with information of particular interest to them, rather than with specifically identified areas of inquiry. Open questions require respondents to be actively involved in the interview process and to organize and structure their thoughts before responding. An interviewer controls the general subject area, but the range of possible responses rests with the interviewee; thus, the client provides much of the direction for the question.

Open questions
Questions that have multiple possible responses.

Because the object is to draw a client out, care should be taken to frame open questions so they cannot be answered with a simple "yes" or "no" or with only a short response. Frequently, the interviewer will begin an open question with a phrase like "Tell me about…" or "What are…," as in the following examples:

- "Tell me about Felicia's speech."

- "What are some of your concerns?"

- "Can you describe how your daughter's friends react to her speech?"

These examples illustrate how the general frame of reference (Felicia's speech; the interviewee's concerns) is provided by the interviewer. The interviewee, however, may respond in a number of possible directions (Felicia's sound errors, correctly produced sounds, intelligibility, frustrations about speech, communicating with others, effects on academics, parental frustrations, effects of treatment, etc.).

Another open-ended method of securing information is to repeat a respondent's key words:

CLIENT: I'm concerned about problems with the tongue.
CLINICIAN: The tongue?

CLIENT: I think my son may have a speech problem.
CLINICIAN: A speech problem? Tell me about it.

CLIENT: I think my hearing has gone downhill.
CLINICIAN: Downhill?

Several advantages of open questions include the following (Morrison & Anders, 2001; Stewart & Cash, 2003):

- Encouraging the party being interviewed to talk
- Communicating interest in the other party
- Encouraging clients in a nonthreatening manner by providing more than one response option
- Learning the issues and concerns that patients feel are particularly important
- Allowing the other party to provide information that might otherwise not have occurred to the interviewer
- Helping reveal clients' knowledge or understanding about certain matters
- Revealing topics about which interviewees or counselees have feelings and questions
- Revealing respondents' frames of references, prejudices, and stereotypical attitudes

A further advantage of open questions is that they tend to elicit responses that are more accurate and reliable than many responses to closed questions (Enelow & Swisher, 1986). Open questions are also useful in helping many individuals from linguistically and culturally diverse backgrounds express themselves more freely. For example, Lian and Abdullah (2001) comment that when working with Malaysians, "presenting direct questions to gather personal information may be interpreted as intrusive and disrespectful. A clinician should be prepared to explain the importance of obtaining relevant information and should use indirect open-ended questions to gather information" (p. 7).

Open questions, however, do have some disadvantages. Using them can be very time-consuming. They may elicit overly long and unorganized answers that require follow-up questions. Respondents may end up addressing information and feelings that are not particularly pertinent, they may fail to provide important information because they think it is incidental or unimportant, or they may get sidetracked on another topic. Another potential disadvantage is that the use of open questions requires a considerable degree of skill. Inexperienced interviewers often find it difficult to control conversational directions with open questions (Shipley & Wood, 1996; Stewart & Cash, 2003). Despite these potential difficulties, however, skillfully asked open questions help interviewers gain important information and insight that is simply not possible when interviewers rely too much on closed questions.

Closed Questions

Closed questions are much more highly structured than open questions because they focus or limit an interviewee's responses. They are typically used to obtain specific increments of information. These types of questions are particularly helpful when interviewers need to check their impressions against those of their interviewees. There are three basic levels of closed questions: moderately closed questions, highly closed questions, and bipolar questions (Stewart & Cash, 2003).

Closed questions
Questions for which responses are limited.

- *Moderately closed questions* require clients to provide specific pieces of information (e.g., "Have you had ear infections?" "How many ear infections have you had?" "Have you ever considered speech therapy?" "How frequently does your child stutter?" "Would you like a referral for _____?").
- *Highly closed questions* allow interviewees to choose among alternative answers (e.g., "Did you have 1, 2, or 3 ear infections last winter?" "Does your child stutter occasionally, frequently, or all the time?" "Would you like a morning, afternoon, or early evening appointment?").
- *Bipolar questions* offer only two response choices (e.g., "Do you have ear infections?" "Does your child stutter?" "Did you do your homework?" "Did you contact the doctor?" "Would you like to schedule an appointment?").

Responses to these different types of closed questions differ. Moderately closed questions offer respondents the most response options, followed by highly closed questions. Responses to bipolar questions are the most restrictive, resulting in responses such as *yes* or *no, like* or *dislike, approve* or *disapprove, agree* or *disagree,* and so forth. Knowing that each question type produces a different type of response, interviewers should vary their use of closed questions according to the type of information needed.

Closed questions have a number of advantages. They are relatively easy to control and thus easy for beginning interviewers to use. They tend to result in short answers that are easy to analyze; thus, a large number of closed questions can be asked in a short period of time. Further, closed questions are generally easy for interviewees to answer because they do not require detailed explanations (Stewart & Cash, 2003). Closed questions can also be useful to "rein in" verbose interviewees (Morrison & Anders, 2001).

Relying on too many closed questions, however, can be detrimental to a relationship or can result in clinicians not understanding some of an interviewee's major areas of concern or interest. It is not uncommon for student clinicians to have difficulties establishing rapport during initial interviews, at least in part because of insufficient knowledge of or experience with closed questions. Clients can also feel that clinicians are performing a "robot-like" interview in which a question is asked and the answer is given, another question is asked and this answer is given, and so forth.

Open and closed questions each have their own strengths and weaknesses in interviewing. Open questions tend to produce longer responses that contain a good deal of general information, whereas closed questions tend to produce shorter responses containing specific pieces of information (Shipley & Wood, 1996). Both types of information are useful in working with communication disorders, and a clinician's ability to employ both types of questions skillfully is important for effective interviewing.

Primary questions
Questions that introduce new topics or new areas within a topic.

Secondary questions
Follow-up questions that elicit more detailed pieces of information.

Primary and Secondary Questions

Primary questions introduce new topics or new areas within a topic. The introduction of a primary question does not require any preceding contextual cues. For example, an interviewer might ask, "Do you think your daughter might have a hearing loss?" When the interviewee responds to the primary question, the clinician may then need to follow up with one or more secondary questions to elicit more specific or detailed information. The interviewer might ask, "What leads you to feel that way?" or "How long have you noticed this?" or "Are there times she seems to be missing what you're saying?" and so forth. Thus, secondary questions are follow-up questions that help elicit detailed pieces of information.

Neutral and Leading Questions

Questions can be distinguished as neutral or leading, depending on whether they are framed in a way that could influence an interviewee's response (Donaghy, 1990). Neutral questions are unbiased, allowing respondents to choose their answers without being unduly influenced by the interviewer. Questions or statements such as "How do you feel about _____?" or "Tell me about _____" are, in general, unbiased because they allow clients to respond within their own frames of reference. Conversely, leading questions tend to encourage specific responses. For example, an interviewer might ask, "Based on our conversation, do you see why I am suggesting this hearing aid?" or "Based on these findings, when would you like to enroll for therapy?"

> **neutral questions**
> *Questions that are not intended to influence the interviewee's response.*
>
> **Leading questions**
> *Questions that encourage specific responses.*

There are times when a leading question may be appropriate, for example, when the clinician truly feels that the individual should enroll for services, complete the home activities suggested, or follow through with a referral. However, there are other times a question with bias is inappropriate, such as when trying to collect information for a case history or understand the patient's real feelings. Leading questions make honesty difficult when they lead interviewees to respond in ways that differ from their true feelings.

Points to Ponder #9

You have taken a new job in a skilled nursing facility in which some residents have language and cognitive problems related to Alzheimer's dementia. You need to interview the patients and their families so that you have a firm foundation for assessment and treatment of those patients. Describe four factors that will help these interviews to be optimally effective.

Reporters' Questions

Many interviewers and counselors also find it useful to distinguish between questions in the manner used by journalists. The well-known *wh* questions—*who, what, when, where, how,* and *why*—as well as *is* or *was, could,* and *should* all produce different types of responses. Ivey (1994) offers the following comments:

Reporters' questions
Questions including the words who, what, when, where, how, why, is, was, could, *and* should.

- ***Who*** *is the client? What is the client's personal background? Who else may be involved?*
- ***What*** *is the client's problem? What is happening? What are the specific details of the situation?*
- ***When*** *does the problem occur? When did it begin? What immediately preceded the occurrence of the problem?*
- ***Where*** *does the problem occur? In what environments and situations?*
- ***How*** *does the client react to the problem? How does the client feel about it?*
- ***Why*** *does the problem occur?*

Needless to say, the who, what, when, where, how, why *series of questions also provides the interviewer with a ready system for helping the client elaborate or be more specific on an issue at any time during a session. … Often, but not always, key question stems result in predictable outcomes.*

- ***What*** *questions most often lead to facts. "What happened?" "What are you going to do?"*
- ***How*** *questions often lead to a discussion about processes or sequences or to feelings. "How could that be explained?" "How do you feel about that?"*
- ***Why*** *questions most often lead to discussion of reasons. "Why did you allow that to happen?" "Why do you think that is so?"*
- ***Could*** *questions are considered maximally open and contain some of the advantages of closed questions in that the client is free to say "No, I don't want to talk about that." Could questions reflect less control and command than others. "Could you tell me more about your situation?" "Could you give me a specific example?" "Could you tell me what you'd like to talk about today?"* (p. 56)

Different questions do result in different types of information. Interviewers should be particularly careful when asking *why* questions because they put many respondents on the defensive. *Why* questions may also be perceived as prying, or they may engender feelings of guilt (Dillard & Reilly, 1988a). *Is* or *was* questions can also present problems by putting interviewees on the spot. A good alternative is to use *could* questions, which tend to be less judgmental and more tentative. Consider the difference between "Was the car traveling too fast?" and "Could the car have been traveling too fast?" The *could* question is more tentative, suggesting a possibility without requiring an absolute commitment of "yes" or "no." *Could* questions also provide interviewees with some degree of freedom and control in an interview. For example, if asked, "Could you tell me more about that?" the interviewee might feel free to say, "I really don't have anything more to add." For these reasons, *could* questions can be very useful in clinical interviewing and counseling (Shipley & Wood, 1996).

The question categories that have been discussed here—open or closed, primary or secondary, neutral or leading, and the *wh* or reporters' questions—are not mutually exclusive. Any particular question asked can be open and neutral, open and leading, open and primary, closed and neutral, or closed and leading; any combination is possible in the framing of questions. Interviewers need to be aware that each question type has a different use and that the different combinations will evoke different responses. Figure 4.1 shows a Sample Interviewer Checklist that can help interviewers to identify the types of questions they ask during interviews.

The Sequencing of Questions

Stewart and Cash (2003) describe four general sequences of questions in interviews. Two of these—the funnel sequence and the inverted funnel sequence—are seen in many speech and hearing interactions. The *funnel sequence* begins with general, open questions and proceeds to more closed types of questions. This sequence is used most frequently in information-getting interviews. The entire interview can proceed in this fashion as the discussion becomes more and more specific. More commonly, the funnel sequence can be used for each new primary question before moving on to the next primary question. The *inverted-funnel sequence* moves in the opposite manner—from very specific, closed questions to open questions. Both sequences are used in information-giving interviews.

Funnel sequence
An interview question sequence that begins with general, open questions and proceeds to closed questions.

Inverted-funnel sequence
An interview question sequence that begins with specific, closed questions and proceeds to open questions.

Sample Interviewer Checklist

_____
(Date)

_____   _____
(Name of Interviewer)   (Name of Person Completing Form)

Instructions: List below as completely as possible the questions asked by the interviewer. At a minimum indicate the first key words of the question (*what, why, how, are,* and so on). Indicate whether each question was open (O) or closed (C).

_____ 1. _____

_____ 2. _____

_____ 3. _____

_____ 4. _____

_____ 5. _____

_____ 6. _____

_____ 7. _____

_____ 8. _____

_____ 9. _____

_____ 10. _____

1. Which questions seemed to provide the most useful client information?

2. Provide specific feedback on the attending skills of the interviewer.

3. Cite your impressions of the interview.

_____

_____

FIGURE 4.1. Sample interviewer checklist. *Note.* From *Intentional Interviewing and Counseling: Facilitating Client Development in a Multicultural Society* (3rd ed., p. 66), by A. L. Ivey, 1994, Pacific Grove, CA: Brooks/Cole, a division of International Thomson Publishing, Inc. Copyright 1994 by Brooks/Cole Publishing Company. Reprinted with permission.

Behaviors in an Interaction

Interviewing is often considered an exchange of specific information in a question-and-response form. However, there is more to an effective interview than simply determining the right questions to ask or comments to share and then wording these verbalizations skillfully. There are, in fact, a number of verbal and nonverbal behaviors that can enhance or disrupt communication. These include verbal behaviors, vocal behaviors, nonverbal behaviors, and combinations. Although these behavior types are considered individually here, clinicians usually employ them in combination.

Verbal Behaviors

Encouragers

Encouragers are described in most texts dealing with effective interviewing and counseling (e.g., English, 2002; Ivey, 1994; Moursund, 1993; Okun, 2002; Stewart & Cash, 2003) as behaviors that signal an interviewee to continue talking about the subject under discussion. There are

Encouragers
*Behaviors that signal
an interviewee to continue talking about
the subject under discussion.*

many examples of verbal and vocal encouragers—words or phrases such as "fine," "I see," "that's helpful," "good," "yes," and "keep going," or vocalizations such as "mmm" or "uh-huh." Using these encouragers serves to increase patients' verbalization, decrease their silences, nurture positive client feelings toward clinicians, and help generalize behaviors and attitudes outside the interview or counseling situation. In operant terms, encouragers are social reinforcers. Some years ago, Richardson, Dohrenwend, and Klein (1965) provided an excellent discussion of the uses and effects of encouragers in interviewing. They commented that when encouragers are used purposefully and near the end of interviewee utterances, interviewees are more verbal and discuss a wider range of the topics of interest to interviewers. It is important to develop and use encouragers because of their powerful effects in influencing client behavior (English, 2002). Effective and experienced counselors use encouragers significantly more often than ineffective or inexperienced counselors (Pederson & Ivey, 1993).

Orientations

Orientations are verbalizations that provide direction or structure to interviews and counseling sessions and focus to conversations. They introduce what should be discussed, encourage all parties to stay on task, and lessen the chances of

Orientations
*Verbalizations that
provide direction or structure to interviews and counseling sessions.*

digressing into irrelevant topics. When a digression does occur, orientations get the discussion back on track.

Examples of orientations include specific instructions or directions, explanatory statements, summaries, and paraphrases. Orientations can occur at any time during an interview. The following is an example of an orientation at the beginning of a meeting with parents in a school setting:

> "Thank you for coming today. In this meeting, we will start by discussing your concerns about Suzy's language skills. Then, Suzy's teacher, Mrs. Snow, will share her opinion about Suzy's language skills as well as Suzy's academic performance in the classroom. Finally, our resource specialist, speech–language pathologist, and psychologist will ask questions of both you and Mrs. Snow to clarify whether a full psychoeducational evaluation is warranted for Suzy. We have 45 minutes for this meeting today, but we can schedule a follow-up meeting, if needed."

Authorities on interviewing and counseling (Kennedy & Charles, 2001; Lang, van der Molen, Trower, & Look, 1990; Stewart & Cash, 2003) advocate beginning an interaction with a clear statement of the purposes of the meeting such as that given above, and concluding the meeting with a summary of the major points discussed and a clear indication of future activities. For example, at the end of the meeting with Suzy's parents, the session leader could say the following:

> "Thank you all for coming. In this meeting, we have discussed your concerns as well as Mrs. Snow's concerns about Suzy's language skills and academic performance. Our resource specialist, psychologist, and speech–language pathologist have stated that they would like to have you sign a request for assessment so a formal psychoeducational evaluation of Suzy's academic and language skills can be carried out. After the formal evaluation is finished, we will call you to schedule a meeting to discuss an IEP to meet Suzy's needs."

Preinterview or precounseling orientations provide clients with a sense of what to expect during the encounter. These orientations let interviewees know the purposes of an interaction, what to expect in a general sense, and approximately how long it might take (Shipley & Wood, 1996). Without such orientations, clients may experience unnecessary uncertainty, concern, and anxiety about a forthcoming encounter. Clients who are given fairly complete information about what to expect (such as in the example above) tend to engage in more discussion of personal matters than clients who do not receive such information (Doster, 1972). It has also been found that patients tend to be less cooperative and to terminate services earlier when their expectations for an interview differ from what actually occurs (Clemes & D'Andrea, 1965). These negative factors—discussing less personal information, cooperating less, and terminating earlier—are important reasons to consider providing appropriate presession orientations to clients and/or their caregivers.

Once a session begins, clinicians use orientations to direct or redirect portions of the discussion. The characteristics of any interview depend, in large part, on how the interviewer structures the session. The interviewer's instructions and directions define the areas to be explored. *Instructions* help interviewees understand what is expected of them and how to proceed. *Directions* tell the client what to do or talk about next, or what actions are necessary (Ivey, 1994). Directions or instructions do not have to be complicated or lengthy. For example, interviewers could use the following:

Instructions
Orientations that help interviewees understand what is expected of them and how to proceed.

Directions
Orientations that tell the interviewee what to do or talk about next, or what actions are necessary.

 "I'd like you to tell me about how the stuttering developed."

 "Talk about what the doctor said. Then we'll address what you are doing at home."

 "I want you to call the teacher this week and discuss _____."

Care should be taken about how directive a direction really is, particularly with some culturally diverse clients. Among some cultures (e.g., Filipino, Japanese, and Malaysian), very direct, command-like statements can be offensive. A more subtly worded request is preferable with such clients (Lian & Abdullah, 2001).

Explanations describe how and why certain information or activities are necessary, which help clients understand requests or suggestions. Explaining why some types of information are needed is particularly helpful with more sensitive or personal subjects. It can also be extremely helpful to say something like "These are routine questions that we ask all of our patients."

Summaries and *paraphrases* clarify topics of discussion and signal that interviewees are being heard and understood. They act to stimulate

Explanations
Orientations that describe how and why certain information or activities are necessary.

Summaries or paraphrases
Orientations that clarify topics of discussion and signal that interviewees are being heard and understood.

interviewees' verbalizations and also help ensure that clinicians understand information correctly. Clients can correct any information that may have been misunderstood or misinterpreted. A summary or a paraphrase also acts as a transition point when clinicians want to move on to other discussion topics. Clinicians summarize or paraphrase what has just been discussed, then introduce the new topic for discussion. For example, in a meeting such as the one described in the preceding example, the meeting leader could say the following:

 "Mrs. Snow, thank you for sharing your impressions of Suzy's classroom performance. Mr. and Mrs. Landis, we appreciate hearing your concerns about Suzy's language skills. Let's have our speech–language pathologist, Bill Lopez, ask some specific questions regarding Suzy's language development history."

High- and Low-Specificity Stimuli

Open and closed questions were described earlier in this chapter. Closed questions are examples of high-specificity stimuli in that the question requires a rather specific type of response, or a high degree of specificity. Open questions are just the opposite, allowing interviewers to field these questions in a number of ways because there is a low level of specificity required. Like questions, directives are also high or low in the level of specificity required. Consider the following examples:

 "Tell me about some of your concerns." (low specificity)

 "Describe your conversation with ＿＿＿＿＿." (high specificity)

Open, low-specificity stimuli result in longer responses that cover a wider range of topics. Closed, high-specificity stimuli result in shorter, more focused responses (Brammer, 1993; Dainow & Bailey, 1988). Open and closed stimuli, whether questions or directives, are used at different times during a discussion. For example, when specific information is needed about the chronology of a problem, clinicians may use a closed stimulus (e.g., "Tell me about the ear infections"). But if the events of the particular time period need to be discussed, clinicians can use a more open stimulus (e.g., "Three months ago? What was going on three months ago?").

Interpretations
Verbalizations that describe why behaviors, events, or feelings have occurred.

Interpretations

Interpretations are verbalizations that describe *why* behaviors, events, or feelings have occurred. They are aimed at providing new perspectives for a client's consideration (Shames, 2000). In a psychological sense, interpretations are used to help provide meaning for dreams, thoughts, or behaviors. However, interpretations are sometimes used to get at other kinds of realities (physical, social, spiritual) expressed by feelings, symptoms, and behaviors. For example, the clinician could say the following to an older adult with a hearing impairment:

 "You said that you don't like to go to parties anymore because you just don't like to stay out late. But I'm wondering if perhaps part of the reason you avoid parties these days is because it's difficult for you to hear when it's noisy. Is that possible?"

In another example, a clinician might say the following to an adult stutterer:

 "You have said you would like to go to college to become a teacher, but finances are a major problem. Is it possible that part of the reason you aren't going to college to study teaching is that you're afraid your stuttering will hinder you from actually realizing your goal?"

The following are basic principles for using interpretations:

1. Look for the interviewee's basic message.
2. Provide the interviewee with a paraphrase of what you think the message means.
3. Convey your understanding of what the message means in terms of your theory or your general explanation of motives, defenses, and needs.
4. Keep your language simple and similar to that used by the interviewee. Avoid wild speculation and statements in esoteric wording.
5. Use statements that indicate you are offering tentative ideas about what the client's words or behaviors mean. "Is this a fair statement?" "The way I see it is _____." "I wonder if _____."
6. Solicit interviewees' reactions to your interpretations.
7. Teach interviewees to do their own interpreting. You cannot give insight to others; they must make their own discoveries. (Adapted from Brammer, 1993, p. 95)

Some cautions are in order regarding the use of interpretations. First, bear in mind that interpretation is based on a clinician's expertise, experience, insight, and personal frame of reference. It is possible that another clinician would formulate an alternative interpretation. The accuracy of a particular interpretation can be culturally related. For example, it is relatively common in U.S. culture to view extended silence as a potential sign of anger, resentment, disagreement, confusion, or lack of understanding. However, extended periods of silence during interactions are within normal communicative expectations in some Middle Eastern cultures (Dwairy, 1998). Silence, which a clinician might interpret as a possible indication of noncooperation, resentment, hostility, or even the withholding of information, may simply be a normal communicative style with individuals from these cultures. Second, remember that psychologically based interpretations are beyond the boundaries of the training and experience of most speech–language pathologists or audiologists. Finally, realize that interpretations have powerful effects that tend to inhibit clients' immediate verbalizations and that the memory of having been interpreted may remain a factor in future interviews (Brammer, 1993; Kanfer, Phillips, Matarazzo, & Saslow, 1960). The act of interpreting why something has occurred can significantly, and sometimes negatively, affect an interaction. This may occur irrespective of whether the interpretation was correct or incorrect. The point is, be careful with the use of interpretations. Clinicians need to be aware of these verbalizations and not use them inadvertently.

Evaluations

Evaluations are positive or negative judgments and comments about someone's actions, behavior, feelings, statements, or questions. They are needed in many instances such as when providing feedback about the mastery of a target behavior or when evaluating someone's assistance with generalization efforts. However, even when evaluations are necessary and offered for the right reasons, they can still inhibit or shorten interviewees' and counselees' responses immediately following the evaluation (Johns, 1975). A conventional expectation is that positive evaluations should increase a client's verbalization. In actuality, however, an evaluative comment, whether positive or negative, typically inhibits interviewees' subsequent verbalization. This phenomenon is similar in some ways to receiving a compliment. Many individuals, although pleased, say little other than "Thank you" or "Thank you, I'm glad you like it" immediately following a positive evaluation.

In some instances, patients or families may view certain evaluative statements as demonstrating a lack of interviewer sincerity and understanding, or as evidence that an interviewer

Evaluations

Positive or negative judgments and comments about someone's behavior, feelings, statements, or questions.

is acting in a superior or judgmental manner (Powell, 1968). The emergence of these feelings is particularly possible with some clients from linguistically and culturally diverse backgrounds that differ from the clinician's. Clinicians would be remiss if they did not provide appropriate evaluative comments as needed in their clinical work. However, they also need to realize the possible effects evaluations may have so they can use them constructively and not be surprised by their effects.

Neutral or Social Verbalizations

Verbalizations that do not relate directly to an interview and its purposes are referred to as *neutral* or *social*. Perhaps the most common example of a neutral or social comment is what Molyneaux and Lane (1982) have called "nonpertinent small talk." Such small talk might include comments about the weather, difficulties finding parking, or what the participants did for recreation over the weekend. Several observational and self-analysis systems used to study clinical treatment in communicative disorders have included sections that look at clinicians' neutral or social verbalizations (e.g., Boone & Prescott, 1972; Molyneaux & Lane, 1982; Prescott & Tesauro, 1974). It is important to identify the presence of these verbalizations because, when used excessively, they reduce overall effectiveness in clinical sessions.

neutral or social verbalizations
Verbalizations that do not relate directly to an interview or its purpose.

Neutral and social comments do not relate directly to the tasks at hand, and many of them take up important time. Rache, Bernstein, and Veenhuis (1974) studied the interviewing skills of medical students and found that "social conversation skills ... must be replaced by responsible communication if the [physician–patient] relationship is to be productive" (p. 591). They also commented that unless medical students received specific training in interviewing, they tended to use too many social comments, to the relative exclusion of more purposeful or insightful interaction. The same holds true for students learning to work with communicative disorders.

Still, neutral or social comments are not always inappropriate. For example, a brief period of social conversation is often helpful when two parties are establishing a relationship. Similarly, two parties who have interacted before may have a relationship that calls for more than "getting right down to business." These brief periods of exchanging social pleasantries (called *platicando* in the Hispanic culture) are important prerequisites to further interaction. However, neutral and social interactions do need to be controlled. The interviewer should strive to use them only as vehicles for increasing patient comfort and interview communication. There is usually little, if any, need for such conversations once a meeting is under way; those that occur during an interaction generally signal that the participants are off task.

Points to Ponder #10

In your new job at the skilled nursing facility, you discover that many family members long to talk at length about the problems they have with the elderly family member with Alzheimer's dementia. Although you feel very sympathetic, you find that these conversations take a great deal more time than you are allotted by your supervisor. You are falling behind in your report writing and other necessary paperwork. Discuss how you might meet the family members' needs for discussion and simultaneously be more efficient during these conferences.

Nonverbal Behaviors

A number of nonverbal behaviors have an effect on interview communication (Corey, 2001; Kennedy & Charles, 2001; Mehrabian, 1972). McClain and Romaine (2002) state that words account for 7% of the communication process, 38% of the communication process is accounted for by tone of voice, and body language and nonverbal cues account for 55% of the communication process. Whether they realize it or not, interviewers and counselors influence their interactions by using nonverbal behaviors such as facial expressions, head nodding, specific postures, eye contact, and touches.

Facial Expressions

Facial expressions convey anger, disgust, fear, sadness, or happiness (Hackney & Cormier, 1994). They also can convey agreement, disagreement, surprise, confusion, or bewilderment. There are a number of potentially important feelings and messages conveyed by facial expression. Glass (2002) states that approximately 55% of nonverbal communication is facial. Scheuerle (1992) considers facial expression to be as important as eye contact in maintaining interpersonal communication. The messages communicated by facial expressions can reveal possible insights into clients' reactions and their inner feelings. Careful observation of the facial area can be important.

Positive and Negative Head Nodding

Head nodding communicates a message. Vertical, up-and-down head nods indicate pleasure, approval, or agreement in the Western culture. Horizontal, or side-to-side, nods suggest displeasure, disapproval, or disagreement. But this is not the case in all cultures. Russians, for example, nod in just the opposite fashion; up-and-down indicates "no" and side-to-side suggests "yes" (Ivey, 1994).

Head nods, whether positive or negative, tend to occur in combination with other behaviors, such as statements of approval or disapproval and accompanying facial expressions. There is a considerable amount of evidence to suggest that head nodding, particularly in combination with other behaviors, influences interviewees' verbal behavior during interviewing and counseling (Burgoon, 1994; Fretz, 1966; Mehrabian, 1972; Rosenfeld, 1967). Unless they are overused, positive head nods communicate that an interviewer is attending, convey a positive attitude toward the other party, and signal interviewees to keep talking. However, too much head nodding can indicate that a person is insecure and overeager to be liked (Glass, 2002). Positive nods are also associated with truthfulness, although this can be deceptive. Conversely, negative nodding acts to discourage or inhibit communication. It indicates that information is not being understood, that there is disagreement, or that the topic of discussion should not be pursued further. Negative nodding also can be interpreted as being judgmental.

Clinicians should use head nodding purposefully to communicate messages such as agreement, keep on talking, disagreement, and so forth. Many clinicians, particularly those who are beginning or are less effective, are not aware of their use of head nods. These are powerful behaviors that need to be used consciously and purposefully.

Body Posturing and Leaning

Body leaning and the general posturing of people in interview situations are indicators of what is happening during an exchange (Shipley & Wood, 1996). Postural shifts are not personality indicators as much as communicative events. The postural change discussed most frequently in interviewing and counseling literature is leaning the body forward or backward.

Forward leans usually indicate interest, affirmative response, respect, and liking (Glass, 2002), and they are presumed to facilitate communication. Backward leans, on the other hand, are considered signs of disinterest, negative response, and unfavorable feelings, and they tend to inhibit interviewee verbalizations and communication (Mehrabian, 1972). Like head nods, body leans tend not to occur by themselves but in combination with positive or negative head nods and comments.

Many clinicians purposefully lean forward to indicate interest or when making a point. Similarly, many interviewers and counselors carefully observe patients' body leans as an indication of interest or agreement, and as a way to judge how well information is being received. Culture, however, plays a role in interpreting what body postures actually indicate. For example, in some Appalachian communities, a relaxed, backward, "belly first" posture is associated with genuine interest, whereas a forward-leaning posture suggests that the other party may be somewhat unnerved (Keefe, 1988).

Eye Contact

It is generally agreed that good eye contact facilitates communication in interviewing and counseling situations (Luterman, 2001; Shames, 2000). However, the frequency and duration of eye contact reflect other factors besides just the quality of a relationship and its communication. Eye contact is related to such factors as the genders of the participants, either party's attitude toward the other party, the participants' attraction to each other, the participants' personalities, the decor of the setting, and the nature of any verbal and nonverbal communication (Donaghy, 1990; Glass, 2002; Pachter & McGee, 2000; Shipley & Wood, 1996).

The use of eye contact is culturally related. Direct eye contact during communication is characteristic of White, middle-class culture in the United States. African Americans tend to use more eye contact when talking and less when listening. Some African American children make little eye contact with adults because it is considered disrespectful. Among some Hispanic and Asian groups, eye contact by the young is also considered disrespectful and is therefore discouraged (Roseberry-McKibbin, 2002; Sue & Sue, 2003). Many Muslim males do not establish eye contact with females or, to show respect, avert their gaze (Nellum-Davis, Gentry, & Hubbard-Wiley, 2002). Many other examples could be noted.

Eye contact is important to consider, but it interacts with many other variables. Thus, guard against inferring information based on the presence or absence of eye contact. The interviewer should strive to maintain good eye contact, but not to a degree that an interviewee feels stared at, feels inspected, or feels violated.

Touch

Touching an interviewee or caregiver can have positive or damaging effects on a relationship and on communication. The effects depend on when and where a touch is given, and how the other party perceives it (Shipley & Wood, 1996). Touch in the form of handshaking is a customary way of welcoming people, of expressing pleasure at meeting and getting to know them. At the close of a meeting, a warm and somewhat firm handshake with appropriate distance between the parties can appear appropriately "businesslike," indicate enjoyment of or satisfaction with the encounter, and indicate the desire to continue a relationship even though discussions have included disagreement. Some handshakes, however, can be interpreted in different ways. A "more intimate" handshake with too little distance or a clasp of both hands can be perceived as being too personal for some individuals. There are also cultural nuances to consider. Males from certain cultures (e.g., some Middle Eastern cultures) may interpret a handshake from a female as forward, inappropriate, or sexual. Handshakes are interpreted differently across a number of cultures.

There are other cultural factors to consider when touching someone else. Touching the head, particularly of children, is discomforting for many individuals from Asian, Carolinian, Chamorro, and other cultures (Hammer, 1994; Roseberry-McKibbin, 2002). Within the context of these considerations, however, touching in nonintimate, friendly ways can express warmth or understanding during interviewing and counseling sessions irrespective of the gender of the participants (Kleinke, 1986). A caring touch on the shoulder or on the back of the hand can help express empathy and concern to someone in distress and can help to increase client willingness to interact and communicate with the clinician. However, a touch that is interpreted as being more intimate or sexual in nature can seriously impair or even destroy a good working relationship. One question clinicians need to ask themselves is whether a touch is used for the client or for themselves. If there is any doubt about the purpose of a touch, the touch should be avoided. It is important to remember that any touching needs to be done in a fashion that cannot be perceived as being sexual or too personal in nature.

Other Behaviors

Silences

Periods of silence during a conversation are acceptable in some cultures (e.g., the Arabic culture). In Japanese, Chinese, Native Alaskan, and Native American cultures, silence is often used to communicate respect (Sue & Sue, 2003). In the general U.S. culture, silence during conversation can be disconcerting, particularly when two parties are just getting acquainted (Cappannelli & Cappannelli, 2002). Silence is feared by many interviewers because they may feel awkward, lost, or out of control. Periods of silence can express several distinct realities. Silence can result from poor interviewing skills, from poorly framed questions, or indecision. Silence can occur when individuals feel "stumped" or surprised by something said, are unsure of what direction to take next, or are uncomfortable that nothing is happening at the moment. Unfortunately, the inclination is to say something to break the silence; often, this is the worst thing to do.

Hackney and Cormier (1994) offer the following comments about counselors and silence:

> For most beginning counselors, silence can be frightening. It seems to bring the total focus of attention on them, revealing their most glaring weaknesses as counselors—at least this is how many beginning counselors describe their experiences with silence. Typically a question is asked. Often it is a bad question—one that can be answered by a minimal response from the client. The answer to the question is relatively unimportant, since the question was not well thought out by the counselor. The counselor may not even be listening to the answer. (p. 50)

Many times, such periods of silence are best not interrupted prematurely. Exercise discipline and decide how to respond rather than responding too quickly with something that is not particularly productive or may actually compound the problem.

The purposeful use of silence can be a powerful clinical technique. These silences are periods of time when interviewers withhold their verbalizations or vocalizations as a signal for interviewees to respond, to begin speaking, or to resume speaking (English, 2002; Shipley & Wood, 1996). Silences that are relatively short (generally about 5 seconds or less) and that are terminated by an interviewee will act to increase the length of the interviewee's verbalizations. They act as signals to begin or continue talking. The use of short, purposeful silences helps the interviewee for the following reasons:

- Many respondents may need time to formulate their thoughts or responses. If a clinician does not remain silent during that time, the respondent's thoughts and subsequent verbalizations are inhibited.
- Even when interviewees think they have completed the expression of thought, an interviewer's use of purposeful silence indicates that they should continue along that line of thought or expand further.

- If respondents find silence uncomfortable, they may continue by either elaborating on the current subject or introducing a new topic. Silence thus acts to make the interviewee more responsible for providing additional information or new directions.

There are some limitations to silence. Silences that last much longer than about 5 seconds (e.g., 10–15 seconds) are likely to be terminated by the interviewer, and result in shorter verbalizations from interviewees. The excessive use of silences is also counterproductive because clients can resent this technique. However, when used correctly, purposeful silence is a powerful and useful clinical tool.

Interruptions and Guggles
In the White U.S. culture, it is considered rude to interrupt someone who is speaking. Interruptions can create agitation, cut off the other person, and even inhibit further attempts to communicate. One study found that the more interviewees were subjected to interruptions, the less interactive they became (Phillips, Matarazzo, Matarazzo, Saslow, & Kanfer, 1961). If a participant feels a need to add information, an interruption or change of topic may occur (Roseberry-McKibbin, 2002). Other cultures have similar values; for example, among some Asians, interruptions in a conversation are considered very impolite and inappropriate. Among some African Americans, conversations may become competitive, with the most assertive speaker doing most of the talking.

In general, interviewers and counselors need to control their use of interruptions. This does not mean that interruptions should always be avoided because interruptions can be used purposefully with highly verbal patients or in cases where a redirection of the conversation is needed. Emerick (1969) provides an excellent example of a case when an interruption, indeed multiple interruptions, would be appropriate:

Mrs. Griewe was an attractive but rather harried mother of six children, all under nine years of age. Her four-year-old daughter, Mary, was beginning to stutter, and Mrs. Griewe came to the clinic for assistance. The longer she talked, the more she talked about herself rather than the child. Finally, she broke down and said that her problem was her religion, a faith which forbade birth control, but as she pointed out ruefully, did not assist with the child-rearing duties. She revealed that she had a college degree but it was of no use since she operated on the level of diapers and runny noses year after year. She blurted out a lot of other things about the clergy and the trap she felt she was in. I tried desperately to shut off the flow but could not. I never saw Mary again. (p. 26)

The problem in this case was that the interviewee revealed too much too quickly, well before a firm relationship had been established. Had the patient–clinician relationship been more fully established, the two parties might have stayed in contact for a counseling referral for the mother, and the child might have obtained the help she needed for her fluency problem. This example helps illustrate how an interruption, or in this case several interruptions, would be appropriate and necessary. Interrupting the other party or asking a series of closed questions in rapid fashion are ways of disrupting a patient's or caregiver's flow of discussion.

For clinicians who worry about seeming abrupt, there is a way to interrupt without being too offensive. We have said things like "Excuse me, Mary, I hate to interrupt, but we only have 10 minutes left. You were concerned about XYZ topics and I wanted to be sure to address all your concerns before our meeting is over" or "John, forgive my interruption, but there is another client waiting and we haven't discussed your question about digital hearing aids yet. Why don't we wrap up with that, and I will look forward to seeing you again next week?"

Guggles

Behaviors that are less powerful and offensive than overt interruptions but still act to interrupt or redirect conversation.

The term *guggles* has been used to describe interruptive devices that are less powerful and less offensive than overt interruptions but still act to interrupt or redirect conversation (Richardson et al., 1965). Guggles can be verbal, vocal, or nonverbal. They serve to signal an interviewee that "it's my turn to talk" or that some redirection is desired. Clearing the throat or interjecting a short "ah" during a client's verbalization interrupt and signal interviewees in a covert manner. Clinicians can also use physical movements like glancing toward a window, checking the time, taking a deep breath, or shuffling papers as cues for changing or terminating a conversation (Knapp, 1972). Of course, some subtlety is needed when using guggles or they can appear rude.

Encouragers were discussed earlier in this chapter as examples of verbal behaviors that facilitate and encourage communication. The question arises, what if encouragers are used too frequently or are introduced too early during interviewees' utterances? In such cases, what a clinician intends as an encourager actually inhibits or discourages interviewees' verbalizations and their overall levels of communication. Consider the effects of the timing of an interviewer's "I see" in the following examples:

CLIENT: When he was about 3 years old, he started to read and really enjoyed the attention he got from us each night.

CLINICIAN: I see.

CLIENT: When he was about 3 years old—

CLINICIAN: I see.

The timing in the first example encourages the interviewee to continue the discussion. The timing in the second instance is premature and interrupts what is being expressed; it inhibits the interviewee from completing the utterance and probably discourages further discussion. Thus, the same phrase (a simple "I see") can be an encouragement or a guggle, depending on how and when it is used.

Guggles do not reduce overall interviewee participation if used sparingly and with some subtlety; however, the premature or frequent use of guggles or interruptions can be perceived as rudeness, which results in less interviewee participation (Richardson et al., 1965; Shipley & Wood, 1996). Interruptions and guggles should be used consciously and purposefully. Many people are not fully aware of their use of interruptions and guggles and therefore affect other people's communication without realizing it. It is important for interviewers to be aware of their own verbal, vocal, and nonverbal actions, and to control them!

Points to Ponder #11

In your clinical fellowship year, your supervisor calls you in for the 6-month evaluation. He tells you that you have excellent technical skills, but that "you let people talk too much" and "your body language needs improving." He is not more specific than that, but gives you a video of yourself to take home and watch. He asks you to evaluate these areas and submit a written critique of yourself. What specific parameters will you look for in your performance?

Several Fundamental Techniques

Summaries, reflections, clarifications, repetitions, pauses, confrontations, and appropriate types of self-disclosure are techniques that utilize some of the verbal and nonverbal behaviors described in this chapter. These techniques can facilitate communication during interviewing and counseling sessions in a number of ways.

Summaries

Clinicians use summaries and reflections to feed back the essential elements of a client's comments. Summaries facilitate communication by signaling that information expressed by the client has been heard and understood; they mirror back the messages, attitudes, and feelings the client has expressed (Dillard & Reilly, 1988a; Ivey, 1994). A summary also helps highlight the major points made by an interviewer. A good summary uses the clinician's own words, rather than the interviewee's words, and captures the most important topics discussed, essentially hitting the "high spots." Summaries during an interaction keep a discussion moving by encouraging interviewees to explore topics and attitudes in greater detail (Mowrer, 1988). They are also used so both interviewers and patients can "double-check" that the clinician understands what the other party is really saying.

Interviewers use summaries at the end of an interview to wrap up or terminate discussion. A good closing summary highlights the major points discussed, helps the interviewee feel that the parties have accomplished a purpose, and helps interviewees feel that they have been understood, or at least listened to attentively (Purkey & Schmidt, 1987).

Reflections

Reflections are typically shorter than summaries and stick closely to the actual words interviewees have used to express their thoughts or feelings. When employing reflections, interviewers should avoid projecting their own opinions and feelings into the comments (Brammer, 1993). There are three basic types of reflections: (a) reflection of the content of the client's message, (b) reflection of both the content of the message and the feelings the client has expressed about the content, and (c) short reflection or "accentuation," which is a restatement of key words or phrases as questions ("Pain?" "Stuttering?").

Another example of a reflection follows:

CLIENT:	When I talk, sometimes my voice cracks.
CLINICIAN:	Cracks?
CLIENT:	Yes, it's like it breaks and then I squeak. It's really embarrassing.
CLINICIAN:	Squeaking would be embarrassing! Tell me more.
CLIENT:	Well, it often happens at work on Monday after a big weekend.
CLINICIAN:	Big weekend?

Reflections are effective in helping to check whether the clinician has correctly understood and interpreted the information presented. They also serve to promote further discussion. Often, greater understanding occurs for both parties as interviewees or counselees respond to a reflection.

Clarifications

Interviewers and counselors use clarifications to understand a client and the client's difficulties more fully (Schuyler & Rushmer, 1987). When something is confusing or ambiguous, interviewers use a clarification to specify the area of confusion. The interviewer might say, for example, "Tell me more about your father's speech problem" or "What do you mean when you say your child's speech sounds immature?" When clinicians need to clarify a larger segment of information, a summary may be in order. "Let me review what I think you are saying: _____."

Like summaries, clarifications help clinicians understand the content and feelings about the client's subject. Clarifications can be used to find out more about specific behavior or to exchange perceptions regarding what has been said. A tentatively expressed clarification gives clients an opportunity to agree or disagree and to add additional information. The clinician might ask, "Did I understand you correctly when you said that _____?" Such a question can facilitate further clarification if there has been confusion or miscommunication.

Repetitions

Clinicians frequently find themselves trying to maintain interviewees' attention. An interviewee's attention can vacillate between what the interviewer is saying and what the individual is thinking about at that moment. For example, an interviewee who is thinking about the costs of therapy may miss a clinician's beautifully worded description of the communicative problem. The dangers of "drifting" are especially great when interviewees are tired or tense, when there are distractions, or when they must make difficult decisions requiring careful consideration.

Clinicians cannot assume that an interviewee's complete attention can be maintained at all times. Virtually everyone's attention drifts periodically. However, the purposeful use of repetitions helps provide sufficient redundance to enable interviewees to grasp the basic message even if they have missed some particular comments. The words that clients do hear and process may carry enough meaning to effectively communicate the clinician's thoughts. For this reason, deliberate repetitions are extremely useful in interviewing and counseling conversations.

Although repetition in writing is often viewed with disapproval, judicious repetition is essential for effective oral communication. Repetitions help the speaker to avoid losing the listener; the more often information is heard, the more it tends to be understood and retained. The speaker who uses repetition in this way can achieve clarity and emphasis while helping listeners catch more of the message. When using repetitions, clinicians hold an interviewee's interest and avoid the appearance of repeating themselves by varying their wordings each time and, when appropriate, giving bits of additional information with each subsequent repetition (Mowrer, 1988). Planned repetitions are very useful when working with individuals for whom there are language barriers, and for whom the material being covered is unfamiliar. They are also helpful when working with an interpreter present.

Pause
A brief moment of silence.

Pauses

A *pause* is a very brief moment of silence. Pauses during a session provide people with opportunities to ponder and reflect (Moursund, 1993). They do the same for clinicians; brief pauses can be helpful to either party. Because pausing suggests that one is thinking, interviewers who fail to employ pauses may be inadvertently suggesting that interviewees' statements are not being taken seriously. Clinicians, therefore, are well advised to pause occasionally, even if such pausing is not necessary for the formulation of questions or responses.

Pausing is more natural in some cultures than in others. In the White U.S. culture, a pause is a period of silence, which is somewhat disconcerting to many individuals. However, among many Native American groups, etiquette requires a lapse of time between a question and an answer. Some Native Americans feel that if a question is answered too quickly, it may not have been worth thinking about in the first place (Gilliland, 1992).

Confrontations

The word *confrontation* tends to conjure up images of something mean-spirited or hostile, but this is not what is meant by confrontation in interviewing and counseling. Confrontations are powerful techniques that enable clients to face and deal with realities, situations, and behaviors that they are inclined to avoid or deny (Brammer, 1993; Pederson & Ivey, 1993; Shames, 2000).

Clinicians should use confrontation purposefully in a careful manner that expresses empathy for patients and concern for their best interests. An especially accepting tone of voice may be needed (Lang et al., 1990). Mowrer (1988) provides this example of a rather direct confrontation with a high school student:

> Bill has discussed advantages and disadvantages of enrolling in a high school speech class to work on his falsetto voice. He is making no special progress toward a decision so you might say, "Well, Bill, it's up to you, do you want to enroll or not?" or "You've been beating around the bush, Bill, why can't you make up your mind? Is it that you feel like a grade-school kid coming to speech class?" (p. 399)

A "you said _____, but _____" construction is often used with a confrontation. For example:

 "You said you really needed the help, but you have missed your last two appointments."

 "You said you would get the medical clearance, but you haven't gotten it yet."

 "You said that you cannot make a good /r/, but listen to the tape."

Confrontation is an important tool in the professional's repertoire. However, if not used skillfully and appropriately, it can be a blunt instrument that is harmful to patients and to the patient–professional relationship (Shames, 2000). Confrontational techniques should never be used to punish or as expressions of hostility or anger. Confrontation is properly a facilitative technique used to engender greater understanding or necessary action (Pachter & McGee, 2000). Using a confrontation may be unwise if clinicians have doubts about their motives or about the appropriateness of the technique in a given situation, if clinicians cannot reasonably estimate a client's response, or if clinicians are working with an emotionally unstable person. Clinicians should also bear in mind that overusing this technique can make some clients feel that they are being criticized or nagged.

Self-Disclosure

Interviewers and counselors practice self-disclosure when they share some of their personal experiences or feelings with clients. The judicious use of self-disclosure conveys empathy and support to clients and caregivers (McDonald & Haney, 1988), or it lets them see that the clinician is a real person rather than just someone in a role (Hackney & Cormier, 1994). Disclosing something can be useful in the overall development of a relationship, but the disclosure needs to be kept brief. For example, sometimes the second author has said things to parents like "Yes, my little boy has real challenges with fine motor skills and writing. It's been hard to see his frustration with his homework each night. I can certainly relate to your feelings of concern when you see your son struggling with understanding what he hears in the classroom and applying it to his homework assignments." Parents have often been very appreciative of this type of brief, empathetic statement and have been even more open about sharing their own experiences with their child. They have also tended to be more cooperative with the second author's recommendations because they have felt genuinely understood.

Some clients, particularly individuals from culturally and linguistically diverse backgrounds, feel better about a relationship if they know something about the clinician (Hays, 2001). In attempting to get to know the clinician better, individuals from some groups (e.g., the Filipino culture) may even ask what are perceived as rather personal questions ("Are you married? Do you have children? Why not?"). Such questions are not being rudely asked; rather, they are a means of getting to know the clinician better (Roseberry-McKibbin, 1997). Appropriate levels of self-disclosure in these instances can be helpful in facilitating rapport between the parties.

It is important to understand that self-disclosure is a clinical tool that can be used to help clients become more comfortable, to understand particular concepts, to experience empathy that the clinician is feeling, and to understand that clinicians are people. Self-disclosure is not unguided, purposeless, or self-serving talk about the clinician and events in his or her life. Clinicians need to guard against self-disclosures that shift the focus away from the client (Bridges, 2001). Whether some specific self-disclosure is appropriate (i.e., whether it is done on behalf of the client rather than the clinician) usually depends on the answer to the following question: "Whose needs am I meeting—the client's or mine?" (Hackney & Cormier, 1979). Self-disclosure to meet the client's needs is an appropriate facilitating technique; self-disclosure to meet the clinician's needs is inappropriate self-indulgence.

Shames (2000) states that self-disclosure or sharing should be brief and should not result in a prolonged focus on the counselor or interviewer. If sharing is done appropriately, "A very real sense of closeness can emerge from such sharing experiences ... and they can easily have a powerful empathic and emotional effect" (Shames, 2000, p. 59). Examples of appropriate and inappropriate self-disclosure follow:

CLIENT: I was so upset when it really hit me that there was actually something wrong with my child. I'd hoped he would just outgrow his speech problem, and I was shocked when the pediatrician told me to consult a speech pathologist because my son needed therapy.

CLINICIAN: (*inappropriate self-disclosure*) Oh, I understand what you mean. My daughter was premature. What a tough pregnancy I had! Bed rest, constant doctor visits, you name it. Well, when she was born 2 months early, she had to remain in neonatal intensive care for a month. We finally brought her home, and she still had problems. I was distraught a year later when the doctor told me she might have cerebral palsy. We didn't know what to do. So we...

CLINICIAN: (*appropriate self-disclosure*) I've been there. Our daughter was 2 months premature, and they told me later that she might have cerebral palsy. It is so hard to hear that something might be wrong with your child.

Self-disclosure can also have cultural components. For example, in Yugoslavia, it is appropriate and expected for clinicians to talk a great deal about themselves and be like friends to clients (N. Mitrovic, personal communication, April 8, 2002). In the United States, however, this behavior would be considered excessive and inappropriate.

Points to Ponder #12

After watching the video of yourself talking with clients and their families, you realize there are several other areas to improve in terms of your verbal communication. Summarize three techniques you can use during these interviews to be a more effective communicator.

➤ Concluding Comments

An effective interviewer–counselor has a number of tools that affect communication with others. These tools include questions, behaviors, and techniques that influence communication during interviewing and counseling. Verbal, vocal, and nonverbal behaviors are always involved in the communication process whether or not the interviewers are conscious of them. These behaviors can either facilitate or impede the process. As interviewers become more conscious of and gain more control over these behaviors, the behaviors become invaluable tools for structuring, controlling, and providing direction to interactions.

FIVE

Obtaining Information

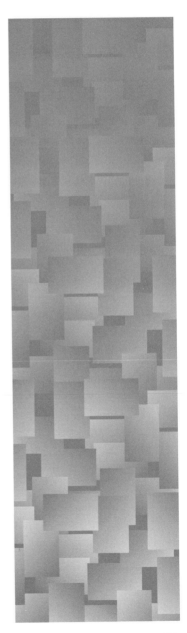

CHAPTER OUTLINE

nformation-getting interviews are an integral part of the diagnostic and treatment process (Clark, 1994b; Haynes & Pindzola, 1998; Peña-Brooks & Hegde, 2000; Shipley & McAfee, 2004). These interviews enable clinicians to gather appropriate information about clients, determine their present and past levels of functioning, identify factors important to the case, and determine clients' potential for improvement. Thus, the functions of information-getting interviews include the following:

- helping in the determination of whether a problem exists
- obtaining information that will aid in understanding the causes of a problem
- assessing factors related to the existence of a problem
- predicting future communicative abilities, with or without intervention
- developing appropriate treatment recommendations, goals, and procedures

Successful informational interviews do not occur by accident or luck. Rather, success occurs in the presence of effective interactional abilities, knowledge of interviewing techniques, skill in asking questions and obtaining information, careful listening, and a knowledge about communicative development and disorders. The absence of any of these qualities or skills can render any interview ineffective, or at least less effective than would otherwise be possible.

Clinicians typically use questions and probes to gather both objective and subjective types of information during information-getting interviews. Because these interviews are performed to gather information and a greater understanding of patients, they are not intended to alter or influence interviewees' behavior or attitudes. In fact, clinicians generally avoid trying to change an interviewee's feelings during these interviews. However, there are occasions during some information-getting interviews when the release and ventilation of patients' feelings and fears can positively change their behavior and attitudes (Haynes & Pindzola, 1998).

Orienting interviewees toward what to expect during an interview is a helpful prerequisite for these interviews. Then, once an interview begins, there are three stages or phases to this interaction: an opening, the body of the interview, and the closing. These three distinct phases cover different types of information and differ in length. The most substantial information pertaining to the case is determined in the body of the interview. This chapter discusses the structure and content of orientation and the three phases of interviews to obtain information.

Presession Orientation

Clinicians set the stage for optimal success by providing presession orientations for interviewees. There are several ways to do this. In settings with support staff, individuals can inform patients about the services to be received. When clients contact an agency or facility to make an appointment, a knowledgeable administrator or assistant provides general information concerning the basic procedures, the professional who will be seen, any fees charged, the length of sessions, and so forth. Of course, support staff members will need to be trained to convey appropriate types of information to clients, their families, and other caregivers.

Another way to orient people is through direct client–clinician contact, typically by telephone. Clinicians can provide basic information concerning the agency or setting and the types of activities that will be involved. This also provides a good opportunity to answer various procedural or general questions clients may have. Such contacts are beneficial because clients and others in their environment are given an opportunity to speak briefly with the clinician prior to a first visit.

Presession orientations can also involve sending written information such as a letter or pamphlet describing the setting, the services provided, or general information about speech and hearing development or disorders. A note or card confirming the time and date of the appointment is also useful.

A case history form is frequently provided to patients or caregivers for completion prior to a first visit. The history form helps to orient clients toward what may be discussed regarding medical, educational, social, or communicative histories. The form also helps clinicians obtain preliminary information about the client and, when returned in advance, it helps clinicians prepare for a session. A release-of-information form is sometimes sent to authorize requests for information from other professionals who have seen a client.

In addition to the specific information provided about the clinical setting, pamphlets or brochures dealing with preparing for a first visit, specific communicative disorders (e.g., hearing loss, voice problems, cleft palate, stuttering), and communicative disorders in general are available through professional organizations like the American Speech-Language-Hearing Association (ASHA), some state speech and hearing associations, many state licensing boards, and commercial publishers in the field. Some of these items, particularly from ASHA, are available in different languages.

The use of such orienting procedures helps minimize clients' uncertainty or anxiety before an appointment, provides information about what will occur during the first visit, and helps engender overall levels of cooperation and rapport. However, there are some factors to consider before implementing these as standard operating procedures. It does little good, and indeed may have some negative effects, when written materials that are provided cannot be read because of illiteracy or because they are written in an unfamiliar language. In some settings and locations, materials in different languages will be needed. Also, be aware that materials sent home with a child, such as from school, may lead caregivers from some cultural backgrounds to an immediate assumption that the child has misbehaved or done something wrong. A clear explanation of what is being sent should precede the sending of such information.

Using an Appropriate Title or Salutation

A tentative relationship between clinicians and clients begins to develop before their first face-to-face meeting. Clients' perceptions of the setting as well as the practitioner's reputation and abilities influence their initial attitudes and behavior toward clinicians (Kennedy & Charles, 2001; Shipley & Wood, 1996).

The title a professional uses also can influence interviewees. Years ago, Gelso and Karl (1974) found that students judged professional counselors' skill levels differently on the basis of the titles they used. These investigators compared students' reactions to various titles—high school counselor, advisor, college counselor, counseling psychologist, clinical psychologist, and psychiatrist—and, not surprisingly, they found that different titles created different initial perceptions. Those who were labeled counseling psychologists or clinical psychologists were perceived as more knowledgeable than those using other titles. This is a factor in our field, particularly in speech–language pathology. Clinicians are sometimes referred to as speech pathologists, speech–language pathologists, speech clinicians, speech and hearing specialists, speech teachers, and so forth. It is helpful for clients to know how to refer to the clinician; clinicians should choose a professional title that is accurate, complies with current acceptable usage, and helps engender appropriate levels of respect.

Clinicians' use of their first name, or their last name preceded by Dr., Ms., Miss, Mrs., or Mr., should also be considered carefully. There has been a trend in the general culture in the last three or four decades toward using first names more frequently than occurred in the early to mid-1900s. However, many older individuals find this disconcerting when initially establishing a relationship, particularly with a clinician who is younger. Likewise, many individuals from linguistically and culturally diverse populations find the use of either party's first names, especially early in a relationship, inappropriate or disconcerting. Many multicultural clients appreciate the use of titles. Malaysians, for example, tend to be particularly respectful of highly educated persons (Lian & Abdullah, 2001).

Occasionally, first-time clients with communicative disorders will inquire about the background of a clinician whom they are scheduled to see. If the clinician has a personal Web site, clients appreciate being able to access the site and check the clinician's background before the meeting, or support personnel or the clinician can provide a brief description of the professional credentials, depending on who is asked. Consider the following examples:

- "You will be seeing Mr. Jones. He is a speech–language pathologist who has worked here with children for more than 7 years. He has worked with many children who have stuttered."

- "Dr. Smith is our audiologist. She has her doctoral degree and more than 10 years of experience with hearing and hearing problems. She works with many people who might benefit from hearing aids."

- "I am Ms. Vang. I am the speech pathologist who will be seeing Vanessa. I finished my Master's degree at Northwestern University and work primarily with preschool children here at _____."

In none of these examples did the individual provide a detailed resume; rather, each statement included the clinician's name and title and a brief notation of professional experience.

Opening an Interview

The opening or beginning phase of an interview to obtain information sets the tone and the stage for the conversations that follow. This phase can motivate interviewees to participate freely and communicate effectively and accurately, or it can hinder an interview early on by limiting free participation and subsequently reducing the flow of information. According to Stewart and Cash (2003), opening an interview involves providing verbal orientations to interviewees and, at the same time, facilitating rapport between the participants.

It also behooves clinicians to remember that some families may distrust authority figures initially because they have had negative experiences with authority figures in their home countries (Domyancic, 2000; Saenz, Huer, Doan, Heise, & Fulford, 2001). If clinicians begin an interaction on a friendly, personal, and informal note, these families may ultimately be more comfortable than if the interaction begins immediately addressing business.

Developing Rapport and Setting the Tone

As indicated in Chapter 2, rapport means establishing a harmonious relationship between the parties. The development and maintenance of rapport are important at all times during interviewing and counseling sessions. Ivey (1994) comments that rapport is important because, "unless the client has some liking for you, you won't go very far" (p. 152). Rapport is expedited by clinician punctuality; an attractive and comfortable setting; and clients knowing, at least in general terms, what to expect during the interview and from the relationship.

Rapport also is assisted by a host of other interviewer characteristics, verbal and nonverbal communicative skills (addressed in Chapters 2 through 4), and by cultural sensitivity and knowledge when working with clients from other cultures (see Chapter 8).

Initial comments during the opening of the interview orient interviewees by defining the participants' roles and indicating some of the activities that will follow. The tone of the interview is affected by the attitudes an interviewer projects. Peterson and Marquardt (1994) note that clinicians and clients are not on "equal ground." Rather, interviewees typically have come to clinicians for help and direction, so clients expect that most of the questions and direction will come from the interviewer (Shipley & Wood, 1996).

The opening phase is structured as clinicians introduce (or reintroduce) themselves, briefly describe their roles, and convey the purposes of a meeting. Clinicians should not assume that clients understand the specific purposes of an interview or the nature of the information that may be requested (Peterson & Marquardt, 1994). Effective interviewers describe in general terms what will be expected from interviewees and any limitations to the services that will be provided. During this opening phase, it is also helpful to tell clients how any information obtained will be used, why the information is needed, and to whom it may be revealed. Finally, it is a good idea to remind clients how much time an interview is expected to take.

As Donaghy (1990) states, the beginning of the opening phase may include the following:

- Introductions or reintroductions and a reminder to the other party of the clinician's role in the setting
- An indication of any titles preferred
- Any information that has been obtained from other persons, or any work or preparation already done
- The degree of confidentiality to be maintained
- The nature of the roles to be assumed

It is worth remembering that many people have difficulty recalling names after just one or two meetings. Names that are unusual or difficult to pronounce present additional problems. A business card, a name tag, or a conspicuously placed desk plate can help people remember names. Regarding personal titles, it can be embarrassing for clients to discover that they have referred to an interviewer as Mr. or Ms. when Dr. would have been more appropriate and, conversely, embarrassment or even feelings of disillusionment or betrayal sometimes occur when patients learn interviewers whom they have called Dr. do not hold such a degree. Knowledge of the clinician's title and role in the setting (e.g., clinical supervisor, speech–language pathologist, audiologist, intern, student teacher) prevents con-fusion so clients are less likely to make erroneous assumptions about the interviewer's authority or capabilities.

The following illustrates what a clinician might say when meeting a couple for the first time in a private waiting area:

> "Mr. and Mrs. Wallace, I am Ms. Sandoval, one of the speech–language pathologists at the center. I will be evaluating John's speech today. Before I see him, I'd like to spend a few minutes with both of you to get an idea of the things you have noticed about his speech. Once we've finished, I will see John by him-self and later we'll talk about some of the things I've found. Please follow me to my office."

Once the clinician and couple have arrived in the office or con-ference area, it is appropriate to reiterate and expand on some of the general points made just moments earlier.

> "Again, my name is Ms. Sandoval and I am a speech–language pathologist. I'd like to spend the next few minutes getting your impressions of your son's speech. Then I'll see John and evaluate his speech. After that, we'll talk again. I'll share my findings and impressions with you at that time. The entire process should take about an hour and a half."

These examples help illustrate how a brief and succinct open-ing phase can serve to orient the party being interviewed. An opening phase should, of course, be modified according to any particular setting or clinical needs. A period of brief chitchat may be useful with some interviewees, particularly those from culturally diverse backgrounds (Sue & Sue, 2003). This can be done at the beginning of the opening phase.

Transition from the Opening to the Body of the Interview

The opening phase of the interview is usually a brief introduction about what to expect. It also sets the stage for the body of the interview. During the body of the interview, clinicians focus on understanding the client, reviewing appropriate histories (medical, developmental speech, educational, etc.), and discussing a client's perceptions of the communicative difficulties being experienced. The actual transition between the opening phase and the body of the interview occurs when the first piece of information about a client is solicited.

 "Tell me about what brought you here today."

 "I'm interested in learning more about your (or your child's, your spouse's, your parent's) speech. Tell me some of your concerns."

Donaghy (1990) comments,

> *The opening question would encourage interviewees to give information. It should be nonthreatening and request information which the interviewee can easily answer. Usually, the opening question is quite general because general questions are less stressful and help interviewees relax. They allow respondents to ease into the body of the interview. The opening question should assume consent on the part of the interviewee—you should use positive phrasing such as, "Suppose you tell me about _____" rather than, "I wonder if you would tell me _____." (p. 92)*

The first few words and thoughts an interviewer expresses can be particularly significant in that they often reveal focuses and degrees of concern very early in an interview (Donaghy, 1990; Garrett, 1982). Several examples of initial statements from parents, with possible interpretations of the concerns expressed, illustrate this point.

 "John's speech is very unclear and he's withdrawing from everyone. He's just clamming up! We hate to see this happen. It's killing us inside to see him just clam up." (There is a high level of concern, a focus on the child's emotional reactions, and another potential focus on the parents' reactions.)

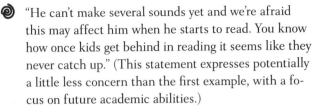 "He can't make several sounds yet and we're afraid this may affect him when he starts to read. You know how once kids get behind in reading it seems like they never catch up." (This statement expresses potentially a little less concern than the first example, with a focus on future academic abilities.)

"I had a cousin who stuttered real bad and we just want to make sure that Julia is not developing this type of problem." (Concern is present because stuttering has occurred in the family, but the level or focus of that concern is unclear.)

"Jennifer's speech is okay, but the doctor insisted that we come see you anyway." (Parent does not appear to be very concerned. This person may be following through out of politeness to someone else or was coerced into it. It is also possible that more concern will come out later.)

In these examples, there are very different focuses of concern (from "clamming up" to learning to read) and degrees of concern (from "it's killing us inside" to no apparent concern). Interviewers should make a mental note and then add to or modify these impressions throughout the session.

In addition to information about levels and foci of concern, interviewees' beginning statements can help provide insight into clients' educational backgrounds or problems. For example, the parents who express concern about their child's sibilant distortions may have a considerably different amount of information than the parents who just know their child "talks funny." During clients' statements of the problem, clinicians listen for information concerning what clients think the difficulties are, their feelings about potential causes of the problem, and the ways they have tried to resolve the problem.

Getting started is difficult for some interviewees. In such cases, it is helpful to note briefly that it can be difficult to know where to begin (Benjamin, 1981). An interviewer might help with a comment like, "I know it can be difficult to decide where to begin, but I need to know about your voice and the problems you are having." When a client has problems with a statement of the concern, the clinician should take care to phrase an open question that is neither too ambiguous nor too specific (e.g., "Tell me a little about your speech problem") and the response will then determine how the interviewer should continue. By phrasing the opening question in an open-ended manner, clinicians avoid inhibiting or restricting clients. This can be particularly useful with individuals from diverse backgrounds.

In the event of more extreme problems getting started, it is sometimes helpful to employ closed questions that are not in particularly sensitive or emotion-laden areas. Open questions are then asked once the patient has started opening up.

Important clues about interviewees' attitudes toward an interview situation or even toward the interviewer may be revealed (Garrett, 1982). These feelings may include ambivalence, confusion, fear, or even hostility. For example, patients sometimes tell clinicians, "I don't need to be here but _____ is making me"; inquire immediately if a doctor is really any good; or seek reaffirmation that nothing in the session will hurt. An indication of hostility or anger in a client's opening statement may warrant a quick change in approach, or at least alert the interviewer to problems that may need to be addressed further.

Points to Ponder #13

You have taken a job in an urban hospital where there are many older, multicultural clients with swallowing disorders (dysphagia). You know that cultures have different beliefs about foods. However, when you try to set up meetings to interview family members about a patient's food preferences and other background information, they either do not show up or they seem very uncomfortable at the beginning of the meeting. What can you do to (a) help encourage family members to attend the meeting and (b) make them more comfortable when they do attend?

Body of the Interview

During the body of the information-getting interview, an interviewer gains potentially important information about the client, including information about the development and present status of the client's communicative skills and appropriate medical, educational, therapeutic, and social histories (Peterson & Marquardt, 1994). Discussion often includes items of particular significance from the written case history form. In the following sections, the sequence of the interview is considered first; this is followed by the content applicable to the body of many information-getting interviews.

Sequence of the Body

The different types of open and closed questions, and primary and secondary questions, were described in Chapter 4. The general sequences of interviews—the *funnel sequence* and the *inverted-funnel sequence* (Stewart & Cash, 2003)—also were discussed in that chapter. Recall that a funnel sequence moves from open to closed questions, from primary to secondary questions. This structure allows interviewers to move from more general to more specific types of information. A funnel sequence is useful when obtaining information in initial interviews. Clinicians begin by asking an open question about a topic, then narrow the topic down into specific details. Different subareas of discussion can also be addressed in this manner when an open question is used first and closed questions then help generate the information needed in that subarea. If the topic has been discussed adequately, an open question is then used to introduce the next subarea of discussion (e.g., "You also mentioned concern about hearing"). Obviously, closed secondary questions then allow more extensive discussion of the topic before moving on to the next subject.

The inverted-funnel approach, which moves from closed to open questions, is less useful for most information-getting interviews, but it can be helpful in some instances. This approach can be used when working with reluctant clients who are reticent to share their real feelings and with patients who are not talking much. This sequence also is helpful with clients who may not feel there is a problem or who are unsure what the problems really are. By asking questions requiring specific types of information first, inroads are sometimes made as these clients begin to see that there really is some reason for concern or begin to see the potential areas of difficulty.

Content of the Body

The major items that have been noted on a written case history are often discussed and considered in detail during the body of the interview. Most diagnoses, estimates of prognosis, and initial plans for remediation or treatment result from at least two sources, and often three. These sources are the information-getting interview; any diagnostic assessment testing and observations performed; and, when available and appropriate, information from other professionals involved with the case.

The following are some of the topics discussed in information-getting interviews:

- *Identifying Information.* A clinician may need to confirm data (addresses, telephone numbers, insurance companies, etc.) that identifies the patient.
- *Family histories.* Disorders such as stuttering and hearing loss tend to run in families. Clinicians may need to determine any possible environmental or genetic links related to diagnosis and subsequent treatment. Clinicians should also determine how family members react to and feel about the communication problem.
- *Developmental and motor histories.* When clinicians are treating children and adolescents with communication disorders, it is important to know about the client's prenatal, natal, and postnatal histories. This knowledge can aid in determining a diagnosis and, sometimes, in the isolation of an etiology. Information about motor development is important because speech is a motor function. Problems with muscle tone, coordination, or symmetry may indicate further examination of specific areas of the communication mechanism.
- *Educational and social background.* A child's educational history is usually helpful. It can provide valuable insight into the child's intellectual potential and social maturity, the parents' expectations, and the consistency of the child's performance across settings.
- *Socioeconomic background.* Information about socioeconomic status can be important because it may reveal influences and conditions that impinge upon opportunities available for the client (Roseberry-McKibbin, 2000b). Clients from low-income backgrounds may need additional services that can be recommended by the clinician (Payne, 2003).
- *Speech, language, and hearing histories.* Speech, language, and hearing development and skills are of primary concern to professionals in communication disorders. Thus, there is considerable emphasis in this area during most preassessment interviews.
- *Special case histories.* Most information-getting interviews will at least touch on the general topics noted in the previous section. However, if a client has a specific disorder, a detailed case history form, relevant to the disorder, can be used.
- *Multicultural histories.* Chapter 8 includes a discussion of factors that can be present with linguistically and culturally diverse clients. It is important to ascertain the presence and possible influence of these factors on communication skills.

**Questions To Ask in an
Information-Gathering Interview**

Irrespective of the type of communication difficulty
being assessed, the following are some universally
applicable questions that often need to be asked:

- When and how did the problem develop?
- Has the problem changed since it was first
  noticed?
- Does the problem vary according to time or
  circumstance?
- How does the client react to the communication problem?
- How do others (e.g., caregivers, significant others, friends)
  react to the problem?
- Where else has the client been seen? What did other pro-
  fessionals find or suggest?
- How has the interviewee tried to help?
- Can the interviewee describe or imitate the specific commu-
  nication problem?

The types of information that allow clinicians to make a
diagnosis are beyond the scope of this book and are not considered here. For more specific information regarding diagnostic
and assessment procedures, the reader should consult other
texts such as Haynes and Pindzola (1998), Nation and Aram
(1991), and Shipley and McAfee (2004). Assessment information pertaining specifically to clients from linguistically and
culturally diverse populations is available in such resources
as Battle (2002), Brice (2002), Coleman (2000), Goldstein
(2000), Lynch and Hanson (1998), and Roseberry-McKibbin
(2002).

Closing the Interview

The body of an information-getting interview is concluded
when a clinician has finished obtaining necessary information
about the client, the client's history, and any other pertinent
details deemed necessary to understand the case. The clinician then moves to the last phase of the interview.

The closing segment of the information-getting interview
is relatively brief and concise. Major features of a closing are
(a) providing a summary of what has been discussed; (b) giving

interviewees opportunities to add on any information gained or clarify any interviewer misconceptions; (c) expressing appreciation to the other party; and (d) revealing the next steps in the process.

Interviewers begin by summarizing the main pieces of information that have been obtained. This helps the clinician demonstrate to clients that they have been heard and understood. It also gives those who have been interviewed an opportunity to make clarifications, add information, or make corrections. Once all information has been summarized, and corrected or added to if necessary, clinicians express appreciation for the interviewee's efforts: "I appreciate the information you have provided. It will be helpful in understanding your speech (or your son's speech, your mother's speech)." Finally, the clinician closes the interview by mentioning the next steps. The actual closing statement is sometimes rather general, but provides enough information so that clients know what will be done next.

 "Now I would like to spend some time with your son. I will listen to his speech in several contexts and evaluate the speech difficulty. That should take about an hour. After I finish, we'll talk again and I will share my findings and recommendations with you. Thank you again for your help."

The same model is useful when the person interviewed is also the patient.

 "Now, let's turn our attention to assessing your dysfluencies and whether we can improve your speech. I'm going to have you read some materials and then we'll check your hearing. I'll let you know what I'm finding as we go along. We'll also spend a few minutes at the end discussing what I have found and what we should do next."

➤ Concluding Comments

Professionals working with communicative disorders are routinely involved in obtaining a number of different types of information in their diagnostic and therapeutic interactions. With first-time patients and families, an information-getting interview should be preceded by an appropriate presession orientation for interviewees. The actual interview proceeds through three distinct phases: the opening, the body, and the closing. Interviewers orient interviewees to what will occur during the opening phase, while simultaneously helping build rapport. A transition is made from the opening phase to the body of the interview when interviewees provide the first substantial piece of information about the case. During the body of the interview, interviewers gain the information needed about a client and the client's communicative difficulty, including background information about speech, language, and hearing or other appropriate histories. Then, in the closing phase, clinicians summarize what has been said, allow clients to clarify any misconceptions and add anything needed, express appreciation to the interviewee, and direct or orient interviewees toward the activities or interactions that will follow.

The opening and closing phases are rather short and succinct; the body of the interview is much longer and is really the "meat" of the interview. Successful information-getting interviews result in an adequate depth and scope of information that, when combined with information from a diagnostic session, will provide an excellent overall picture of the communicative problem and its various ramifications.

Interviews to obtain information are also conducted when a client is enrolled for ongoing treatment to gain information about medical, educational, or psychological testing done elsewhere; to find out if communicative behaviors are generalizing outside the clinical or educational environment; to learn more about a client's progress; and so forth. These interviews use the same basic structure, including opening, body, and closing phases, but the content of the body is about specific topics, compared to the large body of information gathered during assessment-related interviewing.

SIX

Providing
Information

CHAPTER OUTLINE

Imparting accurate, understandable information about clients and their communicative disorders is an important responsibility of clinicians in all settings. Sharing information often occurs after assessment sessions with children, and during or after many assessment sessions with adults. Information regarding treatment progress is, or should be, shared on an ongoing basis when the client is enrolled for ongoing services. There are also occasions when information is shared with others who are involved with the case such as teachers, physicians, or mental health professionals. Of course, this is done with the client's or caregiver's permission. The importance of providing accurate and appropriate information cannot be understated because it is a very important professional responsibility.

Cunningham and Davis (1985) relate that the most frequent complaint cited by parents of children with special needs concerns unsatisfactory communication with professionals. Too often, professionals provide insufficient, inaccurate, or even excessive information, causing real problems for individuals needing services (Luterman, 2001; Rossetti, 2001). Haynes and Pindzola (1998) suggest that the most common complaint of patients in hospital and clinic settings is that they have not been kept well informed of their conditions or progress.

Clinicians may not be fully understood because of ineffective presentation techniques or the inappropriate use of technical language. When confusion or misunderstandings occur, relations between clinicians and clients or their caregivers suffer and rapport is undermined.

A clinician's effectiveness in providing information is related to the various factors discussed in the preceding chapters. Especially important are the enabling conditions—sensitivity, respect, empathy, objectivity, listening skills, motivation, and rapport—discussed in Chapter 2. The ability to communicate effectively—knowing what to share, when to share it, and how to share it—is very important.

Conveying Information

Information is typically provided in person to clients or their caregivers. There are instances when this occurs by phone or correspondence with other professionals. In the following sections, conveying information is discussed primarily in the context of a postassessment interview. However, the same principles apply to other circumstances, such as providing information during an assessment session with adults or providing information about progress in therapy. These principles are simply modified as appropriate for other circumstances.

Like information-getting interviews (discussed in Chapter 5), an information-giving interview usually proceeds through three stages or phases: an opening, the body, and a distinct closing. Before describing these phases, the always-important area of preparation needs to be considered.

Preparing To Give Information

Adequate preparation is needed before opening any interview (Shipley & Wood, 1996), and it is particularly important for an information-giving interview. An interview room should be free from clutter, appear professional, and be arranged appropriately for a serious discussion. Confidential materials, patients' folders, or any other materials that could violate privacy or be distracting should be removed from sight. Appropriately sized chairs should be available for everyone involved. This is of particular concern in settings where clinicians work with children.

If a client has been evaluated during a diagnostic session, it is important to allow adequate time for materials to be collated, scored, and evaluated so that clinicians can share results in the information-giving interview. If insufficient time has been allocated, information may not be available, rushing may result in scoring tests incorrectly, and assumptions may be based on inaccurate information. Taking the time necessary for accurate, reliable test scoring and interpretation is important, particularly when results influence a clinician's judgment about the presence or extent of a problem.

For both inexperienced and experienced, but cautious, interviewers, it is helpful to list in advance the major findings that need to be addressed in an information-giving interview. This listing helps clinicians develop a sequence for the interview, and it prevents inadvertently forgetting to share important information. However, clinicians should avoid relying on a checklist for each point and comment made during an interaction (Enelow & Swisher, 1986; Shipley & Wood, 1996) because a "checklist interview" is often very noncommunicative and inflexible.

Opening the Interview

Most information-giving interviews are conducted separately from the diagnostic session, although many sessions include both, particularly with adults. When these are separate occasions, clinicians usually begin the interview with a brief, general orientation statement about what will be discussed.

 "I have evaluated your son's speech, and I want to share my findings and some suggestions with you."

"Having talked with your physician and evaluated your hearing, I'd like to share some of my findings and recommendations with you."

 "I finished evaluating Javier's language on Friday and talked with his teacher today. I'd like to share some of the information I have with you."

It is also helpful for the clinician to indicate approximately how much time will be involved and to report whether a satisfactory, representative sample of the client's communicative behavior was collected during the assessment session. Many interviewees are concerned about time constraints: whether there will be enough time on the parking meter, whether there will be enough time to pick up another child, and so forth. Many interviewees, particularly parents, are concerned about a child's behavior and whether the communicative behavior of concern was exhibited during the diagnostic session. Such concerns, which frequently go unsaid, can affect the concentration of the interviewee. A positive statement about how the client interacted or cooperated during the assessment can be helpful, particularly with caregivers of "feisty" adults who were evaluated or with parents.

The second author, who works part time in a public school setting as well as in a university clinic, has frequently found that parents genuinely appreciate a positive statement at the beginning of the interview. A clinician might open an information-giving interview with a statement such as the following:

 "Ben was very cooperative and worked hard during the whole session. I was able to get a good sample of his speech and how he's making his speech sounds. I want to take the next 10 to 15 minutes to share the results with you."

In this brief statement, the clinician describes the general behavior of the child, indicates that a good speech sample was obtained, notes the purpose of the interview, and suggests the approximate time anticipated for the discussion. Of course, the actual time may vary from the clinician's estimate, depending on the interviewee's needs.

The same basic content areas apply to discussions of ongoing treatment.

 "I have now seen your mother three times and she is working very hard. I'd like to talk about what we are doing and the progress I'm seeing. I also have some

suggestions for use outside the clinic. Let's take about
15 minutes and I'll share this with you."

This model can be adapted with different situations. Three
different examples follow.

    "Maria was quite active during the session, but she
did work hard on several tasks. I was able to get some
of the information needed, but there are things that
still need to be completed and I will need to see
Maria again to finish the evaluation. Before scheduling her for another session, I do want to take about
10 minutes to share my impressions with you."

    "Like many stroke patients, your father was very agi-
tated and sometimes confused. But he cooperated
with much of the testing and I have a pretty good idea
of what needs to be done. In the next few minutes,
I'd like to share some of my findings and suggestions
with you."

    "Mrs. Knight, I know that some of the sounds you
were listening for were difficult to hear and that it
was hard to hear all the words I was saying. But
you stayed with it and responded very consistently.
Let's take the next few minutes and talk about your
hearing."

These short statements follow the same model of describing
a client's general behavior during the assessment session, the
adequacy of the behavior sampled, the time needed to discuss
the findings, and the purpose of the present conversation.

    Impressions of a client's behavior should always be a de-
scription of what actually took place; that is, do not say a client
worked well if this is not the case. However, it is possible to
put positive and negative aspects of behavior in perspective in
an objective and nonthreatening manner. It is also true that we
can find something positive in every individual.

    "Julia worked well the first 5 to 10 minutes, and then
seemed to tire."

    "John was quite active, but I did get several things
accomplished."

    "Jennifer was pretty upset at first, but she did even-
tually calm down. Once her crying subsided, I was
able to _____."

The same general framework is used with reporting progress about ongoing treatment.

> "Jennifer had a few difficulties adjusting to what I was asking her to do the first two sessions, but she has now adjusted and is working hard. She seems to be enjoying our time together and is starting to progress in several areas. Let's take the next few minutes and I'll share some of what we are doing."

Statements of behavior that draw conclusions or that consist of a clinician's feelings about a client are unproductive. For example, statements such as "He's really uncooperative!" or "She really behaved poorly" or questions such as "Is he always like that?" frequently do no more than engender negative feelings. Care also is necessary here with parents who might punish a child for "misbehaving." Some children may be punished, sometimes physically, for not cooperating fully or for not meeting a parent's expectations. In one situation, the second author talked to a mother who said, "If Britton doesn't do his speech homework, I just shake him until he does it!" Needless to say, the second author conversed with this mother about more positive ways to work with her child.

The opening of interviews to provide information is usually very short. Clinicians then move immediately into the most important part: the body of the interview.

Body of the Interview

Structure of the Body

The concepts of funnel and inverted-funnel sequences were introduced in Chapter 4 in relation to how open and closed questions are sequenced. These two sequences were discussed again in Chapter 5 as they apply to the sequencing of information sought in information-getting interviews. Recall that a funnel sequence starts with open comments or questions before moving into more closed types of stimuli. An inverted-funnel sequence is just the reverse, moving from closed to open. The same principles apply to conveying information, particularly in postassessment interviews. General, overall, or conclusive comments can be provided first, followed by more specific details or findings in a funnel sequence. Conversely, an inverted-funnel sequence involves providing more precise details or findings first, and then general information or overall conclusions. Both sequences are useful when conveying information to others.

While preparing for an information-giving interview, clinicians should try to judge how anxious an interviewee is about the communicative problem or any information that might be conveyed. When an interviewee is anxious or concerned, it is best to share major conclusions (sometimes referred to as the "bottom line") at or near the beginning of the interview.

 "Mrs. Smith, John does have problems making a number of his speech sounds. He is going to need therapy to learn to make these sounds. The first thing I found was _____."

 "Mr. Richards, you do have a significant hearing loss and would benefit from a hearing aid. Here are some of the things I found: _____."

Certain highly anxious clients are so concerned about learning the major conclusions that they are unable to effectively listen and process other information until they have heard those conclusions. A highly anxious student often hears little of an instructor's feedback about the strengths or weaknesses of a given test or project because the real area of immediate concern (the bottom line) is the grade. For such students or such clients, sharing the bottom line (e.g., the grade) before providing specific feedback about *why* allows opportunities for greater understanding of both the specific findings and the conclusions drawn.

Conversely, with less anxious and less concerned patients, or with individuals who have doubts regarding the existence or severity of a communicative difficulty, it is often helpful to present the more detailed, specific findings first (e.g., the results from a hearing test or the articulation testing) before sharing the overall or bottom-line conclusions. This order of presentation helps build a case for the conclusions offered and allows individuals to understand how these conclusions were reached. When clinicians build a case this way, there is less chance that interviewees will reject the clinician's conclusions, either verbally or silently, before at least hearing all the details underpinning these conclusions.

Content of the Body

Whether the bottom-line conclusions are presented at the beginning or at the end of the body of an interview, the major content includes the most important items that need to be shared. This typically includes information derived from an information-getting interview, observation, and any formal or informal testing performed. Before beginning this type of interview, clinicians should determine the most salient points that they want interviewees to understand.

Clinicians overwhelm many interviewees with too much information too quickly, causing a lack of understanding and confusion (Luterman, 2001). Using a general guideline of three to five major points to share is helpful because clinicians are forced to identify and then convey the major points, and interviewees are allowed to focus on and truly understand these points. Providing three to five major points is a general rule; there may be only one or two major points in some interviews, and six or seven in others. However, more than four or five important points is "stretching it" in many interactions. Of course, more than one or two points can stretch the limits with some clients, particularly with difficult-to-deal-with information, for an interviewee who does not comprehend what is being said, in the presence of language barriers, and so forth.

When clinicians present more than three to five major points, it is difficult for many patients to process them, let alone to recall them later. Sticking to a smaller number of points and limiting discussion to the framework of those points help ensure that the most important points are discussed. Presenting more points often creates confusion regarding which points are really important and which are of secondary importance. Determining the major points to convey is relatively easy—list the points that need to be shared and then rank order them in importance. Many times, clinicians find that some of the items they write out initially fall under other points. Some clinicians literally draw a line after the four or five most important points, saving items below the line for another occasion.

For a long report with many critical points, it can be helpful to say something like, "I am going to hit the highlights of this lengthy report. I will give you a copy. After you get home and read the report, if you have questions about anything I did not cover to your satisfaction, please e-mail me or give me a call. I'd be happy to answer any questions." The second author has found this to be highly successful with parents in long IEP meetings where the parents are given a great deal of information by various professionals.

Using three to five major points is helpful even if a client's speech, language, or hearing skills are fine and there is no need for concern. In this case, the three to five major points might be positive findings having to do with normal speech-sound production, language, oral structure and function, and hearing.

A majority of the information during information-getting interviews is provided by interviewees. With information-giving interviews, most of the information is provided by the clinician. When conducting an information-giving interview, however, clinicians still can seek additional, clarifying information. Clinicians should also allow interviewees sufficient opportunities to seek additional information they need or desire. The point is, interviews intended primarily to provide information are not "one-way streets."

Points to Ponder #14

You work in a public school setting where there are many children with speech–language disorders. You are not having great success with information-getting or information-giving interviews; many parents work and can't be bothered to attend your meetings. The few who do come seem very reticent about sharing information with you. Describe the strategies that you can use to motivate parents to attend meetings and share pertinent information during the interview process.

Closing the Interview

Once the major points have been discussed and the clinician is confident that the other party has understood the points, the interviewer moves into the closing phase. This phase allows the clinician to terminate the interaction systematically and smoothly. A good closing prevents the kind of awkward terminations that occur when "there doesn't seem to be anything else to talk about, so we might as well stop." An appropriate closing consists of the following:

- Summarizing the main points discussed
- Asking if there are any questions
- Expressing appreciation for the interviewee's time, help, and interest
- Sharing the next steps that will be taken

Clinicians summarize the major points discussed, repeat any conclusions drawn, and reiterate the major suggestions or recommendations provided, as in the following example:

> "I'm pleased we had this chance to talk. Again, our major findings were _____. This is why I believe that _____. What we need to consider doing next is _____."

This model allows clinicians to repeat main points in an easy-flowing, systematic manner. The major points, which were determined prior to the interview, are often the same items that end up being summarized in the closing phase. Additional points may have become important, and these are also included in the final summary.

Opportunities to ask questions are provided throughout the body of the interview and, hopefully, clients will take advantage of this. In the closing, there is a final opportunity to seek additional information or clarification.

 "We've talked about a number of things. Let me stop for a moment. You may have additional questions about some of the things we've talked about."

 "We've talked about several aspects of your voice. If you had one or two questions you really wanted to ask (or want me to go over again), what might they be?"

 "Is there something else you really want an answer to, or something that isn't very clear?"

In some cases, particularly when difficult-to-deal-with information has been covered, interviewees need time to collect their thoughts and to think about the information conveyed. We sometimes recommend calling a "time-out" for this purpose.

 "There's something I need to grab from the next room. Why don't you think about anything we need to discuss further, or questions you still have. I'll be back in a minute or two and we'll discuss your questions."

This type of time-out allows clients to think and then ask questions to clarify points that were not completely understood.

Another technique for stimulating questions is to tactfully ask patients for a summary of the major points discussed.

 "Suppose your wife (husband, parent, child, employer, physician, insurance company, one of my colleagues) were to ask you to talk about the most important things we discussed. What might you share?"

This request helps clinicians assess what information interviewees have and understand; it also allows the other party to discover areas that are still unclear. Thus, asking patients for this type of summary sometimes triggers clarifying questions.

Once all questions are satisfactorily addressed, clinicians thank those who were interviewed for their time, interest, or whatever else is appropriate. People are busy, and we believe it is always appropriate to thank them for their time. Any next steps in the clinical process are then briefly addressed. This can be as short as, "I'll be seeing Mark again Thursday, and you and I will talk again in about 2 weeks," or it may be more detailed, depending on the circumstances.

Basic Principles of Human Nature and Sharing Information

Ten Principles of Human Nature

Many variables influence how people receive and react to information shared. A few of these include the interviewer's personality and communicative style, the types of information shared, the manner in which information is conveyed, and individual differences among those who are interviewed. Donaghy (1990) writes about 10 basic principles of human nature that affect interactions. In the information that follows, the italicized comments are Donaghy's (1990, pp. 19–21); the nonitalicized comments are adaptations of his thoughts.

1. *No two people are alike.* People react differently to information; two individuals who receive identical information may not respond in the same manner.
2. *People are conditioned by their environment and past experiences.* Experiences that interviewees bring with them into an interaction affect their feelings about an interviewer, the situation itself, and any information conveyed.
3. *People behave both verbally and nonverbally on the basis of their needs.* Specific needs that clients bring into interactions will influence their behaviors. What needs do interviewees and counselees have that must be considered or addressed in the interview (to defend, to confirm, to be reassured, to be comforted, or other)?
4. *Needs may be conscious or unconscious.* Are interviewees aware of their needs? Are there unconscious needs that must be met?
5. *Needs have both logical and emotional elements.* Many times, an individual's first reaction and overriding feeling about someone or something occur at an emotional level. Logical or rational thinking may occur later. Clinicians who focus primarily or exclusively on rational levels are often unsuccessful, at least initially, when their clients are dealing on more emotional levels.

6. *A person's needs can distort their perceptions and recollections.* An individual's needs may influence or distort what interviewers convey or suggest. This is a primary reason why an expression such as "but that's not what I said to them" occurs.

7. *People need the recognition, acceptance, and approval of others.* This is important for clinicians to remember: successful interviewers and counselors recognize and affirm others.

   For example, the second author said to the grandmother of a child in therapy, "I know that it takes 4 to 5 hours a week of your time to bring Raymond for therapy. That's a lot, and he is fortunate to have a dedicated grandma like you." People greatly appreciate being acknowledged.

8. *People have a need to organize and structure the world.* Donaghy suggests that this is helpful in interviews; it is one reason people are willing to participate in the interviewing and counseling process. Clinicians benefit from people's needs for structure by their participation in these interactions, as well as their assistance in implementing suggestions. However, interviewees' needs to structure are unproductive if the ways in which they "organize" the world are by stereotyping kinds of attitudes (racially, culturally, genderwise) or in attitudes such as "therapy is a waste of time," "physicians are only out to make money," and so forth.

9. *People have a need to influence the world.* This is a powerful principle. People need to be heard and feel they are influencing the interaction. Interviewees who are brought into the clinical treatment process are helping shape their worlds. For example, a clinician could say to the wife of an Alzheimer's patient, "You were right. Fred loves *Sports Illustrated.* I've been using it in therapy, and he's responded well. Thanks for the suggestion!"

10. *Constructive and lasting changes usually come from satisfying, successful experiences.* One of our critical tasks is to help bring comfort and satisfaction to often troubled situations. Our clients and their families need to feel that what we are doing is actually making a positive difference.

Donaghy (1990) correctly notes that these basic principles only "scratch the surface" of human nature. These principles hold important implications for clinicians' interviewing and counseling activities. The discussion of motivation in Chapter 2 also is applicable here with regard to human nature and working effectively with people.

Specific Suggestions for Conveying Information

The following suggestions apply to all interviews in which information is conveyed. This includes discussions following assessment sessions as well as intervention efforts.

≋**If more than three to five important points need to be made, consider alternative methods for conveying the information.** Another session should be scheduled when there are many points to be made or there is a series of complex or difficult areas to discuss. Providing a list of the important areas discussed, including a brief comment about each, is useful, as is sending a follow-up letter (Martin, 1994). In some settings, an audiocassette recording can also be sent home with participants.

≋**Try to "sandwich" positive and negative points.** A "which would you like first, the good news or the bad news?" approach is generally inappropriate. Conveying all the "good news" first means all the negative information is provided at the end, and that may be what the client retains. On the other hand, if only "bad news" is conveyed first, the interviewee may not hear more positive aspects that are shared later on.

More important, receiving all the positive or the negative aspects at one time hinders developing a true picture of the communicative disorder. Sandwiching the information, on the other hand, allows clients to understand how various findings and factors relate to each other. For example, if a client has a speech problem because there are too many atypical speech sound errors (an example of bad news), the clinician can affirm that the client's hearing appears normal and does not account for the problem (an example of good news). By integrating this and additional information, clients begin to get an accurate picture of where the problem lies, what factors are or are not contributing to the problem, and so forth.

≋**Keep language use simple and appropriate.** As previously discussed, professional terminology is complex and not readily understandable for persons without advanced levels of education in the field. The extent of this terminology is illustrated by reviewing Nicolosi, Harryman, and Kresheck's (2004) *Terminology of Communication Disorders,* a dictionary that contains over 340 pages of definitions for terms used in the field. Of course, this source does not include all the medical, psychological, and educational terminology sometimes used by members of the professions.

Clinicians often use technical terminology on a day-to-day basis and are sometimes unaware of when or even how often they use it. Clinicians create confusion when they use acronyms, idiosyncratic terms, or terms that are used differently by different specialists (e.g., *developmental apraxia* and *dyspraxia, central auditory processing,* or even terms such as *mild, moderate,* and *severe*). To minimize confusion, an absolute minimum of technical terminology should be used in conversation with clients because most clients become confused by professional language. When such terms are necessary, or are used inadvertently, they should be defined in everyday language immediately.

 "Johnny's *articulation,* his speech sounds…"

 "Her *diadochokinetic rates,* how quickly she makes rapid speech movements…"

 "The *rugae,* those prominent ridges right behind his upper teeth…"

Be aware that language is not a static entity. Rather, word meanings depend on their context, current usage, and how a listener defines them.

≋ **Avoid relying on test names and protocols.** In a majority of cases, people are concerned more with the evaluation or treatment results than with the specific instruments that were used. For example, parents are interested in the fact that a clinician sampled how their child makes speech sounds, but it is meaningless to them whether the clinician used the *Arizona, Goldman–Fristoe, Photo Articulation Test, Templin–Darley,* or some other tool for this purpose. The use of test names can also be highly noncommunicative. Saying, "I gave Johnny the *Goldman–Fristoe Test of Articulation* and found three sound errors" can be stated more simply as, "I evaluated Johnny's speech sounds and found three sounds that he can't make." The same principle applies to procedures and tests used to assess fluency, hearing, language, and voice.

Some clinicians feel, perhaps naively, that sharing test protocols (scoring sheets) with clients somehow enhances understanding, but this usually does just the opposite by confusing them. What these clinicians fail to realize is that such materials do not mean anything to untrained persons. For example, remember your own confusion and uncertainty the first time you viewed an audiogram, a tympanogram, or the scoring sheets from language tests.

Luterman (2001) feels that it takes parents of children who are deaf or hearing impaired about a year to really understand an audiogram. Similarly, Martin (1994) suggests that most graphs tend to confuse patients. Throwing out fancy titles or showing test materials or score sheets is certainly no substitute for appropriate, communicative explanations of findings. This does not mean that test forms are never to be shared— just do not assume that what is interpretable by a clinician is necessarily understandable to someone else.

≋**Continuously watch for signs of misunderstanding or resistance.** Throughout a session, clinicians need to carefully observe interviewees for verbal and nonverbal signs that interviewees do not understand or are resisting the information being shared. Often, an interviewee's facial expressions or body posture will signal that some information is confusing or is not being fully accepted. Such signals are only caught by attending to such factors.

Points to Ponder #15

Because you are a new clinician, you feel very nervous about conducting information-giving interviews. Many of the parents are older than you are, and some are highly educated (e.g., attorneys, physicians). Discuss ideas that you will implement to conduct these interviews successfully.

≋**Accept emotional responses professionally, supportively, and matter-of-factly.** Being told that there is a problem is an emotional moment for people. Suppose you were told your last five checks had bounced, that your car needed $2,000 worth of repairs, that the one class you needed to graduate had been cancelled, or that the pay raise you were hoping for was denied. All of these are problems that could cause any of us a good deal of emotion at the moment. Now imagine the emotion involved in being told that a loved one's stroke has caused severe problems understanding others, that a child cannot hear, that a hearing aid will not help, that one's child has autism, or that long-term therapy is needed. These types of situations are typically accompanied by considerable emotion.

Conversely, consider the opposite range of feelings, those of absolute delight, exhilaration, or relief. People cry at joyous occasions and in pleasant situations, such as at births, graduations, and weddings; when they win the lottery; and when they watch a touching story on television or at the movies. Now consider potential reactions when people are told that there is no problem with a loved one's speech, that a hearing aid can help, or that certain problems could be overcome with assistance. Good news can trigger an emotional release from many people.

Tears and other signs of emotion, whether they are the result of good news or bad news, should be handled matter-of-factly, supportively, and certainly without any criticism (Shames, 2000). Such expressions of emotionality do not suggest weakness. Clinicians need to have facial tissues available to offer to clients who are affected emotionally. It is also helpful to let the other person know that demonstration of such emotion is fine. In most cases, the emotional release is therapeutic.

We have found that when someone starts crying, it is helpful to say something like, "It's okay to cry. This is very upsetting news" or "Go ahead and cry. It's okay. You're facing some very difficult times." People are relieved to be reassured that their tears are accepted, not short-circuited.

Other Factors for Effective Communication

There are several other principles interviewers should keep in mind. The following suggestions, which are based on Emerick (1969) and Haynes and Pindzola (1998), are useful when imparting information.

≋**Be alert for emotional static or confusion that inhibits the ability to understand.** When either clinicians or those who are interviewed or counseled are feeling anxious or emotionally preoccupied, optimal understanding and communication does not occur. Clinicians should be sensitive to such problems within themselves and with their clients.

≋**Refrain from lecturing or being didactic.** Lectures are typically not appreciated in interviewing, counseling, or general conversational situations. Information is obtained from or conveyed to others best when the other parties are treated as "conversational equals." Even better, consider clients and families as partners in the process (Campbell, 1993; Schuyler & Rushmer, 1987; Thornton, 1994).

Do not, however, shirk the responsibility of providing direction and structure in interviewing and counseling situations. A number of clients, including some from linguistically and culturally diverse backgrounds, enter into sessions with the expectation that the authority figure will control the situation. Clinicians will need to provide direction, provide specific counsel, and make appropriate recommendations. However, this can be done in conversational and partnership ways that do not involve a one-sided monologue or lecturing the other person.

≈**Try to provide constructive action for the party being interviewed.** It can be very upsetting for some clients to be told that there is a problem without being given something to do to help resolve the difficulty. This is particularly important if clients cannot be seen for service rather quickly or if a client is placed on a waiting list. It is like telling a student he or she is not doing well in a class. Out of a desire to improve the situation, the student's first question often is, "What can I do to improve my grade?" The client, like the student, wants to do something to improve the situation. This is especially true for parents of children with disabilities (Dodge, 2000). Many times, there are some activities or actions that can be suggested.

≈**Present negative information pleasantly but candidly.** Martin (1994) comments that "the skill with which 'bad news' is initially delivered may have a profound effect on acceptance of the disorder and all the efforts toward rehabilitation that become necessary" (p. 39). It can be difficult to present bad news, but it is inappropriate to provide false assurances or to fail to convey findings and impressions accurately and honestly. Say what needs to be said kindly but candidly. The presentation of negative information sometimes needs to be preceded with more positive aspects of the situation, particularly with some individuals from cultures that place value on degrees of indirectness (e.g., Filipino or Native American).

Some cultures, such as the European American culture, are relatively direct and "to the point." Other cultures are less direct. However, degrees of directness generally refer to how information is conveyed and what information precedes or prefaces certain presentations. Across cultures, clinicians still need to convey what has to be said—the differences are in how and in what order they do this.

Clinicians should share information respectfully, and, when possible, cheerfully (Mowrer, 1988). However, it is not always possible for clinicians to be cheerful, especially when they must deliver bad news. To convey respect appropriately in these situations, clinicians can incorporate the following suggestions (Pachter & McGee, 2000):

- Be direct, honest, and compassionate.
- Try to soften the bad news when possible. For example, a clinician could say, "Your child has an above-average

nonverbal IQ, and this will be quite beneficial to him as he goes through school. However, he does have moderately severe problems with verbal expression, and we will discuss that in this meeting." Or an audiologist might tell a client, "Fortunately, you are able to hear speech quite well when it is quiet. Unfortunately, when there is noise in the background, you have more difficulty."

- Express sympathy if appropriate. For example, when telling a family that one of its members has been diagnosed definitively with dementia, the clinician could say, "I know this must be a difficult time for you and your family. I'm so sorry. I will do whatever I can to support you through this."

It is important that the clinician never say "I know just how you feel" or "I understand what you are going through" (unless, of course, the clinician has been in similar circumstances). Clients and their families may feel disrespected and justifiably angered by this statement, because usually, the clinician has never undergone a similar experience. However, as stated, there are constructive and respectful things that the clinician can say when discussing difficult situations.

≋ **Realize that the "bearer of bad news" may be subjected to an interviewee's anger or other negative reactions.** Anyone can be blamed for something. A physician may be blamed for identifying a serious disorder, an innocent store clerk verbally assaulted for the high costs of products, or a meal server criticized for cooking a bad meal. Clinicians are often the most available people for clients or their caregivers to criticize out of frustration. Confident clinicians are prepared to serve as emotional lightning rods for clients, if need be. Clinicians are aware that many expressions of anger and other feelings, although they may be directed at the professional, are not really aimed at or caused by them (Dodge, 2000). Parents may express anger at clinicians for telling them that their child has a language learning disability. In these cases, the parents are not really mad at the clinician; they are very upset by the information that their child has a problem or challenge that requires intervention.

≋ **Whenever possible and appropriate, provide encouragement to clients and family members.** Interviews tend to result in more positive action when strengths and possibilities are emphasized rather than weaknesses and limitations. Sometimes, a client's acknowledgment that there may be a problem is an important first step toward progress.

≈**Don't be surprised if suggestions are not acted on immediately.** Not everyone will heed advice or suggestions made (Mowrer, 1988; Shipley & Wood, 1996). If well-intended, sound advice were always taken, there would be far fewer unwanted pregnancies, people would not smoke, alcohol and drugs would not be abused, and so forth. The same principle applies to communication disorders. Not every patient will follow exactly what the professional suggests. From time to time, clients will seek confirmation of their own feelings and conclusions, irrespective of what the clinician or other professionals say. These clients fail to accept clinicians' findings and recommendations, and they will continue to seek confirmation of their beliefs elsewhere.

Some clinicians, especially beginning clinicians, are offended when a client or family member wants a second opinion. However, it is important to remember that a diagnosis such as profound hearing loss or aphasia is devastating to clients and their families, and, being human, they hope that this diagnosis is incorrect. An accurate diagnosis like "Your child is profoundly deaf" has such far-reaching implications that families may go to great lengths to find a more palatable diagnosis. We know the mother of a child diagnosed with autism who said, "Any parent worth her salt will get a second opinion." She went to four or five professionals before she was willing to accept the diagnosis. It can be helpful if an exchange can be made along the following lines:

PARENT: My child is not deaf! I am going to get a second opinion.

CLINICIAN: The diagnosis of deafness is really tough to take. I don't blame you. Sometimes a second opinion can be helpful.

PARENT: I really don't think my child needs therapy for his articulation skills. He is still little. I wonder if other speech pathologists would agree with you?

CLINICIAN: I can give you a list of other local speech pathologists if you would like. You might call one of them and arrange for an appointment to get a second opinion.

Often, a confident clinician who is willing to give such a supportive response ends up appearing more credible in the eyes of the client or family member who was initially defensive.

Points to Ponder #16

You are having lunch with the school psychologist toward the end of the school year. You feel quite relaxed with George; he is somewhat older than you and has a great deal more experience. You and George have been in many information-obtaining and information-giving interviews together. You ask George for any suggestions for improvement. He tells you that while you are excellent at asking questions, you have a very difficult time delivering the "bad news" that a child has a speech–language disorder. He says that you get quite flustered when parents get upset with you. Describe several possible things you could be doing ineffectively, and suggest strategies to improve during the next year.

▷ Concluding Comments

An information-giving interview, like the information-getting interview discussed in Chapter 5, can be seen as proceeding through three distinct phases—an opening, the body, and a closing. By approaching the interview systematically in terms of these three phases and working at smooth transitions between the segments, clinicians minimize confusion and reduce awkward moments of undirected conversation.

A clinician's preparation for an information-giving interview is important. The interviewer should carefully choose the major points to be shared with an eye toward avoiding information overload. Three to five points is often a good general rule. Clinicians should also plan the presentation of specific observations and general conclusions in relation to an interviewee's emotional state, such as whether the interviewee is highly anxious about information that will be presented.

Just as important for the success of providing information is the skill with which clinicians communicate their information and suggestions to clients: balancing good and bad news, choosing the language to use carefully, staying alert for signs of confusion or misunderstanding, and dealing professionally with emotional responses. The closing phase of the interview provides a final opportunity for the clinician to summarize and clarify points for the client's understanding.

SEVEN

Counseling

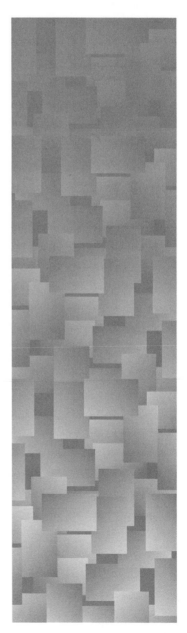

CHAPTER OUTLINE

Counseling is an important aspect of clinical work. In their professional practices, clinicians frequently engage in counseling activities, whether they call it interviewing, helping, or counseling. They discuss communicative disorders, their effects, and their treatment with clients, families, and other caregivers. Clinicians provide ideas and methods for promoting communicative growth and for coping with different problems. They help clients and families release or identify feelings related to communicative difficulties, help people adjust to or cope better with their difficulties, and then face new challenges and develop new skills.

Stated differently, one role of counseling activities is to help clients adjust to current situations—that is, to help them cope with a communicative disorder and its ramifications in life. Another function is to help patients and caregivers release "pent-up" frustrations and deal with their lives in more productive manners. A third basic function is to facilitate learning, which is, in effect, teaching clients or caregivers more about the nature of a particular disorder or its treatment. A fourth function is to help alter or modify people's feelings, attitudes, or behaviors that are helping to maintain a communicative disorder, or are counterproductive to improving the problem.

In other words, clinicians seek to bring about for clients greater understanding of themselves, their feelings, their environments, their communicative disorders and the disorders' effects, and changes that are necessary to improve their situations. Clinicians, therefore, need to develop the skills to enable such understanding and promote changes that are considered appropriate.

Counseling Defined

Counseling in audiology and speech–language pathology has been defined as advising, directing, and exchanging opinions and ideas (Scheuerle, 1992). Counseling has also been considered within the context of informing, persuading, or listening to and valuing others (Luterman, 2001). Counseling is defined here quite simply as a helping relationship that involves one party who needs help, another party who provides help, and a setting that allows a helping process to occur (Cormier & Hackney, 1987). Counseling involves a number of different functions. It is certainly more than a standard set of procedures; counseling is a process that includes a series of caring and purposeful actions to achieve preselected and specific objectives and goals (Purkey & Schmidt, 1987).

Counseling
A helping relationship that involves one party who needs help, another party who provides help, and a setting that allows a helping process to occur.

Characteristics of Good Counselors

An important characteristic of counselors in our field is the willingness to expand personal boundaries, to learn and experience more so that patients and families will benefit. A variety of other skills and attitudes characterize an effective counselor. The characteristics reviewed in Chapter 2—spontaneity, flexibility, concentration, openness, honesty, emotional stability, trustworthiness, self-awareness, belief in the client's ability to change, commitment to helping people change, wisdom, communication skills, and professional competence—are important for effective counseling.

Years ago, Erickson (1950) wrote that good counselors need to use a variety of methods and approaches, be able to shift from one method to another when appropriate, use the tools that work best for the client, be highly skilled, and remain skilled by continued study and self-improvement. These characteristics remain of paramount importance today (Corey, 2001; English, 2002; Hays, 2001).

Counseling in Educational and Clinical Settings

The Need for Counseling

The need for effective counseling as a part of the assessment or treatment of communicative disorders is noted in a number of audiology and speech–language pathology textbooks. Unfortunately, the sections dealing with counseling are often limited, at times simply to the general recommendation to provide counseling if it is needed. There are relatively few discussions of how to counsel, or even the specific areas that should be addressed. The need for counseling is also suggested in a variety of journal articles. Again, however, it is generally assumed that readers will already know what or how to counsel.

Despite widespread agreement about the need for interviewing and counseling abilities, these skills are often neglected in professional preparation programs and clinical and research literature (e.g., Clark, 1994a; Gregory, 1995; Hegde, 1993; Johnson, 1994; Rollin, 2000; Shames, 2000). Stone and Olswang (1989) comment that

> counseling and family involvement in treatment of communication disorders are not new activities per se, though current applications are expanded and innovative. … Despite counseling's historical and continuing place in communicative disorders, many professionals remain uncomfortable with counseling responsibilities.

Uncertainty persists as to where counseling fits into communication disorders works. … Such uncertainty may be because few speech–language pathologists and audiologists receive adequate educational preparation in counseling since counseling courses are significantly underrepresented in standard speech and hearing curricula.… Thus, although most speech–language pathologists and audiologists agree on the importance of counseling they may feel they lack the necessary tools to incorporate counseling into their work. (p. 27)

Webster and Ward (1993) outline the following four major functions of communicative disorders specialists who work with parents: (a) obtaining information; (b) giving information; (c) understanding and clarifying ideas, attitudes, emotions, and behaviors; and (d) offering alternatives for personal behavior, or the behavior of others, and assisting in making these changes (pp. 4–5). These functions apply to the specialists' relationships not only with parents, but also with clients, irrespective of age. Obtaining and providing information are discussed in Chapter 5. The understanding and clarification of ideas, attitudes, emotions, and behaviors, as well as assisting people in making changes, are issues that are addressed primarily in this chapter.

Counseling activities can focus on the past by addressing what has occurred, on the present by addressing what is currently happening, or on the future by determining and promoting what needs to be done. Sometimes counseling is a matter of educating; at other times, counseling is directed more toward helping interviewees ventilate their feelings and reducing "blocks" that aggravate a patient's or family's situation.

Guidance, Counseling, and Psychotherapy

Many clinicians lack formal preparation for counseling and experience uncertainty concerning the boundaries of counseling (Flasher & Fogle, 2004). How, for example, is counseling different from guidance or psychotherapy? Each of these three activities is different, and yet they sometimes overlap, causing role confusion for clinicians.

Guidance, counseling, and psychotherapy should be viewed as activities on a continuum rather than as well-defined, distinct practices (Mowrer, 1988; Rollin, 2000). Mowrer (1988) notes that each of these functions is actually a process. The process of guidance generally involves providing information to people; counseling involves helping people solve problems by doing more than simply providing information; and psychotherapy involves helping individuals make more profound personal adjustments.

Psychotherapy is concerned with the treatment of psychological abnormality, encouraging considerable individual adjustment and sometimes even basic personality changes (Shames, 2000). Using a medical model, Rollin (2000) feels that individuals requiring psychotherapy are "sick" and need help to alter psychopathological feelings and behavior. Thus, psychotherapy generally falls within the province of psychiatry, clinical psychology, or other mental health professions.

Psychotherapy
Treatment of psychological abnormality.

Counseling deals with personal adjustment rather than major personality changes. Counseling helps people examine their methods or styles of interacting with others, analyze their positive and counterproductive behaviors, evaluate and face their values and beliefs, increase their personal awareness and self-knowledge, and achieve self-development. Counseling helps an otherwise normal person make adjustments. English (2002) states that

Counseling
Professional guidance to help a client make personal adjustment rather than major personality changes.

> personal adjustment counseling *attempts to match an affective statement with an affective response—that is, a response that lets a parent or child know that the affect or feeling was heard, and that the listener is attending carefully to that feeling. Instead of the "one-way street" of communication found in informational counseling, personal adjustment counseling uses an "open-ended" approach, which requires that the professional do two very difficult things: (1) stop talking, and (2) listen, or more accurately, listen effectively …, we can follow a process … help people tell their story, help them clarify their problem, and help them challenge themselves to solve the problem.* (pp. 7–8)

Guidance is a method of influencing another person's thoughts or behaviors that is typically less formal than counseling or psychotherapy. Guidance may or may not be provided by someone with advanced or specific training. Generally, guidance involves an educational process in which information is dispensed (Mowrer, 1988). Advice may be given, suggestions may be offered, informational materials may be distributed, and so forth.

Guidance
A method of influencing another person's thoughts or behaviors; typically less formal than counseling or psychotherapy.

Speech–language pathologists and audiologists are ideally suited to provide guidance and many types of counseling because of their intensive training in rehabilitative procedures, and because they work directly and intensively with individuals who have disabilities (Mowrer, 1988).

> *The question sometimes arises, "Can't the speech patholo-gist or audiologist do damage to parents by attempting to counsel with them?" The answer depends in part on how one defines counseling. If counseling means the im-position of prescriptions without care for the person for whom they are prescribed, one may indeed do damage. The nonaccepting, noncompassionate clinician runs the risk of hurting parents; so does the one who focuses con-cern on the child to the exclusion of concern for the par-ents. The speech pathologist or audiologist who leaves to others the interpretation of the information his [or her] field has to offer may do parents great harm. The same can be said for the clinician with limited knowledge who gives faulty information.* (Mowrer, 1988, p. 339)

Professionals who treat communicative disorders need counseling skills in order to serve the best interests of their cli-ents. Counseling is being used more and more in the treatment of communicative disorders and in new and different ways, so clinicians must remain flexible and willing to work with various counseling theories, approaches, and procedures. However, speech and hearing professionals also need to be aware of their limitations as counselors. It is critical that clinicians have the judgment to know when their training and experience will not suffice, and when they should make referrals to professionals with more specialized counseling or psychotherapeutic train-ing. This leads to considering the concept of boundaries.

Boundaries of Counseling

The American Speech-Language-Hearing Association's (1990) *Scope of Practice* specifically mentions counseling as an appro-priate function of speech–language pathologists and audiolo-gists. Stone and Olswang (1989) note that, although there has long been a need for professionals in our field to involve them-selves in counseling activities, there are also somewhat per-vasive "discomfort levels" about counseling. What is it? Who should do it? What should it entail or encompass? When should it be done? Stone and Olswang appropriately note that much of this discomfort originates from two sources: (a) our profes-sions' general lack of preprofessional exposure to counseling and (b) the question of boundaries. What are, for example, the roles and responsibilities of professionals in communicative disorders, and what are the roles and responsibilities of other professionals (psychologists, mental health counselors, social workers)? It is important to understand our roles, as well as those roles that are best served by others (Mathers-Schmidt, 2001). Some of the information in the following paragraphs is based on Stone and Olswang's (1989) contribution.

Knowing one's boundaries does not occur in a single lesson because the boundaries change and (hopefully) expand across time. Boundaries are related to the individual clinician and that person's skills and abilities, the setting in which the person works, and the clients being served and their needs. For example, clinicians working in settings or locations where mental health specialists are not readily available will involve themselves in activities that other clinicians who have greater access to psychologists, counselors, or other mental health professionals will not. The basic goals of counseling include (a) establishing an environment within which change can occur; (b) providing information about communicative disorders and their remediation; (c) providing release and support for those who need it; and (d) assisting in the improvement or resolution of patients' or families' problems, particularly as they pertain to a communicative disorder.

These are all activities that fall within the domain of professionals in communicative disorders. However, counseling intended to make major personality adjustments or change basic response patterns to events in life typically are best handled by an appropriately trained mental health professional (Mathers-Schmidt, 2001). The counseling we do helps people adapt to, live with, and work toward improving a communicative problem and its ramifications.

There are internally and externally defined boundaries that describe roles in counseling. Internally defined boundaries relate to how individuals perceive their own abilities and skills. "I can help with that" or "I need to help my client address _____" versus "I can't talk with clients about _____" or "That's not my job" are examples of internally defined boundaries. Good clinicians work to expand their internally defined boundaries and, thus, serve their patients better.

Externally defined boundaries refer to some limitation placed on a clinician by external forces. Not trying to assist a patient overcome a phobia of heights or of snakes or spiders is an externally defined boundary because such help customarily and appropriately falls within the province of a mental health professional. A restrictive job description or the expectations of colleagues in the work setting are also examples of externally defined boundaries.

Either internally or externally defined boundaries can influence what the counselor does with patients. In general, the role of professionals in communicative disorders is to expand boundaries—whether internal or external—so as to provide the services needed by patients and families. Boundaries change, particularly as clinicians acquire greater skills, abilities, and experience, and as other people see how effective professionals in communicative disorders can be in situations or with problems.

Internally or externally defined boundaries can influence the content of counseling efforts. Attitudes, behaviors, information, and problems associated with communication disorders are clearly within our province. Who else, for example, knows more about these areas than audiologists and speech–language pathologists? Areas that are beyond speech and hearing clinicians' boundaries include subjects such as unrelated medical problems, chronic unhappiness and depression, marital instability, and domestic violence (Stone & Olswang, 1989). Stone and Olswang note that some areas—interpersonal relations between persons with communicative disorders and significant others, a client's deep grieving about a communicative disorder, difficulties adjusting to a communicative disorder, and helping with behavior management with communicatively disordered children—often "test the boundaries" within which we work. However, other authorities (e.g., Leith, 1993) see speech–language pathologists, in particular, as being among the best persons available to assist with these types of problems. Certainly, when such problems are related to a communication disorder, the speech and hearing specialist can be extremely helpful.

Points to Ponder #17

You are working on a team at an audiology clinic that deals almost entirely with adults with acquired hearing impairments. These older adults, who need hearing aids, often express depression, anger, or both when told they need hearing aids. You mention to your colleagues that you have had a class in counseling, and that you might have some useful ideas for helping these older adults adjust to their hearing losses and the need for amplification. Your colleagues, who have never had such a class, say, "That's not our area. We just refer to psychologists. Of course, the clients never go, but hey … our business is dispensing hearing aids, not being shrinks." What will you say to them?

Approaches to Counseling

All approaches to counseling have the person-to-person nature of the work in common. Counseling, as we have defined it, is a helping relationship in which one participant assumes the responsibility of helping the other. It is further assumed that both participants see the welfare of the one being helped as the central concern of the relationship, and that the participants will work together toward solutions to problems that influence that welfare. In the case of a clinician counseling a young patient's parents, it is the welfare of a third party—the child—that is the central concern.

The speech and hearing fields do not have unique or distinctively different approaches to counseling than other fields. Indeed, professionals in communication disorders have relied on different approaches initially developed for use in psychology and other counseling professions. It is beyond the scope of this book to describe all the different approaches that have been developed over the years, and it is not necessary. For readers who are interested in the different approaches, Meier and Davis's (1993) *The Elements of Counseling* contains a brief, clear description of the major counseling types. Other resources containing more information include Brammer (1993), Corey (2001), Flasher and Fogle (2004), Mowrer (1988), Okun (2002), Rollin (2000), and Shames (2000). The approaches most frequently useful in speech and hearing are described in the sections that follow. But first, we describe the notions of directive and nondirective approaches to helping.

Directive and Nondirective Approaches

An important way in which counseling approaches vary is in the degree of direction that counselors provide to clients. In directive (or active) approaches, it is the clinician who takes major responsibility for assessing the problems encountered and for focusing any intervention or treatment (Stewart & Cash, 2003). Counselors taking this approach

Directive counseling
Approach in which the clinician takes major responsibility for assessing the problems and focusing intervention or treatment.

Nondirective counseling
Approach in which clients take a greater role in determining problems and possible solutions.

play an active role in directing the discussions and activities of intervention. In nondirective approaches, on the other hand, the client plays a greater role in determining the problems and their possible solutions. Nondirective methodologies tend to stress the creation of an atmosphere in which clients engage in self-explorations that ultimately lead them to their own healthful conclusions about themselves, others, and the problems at hand.

Nondirective approaches are often associated with the client-centered therapy advocated by Carl Rogers (1951, 1986). In client-centered counseling the client is encouraged to take most of the responsibility for providing direction to the interactions.

Rogers's client-centered approach assumes that clients have the capacity for self-direction and constructive personal change. Specific goals are not imposed on clients; rather, clients develop their own goals (Corey, 2001). This approach is very useful when professionals need to help clients release pent-up emotions, clarify specific feelings, understand certain reactions, and learn to accept certain problems. Rogers's approach can be especially helpful when clinicians are dealing with clients and families soon after the initial diagnosis of a problem (Roseberry-McKibbin & Hegde, 2006).

Directive approaches are useful when clinicians are reasonably sure of a problem and appropriate alternatives for its treatment. Such is the case in most clinical activities in communicative disorders because speech–language pathologists or audiologists typically know what the disorder is and what course of action is needed. In these cases, a form of directive counseling allows clinicians to share information and to work more directly toward modifying certain feelings, attitudes, and behavior that are connected to the disorder.

Client-Centered Approach

It has already been noted that client-centered approaches are typically associated with Carl Rogers's work in psychotherapy. These approaches are generally indirect, placing primary responsibility on clients for providing direction, and even some structure, to interactions. There are clinical situations in communicative disorders for which it is helpful to yield responsibility for direction to clients who need to work out personal feelings and reactions.

When a client or family member becomes emotional (e.g., cries or gets angry), many clinicians make the mistake of trying prematurely to get that person back into a "cognitive role" (Fogle, 1998). It is easy for clinicians to immediately start giving ad-

Client-centered counseling

Approach in which the client is encouraged to take most of the responsibility for providing direction to the interactions.

vice, suggestions, and information to short-circuit the expression of feelings and start trying to change the client's or family member's behavior. But Luterman (2001) emphasizes that for most clients, being listened to and understood is a foundational first step which precedes the clinician's giving advice and suggesting action steps. If a client feels truly understood, he or she is more likely to comply with the clinician's suggestions (Greenberg, Watson, Elliott, & Bohart, 2001). Thus, if clinicians can be patient enough to listen, empathize, and allow clients to express their feelings, clients will be more likely to follow the advice that is given later. Consider this example of Mrs. F, the wife of a patient with Alzheimer's disease:

MRS. F: (*starting to cry*) I'm just so overwhelmed by caring for Wes. He doesn't even want me to leave the house. Our children live far away, and I'm so lonely. And I am *so* tired. Sometimes I just don't know how I can go on much longer.

CLINICIAN: Well, yes, ahem. Here's a tissue. There are lots of things we can do to help both you and Wes. First of all, do you have e-mail? If not, you might consider getting e-mail so you can e-mail back and forth with your children and friends from church. And there is respite care here in Apple City. You just need to be firm with Wes and get 1 to 2 hours a day for yourself. Here, I am going to give you the respite care hotline number.

Although it is the clinician's job to give Mrs. F constructive help and suggestions in answer to her needs, it might have been more helpful to hear and acknowledge Mrs. F's emotions first:

MRS. F: (*starting to cry*) I'm just so overwhelmed by caring for Wes. He doesn't even want me to leave the house. Our children live far away, and I'm so lonely. And I am *so* tired. Sometimes I just don't know how I can go on much longer.

CLINICIAN: It must be so hard on you to feel like you can't even go to the grocery store for half an hour.

MRS. F: It is! Sometimes I feel like a prisoner in my own home.

CLINICIAN: You and Wes were very active members of your community, especially the church, before he had Alzheimer's. This is a major and stressful change in your lifestyle.

MRS. F: Boy, is that true. I feel like my whole world has turned upside down.

CLINICIAN: And you miss your children. I can see that you feel sad and lonely partially because you are rarely in contact with them.

MRS. F: I miss them more than anything. I know they're busy ... I just wish they could pick up the phone once in a while.

CLINICIAN: There are a lot of stressors in your life: feeling cooped up at home, missing your children, being so tired ... I can see how it would be really difficult to make it from one day to the next.

MRS. F: (*starting to cry harder*) I just don't know how I am going to make it. I'm sorry I'm crying. I just can't help it.

CLINICIAN: Mrs. F, it's okay to cry. This is a very sad and difficult time in your life.

MRS. F: (*crying starts to subside after a few minutes*) It is. I just never thought I'd be in this situation.

CLINICIAN: Your feelings are a very natural response to a distressing and trying time in your life. You have every right to feel sad and lonely. I'd like to offer a few ideas that will make things easier for you.

MRS. F: Do you really think you can help?

CLINICIAN: Yes, you bet. I have a few ideas for you. First, we have a respite care center here in Apple City...

In this example, the clinician used elements of the Rogerian approach: She encouraged the client to freely express her emotions, she was warm and accepting, and she listened to and reflected Mrs. F's feelings. It was only after Mrs. F's feelings had been released and empathized with that the clinician began to make constructive suggestions to help Mrs. F cope more successfully with her husband's illness. Again, elements of the Rogerian approach can be helpful when a client or family member is facing strong emotions and needs to release these emotions before moving on to positive action (Dodge, 2000; Roseberry-McKibbin & Hegde, 2006). As English (2002) states, when people feel unconditionally accepted, they are often in more of a "learning-readiness mindset" (p. 44).

Rogers's client-centered approach has some limitations for clients and families from culturally diverse backgrounds. First, some multicultural clients (e.g., Arab, Chinese) expect clinicians to be directive and structured (Corey, 2001; Dwairy, 1998; Lin, 2002). Dwairy states that Arab clients seek guidance and advice and would find a nondirective approach confusing, uncomfortable, and threatening. Members of the Chinese culture are often comfortable with an authoritarian approach; they expect and want the clinician to give advice. Members of some cultures like the Chinese and Arab cultures are socialized to conceal their true feelings in many circumstances (Fung & Roseberry-McKibbin, 1999). Among Asian Americans, self-restraint and reserve are viewed as admirable traits which indicate maturity and self-control (Hays, 2001). Because client-centered approaches strongly encourage the expression of feelings, use of these approaches would be quite uncomfortable for Asian and Arab clients and families. However, the client-centered approach might work well for families from backgrounds where more open discussion of feelings is encouraged. For example, McEachern and Kenny (2002) found that Hispanic families in their study had more open expression of feelings than families from other cultural backgrounds. Clinicians should strive to evaluate each family individually and use the most effective approach or combination of approaches.

Behavioral Approach

When a clinician has allowed the client or family member to freely experience and express emotions, then it is often easier to move into using behavioral counseling to help that client or family member make constructive changes. Behavioral counseling grew out of the work of B. F. Skinner and those who followed him in operant learning and conditioning. The movement toward behavioral counseling is a significant departure from previous counseling approaches, which were for the most part phenomenological (i.e., subjective, intentional, motive oriented). A behavioral approach to counseling is generally distinguished by its focus on specifically identifiable attitudes or behaviors of clients, rather than on presumed "deep" underlying causes of those attitudes or behaviors. The focus is on what can be observed and measured objectively—behavior understood as the outward manifestation of feelings and attitudes—rather than on the subjectively determined, speculative, or unknown origins of a problem. In this approach to counseling, behavior is often defined as including only objectively or publicly observable responses. That behavior is understood as being a response means that it can be learned through the use of operant conditioning methods—that is, through positive reinforcement, negative reinforcement, and/or punishment of responses elicited. This is an important premise of the behavioral approach to counseling.

A behavioral approach to counseling is very attractive to professionals treating communicative disorders because it allows them to focus on areas that affect a client's communicative abilities. In other words, clinicians can focus primarily on feelings, attitudes, or behaviors that pertain directly to communicative difficulties, thus limiting themselves to areas for which they have had proper training and experience. Furthermore, clinicians are already well trained in and knowledgeable about the techniques that effectively promote change. Using a behavioral model, clinicians implement consistent procedures that utilize appropriate shaping techniques and procedures to alter clients' behavior or to influence clients' feelings and attitudes.

A behavioral approach also is appealing to clinicians because the effects of counseling can be measured on an ongoing basis. By evaluating behaviors before and after sessions, or following a series of sessions, clinicians monitor the effectiveness of their counseling efforts. Finally, behavioral approaches are attractive because they are very effective.

Krumboltz and Thoresen (1969), pioneers in behavioral counseling, describe the four essential features of a behavioral orientation: selecting a goal, tailoring specific procedures and techniques to meet the client's needs, experimenting with techniques while simultaneously assessing their effectiveness, and constant monitoring of feedback from the counseling session. These features are fundamental to most clinical intervention activities. Behavioral approaches are well grounded and useful because of the following (Brown & Brown, 1975; Hegde, 1993):

- The basic principles, being empirically derived, are based on observation and experience.
- The effectiveness of behavioral techniques for altering behavior makes them ideal in clinical settings where the effects of specific behaviors can be pinpointed.
- Behavioral techniques produce observable data to support the effectiveness of intervention.

A behavioral approach allows clinicians to select goals and objectives to be achieved through counseling efforts. Whenever possible, counselors and counselees should agree on goals that are attainable and measurable. The orientation does not call for the exclusive use of a single procedure or specific set of procedures. Rather, counselors employ a variety of possible techniques to alter or influence behavior and attitudes. Many appropriate reinforcement or punishment procedures can be employed. Clinicians can also use teaching methods such as direct instruction, modeling, feedback, and providing specific suggestions. Behaviorally based counseling allows clinicians to evaluate different techniques, the effects of which can be determined through the results of counseling efforts on an on-going basis, after one session or a series of sessions, after a week or a month or 3 months, and so forth (Krumboltz & Thoresen, 1969).

Behavioral approaches can work well with multicultural clients who are reluctant to share their feelings and who expect specific advice. Behavioral counseling does not emphasize experiencing catharsis. Rather, it focuses on changing behaviors and developing problem-solving skills and action plans. For some clients and families, such as those from Asian backgrounds, behavioral approaches feel culturally comfortable and appropriate (Corey, 2001).

Cognitive Behavioral Approach

Another effective counseling model is the cognitive approach, often used in combination with behavioral approaches. Ellis (2001) describes rational emotive behavior therapy (REBT), which is a model used by many clinicians (Burns, 1999; Corey, 2001; McMullin, 2000). Ellis's (2001) fundamental premise is that clients need to see that their irrational beliefs play a large part in their emotional dysfunction. Simply put, cognitive approaches stress that thoughts create emotions. A person who has negative emotions needs to change his or her thoughts, and will feel better as a result.

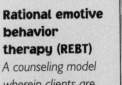

Rational emotive behavior therapy (REBT)
A counseling model wherein clients are encouraged to see that their irrational beliefs play a large role in their emotional dysfunction.

Leith (1993) provides the following example:

> a stutterer who feels that when he stutters, everyone stops what they are doing and looks at him. He will not order food in a restaurant because everyone will hear him, look at him, watch him as he completes his order, and discuss him with others at their table. He feels that he becomes the center of attention when he stutters. If the waitress stands across from him to take his order, he is even more intimidated since, if he speaks up, all of the people in the restaurant will turn and look at him. (p. 208)

With a patient like this, there are two problems: the stuttering behaviors themselves and the rather intense, self-conscious feelings about being dysfluent. It is possible that, even if this client's dysfluencies were reduced or eliminated, at least some of the intense feelings about "always being watched" would remain. Thus, a cognitive behavioral approach is used to modify or eliminate some of these harmful and counterproductive feelings. This is done through counseling by (a) identifying and focusing on the precise problem area, (b) identifying the distorted thoughts (cognitions), (c) confronting the problem area with new thought (cognitive orientations), and (d) changing the thought (cognitive set) by objectively evaluating the new thoughts.

The clinician who uses REBT actively disputes a client's irrational beliefs. Ellis (2001) emphasizes that REBT "insists on homework assignments … and on other forms of active work on the part of the patient" (p. 60). Clients are asked to make lists of their problems, look at their absolutistic beliefs (e.g., "my life is ruined because I stutter"), and dispute those beliefs. In doing homework, clients are encouraged to put themselves in risk-taking situations that will allow them to challenge their self-limiting beliefs (Corey, 2001). Roseberry-McKibbin and Hegde (2006) give the following example of how the REBT approach might be used successfully with a client with spasmodic dysphonia. This client believes that everyone avoids him because of how he sounds, and thus is unwilling to practice therapy techniques that the clinician recommends.

- *Help the client explore his or her thinking.* CLINICIAN: "So you believe that everyone avoids you because of your voice. Does everyone avoid you, or just some people?"
- *Challenge the client to test the validity of his or her old belief through experimentation.* CLINICIAN: "When you go to that barbecue after work on Friday, observe people's reactions to you. Does everyone avoid you, or just some people?"
- *Create a change in thinking through analyzing the data gathered through experimentation.* CLINICIAN: "What happened at the barbecue?" CLIENT: "Lots of people talked to me. A few appeared uncomfortable and moved away." Thus, after the barbecue, the clinician and client compare the client's thinking or old belief to the positive evidence gathered at the party.
- *Create a change in behavior based on new, positive evidence.* The clinician uses the new, positive evidence to motivate the client to take active steps to improve his voice through such techniques as relaxation, easy onset, and others. (Adapted from p. 732)

Burns (1999) discusses the fact that clients and family members may have cognitive distortions about the communication disorder and variables related to it. In using REBT, the clinician looks for and deals with cognitive distortions. These can include the following:

1. *"Should" statements.* "I should always wear my hearing aids." *Should* statements make clients and family members feel coerced, resentful, and pressured. The clinician can help the client change his thinking and wording to "I *choose to* wear my hearing aids." If people feel that clinicians are trying to pressure them to do something, the counseling frequently fails. It is far better to say, "You have two choices. If you choose to wear your hearing aids, you will hear better. If you choose not to wear them, you will miss out on many conversations and be more socially isolated. It is your choice."

2. *Overgeneralization.* If something happened once, it always will. A teenager who stutters may say, "I never go out. I called a girl on the phone once for a date. When I stuttered, she hung up on me. Girls will always hang up when I call." The clinician can gently help this teenager to see that this occurred one time and may not necessarily occur all the time.

3. *All-or-nothing thinking.* This person thinks in absolutes, in black and white. "Because I have Parkinson's disease, my life is over. I'm worthless. I can't go rock climbing, and I can't go to parties because my speech is slurred." The clinician can help this client to see that "Yes, some of your activities like rock climbing are no longer possible. But you can enjoy water exercises in your swimming pool. Strangers may have a little difficulty understanding you at parties, but your friends and family love you and they will make the effort to understand you."

4. *Mental filter.* This involves dwelling on the negatives of a situation and not focusing on the positive aspects of it. "My little Benjy was diagnosed with autism. I'll never get to go anywhere again. My friends don't want to be with me. My older daughter avoids being at home as much as possible." A clinician dealing with this mother's grief can help her to see that "We can provide respite services for you 2 days a month. And there is a support group of other parents who would welcome you to join them. Why don't I talk with your older daughter, and we will help her feel involved in Benjy's home carryover program?"

5. *Emotional reasoning.* The person takes his emotions as evidence of the truth. "I feel angry at you for diagnosing my son with a language-learning disability. Therefore, you must have done something wrong" or "I feel guilty that my baby was born 2 months prematurely; therefore

(because of my guilt), I must have done something wrong." Again, once the clinician supports the person in expressing emotions, the clinician can diplomatically help the person to distinguish between emotions and the facts of the situation.

Cognitive behavioral approaches are used frequently in mental health counseling activities; they are also useful with speech and hearing. Basic thoughts are reshaped into more constructive feelings and attitudes. Because cognitive approaches are helpful for a variety of situations and problems, these approaches are often used in combination with support groups or readings. For example, books such as John-Roger and McWilliams's (1992) *The Portable Life 101* are particularly useful with some patients, particularly those with negative cognitive sets (i.e., those who feel that the glass is always half empty rather than half full).

Cognitive behavioral approaches can be quite successful for some multicultural clients and families. For example, Lin (2002) comments that Chinese expect counselors to be direct, paternalistic, nurturing, and empathic leaders. Counselors are expected to offer advice and information, solve problems, and suggest solutions. As previously stated, members of many cultural groups expect the clinician to be an authority figure who gives practical, straightforward advice and suggestions (Roseberry-McKibbin, 2002). According to Paniagua (1998), most African Americans, Hispanics, Native Americans, and Asians appreciate a therapy process that is directive, active, and structured. Clients and families from these multicultural groups want to know what the problem is, what their role is in the solution to the problem, and exactly what the clinician recommends to solve the problem.

Summary of Approaches

We recommend that clinicians incorporate elements of both the nondirective and directive approaches as situations demand. Using elements of nondirective approaches encourages clients and family members to express feelings and unburden themselves so that they will be able to hear suggestions for changing behavior. When people have been able to ventilate their emotions to a receptive and empathic clinician, they are usually more receptive to the clinician's ideas for constructive changes in behavior. After listening and empathizing, the clinician can then use elements of the directive behavioral and REBT approaches to help clients and families take positive action steps that will change their lives. As Shames (2000) writes,

A very real question is whether a clinician can be the directive authority figure one moment, and then shift to a listener who encourages self-discovery by the client through sharing his innermost feelings with you in the next moment. This is a shift for both the clinician and the client. Both must become aware of and become comfortable with this dramatic shift, back and forth, again and again … for each of them. … Both types of activities (directive and client-centered) are valuable and necessary for an optimum regime of therapy. (p. 16)

Points to Ponder #18

You are having your first session with a 27-year-old man who stutters. He wants to go to law school and is clearly quite intelligent, but he has worked as a custodian all his life. One reason he is seeking treatment is to see if he can become fluent enough to succeed as a lawyer. You discover that he grew up in a large family in which everyone teased him mercilessly about his stuttering, and told him that he would "never amount to anything that involves talking for a living." He gets tears in his eyes as he says this. Throughout your meeting, he says many things like "I'll never get a decent job in law," "my law professors will never call on me," and "I can't even get a date, much less become a lawyer." What counseling approach or combination of approaches will you use in subsequent sessions with this client to help him during therapy?

The Process of Counseling

One function of counseling is providing information, so the processes and techniques of giving information described in Chapter 6 apply to these types of interactions. Activities that are intended to help patients or caregivers understand or clarify their feelings, attitudes, emotions, or behaviors, or activities offering these individuals methods and alternatives for changing behavior, are typically viewed as being in the "counseling" realm. The following sections describe the basic stages or processes for these types of interactions. These basic steps are used irrespective of the counseling approach employed (behavioral, cognitive, cognitive behavioral, or most others).

Depending on the authority consulted, the process of counseling has from 2 to more than 10 steps (see, e.g., Brammer, Abrego, & Shostrom, 1993; Corey, 2001; DeBlassie, 1976; Hackney & Cormier, 1994; Moursund, 1993; Okun, 2002). For example, Okun (2002) views counseling as a two-step process. The first stage involves building a relationship by establishing rapport, developing trust, encouraging client self-disclosure, listening, attending, and so forth. The second stage involves strategic planning, implementation, evaluation, termination, and follow-up.

DeBlassie (1976), on the other hand, outlines the following eight steps in the counseling process:

1. Observing the situation
2. Ordering and assessing observations
3. Predicting the course of events without intervention
4. Predicting the course of events with intervention
5. Formulating tentative hypotheses and alternatives
6. Providing purposeful intervention
7. Observing the effects of intervention
8. Reassessing previous appraisals and reformulating hypotheses (p. 87)

These basic steps provide excellent guidelines for determining the need for counseling, developing and providing appropriate counseling, and evaluating the effects of clinical efforts. It is also worth noting that these eight steps can be applied to any clinical activities, including diagnostic or treatment sessions.

Although authorities have outlined different numbers of stages in the counseling process, these differences relate more to how specific each step is than to actual differences in the process. For example, Okun (2002) includes activities like planning, implementing, evaluating, terminating, and following up in the second of her two stages, whereas other authorities would consider each of these activities a separate stage in the process.

Our preference is to use Cormier and Hackney's (1987) five-stage model for counseling activities (see Figure 7.1). The stages in this model can overlap so that, for example, clinicians may continue to build relationships across any of the stages.

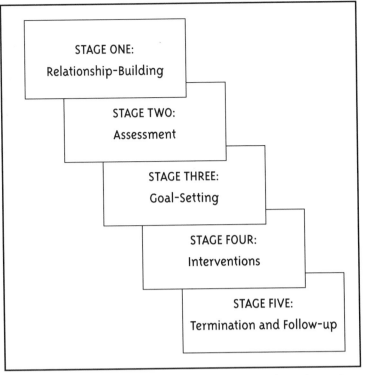

FIGURE 7.1. The stages of counseling. *Note.* From *The Professional Counselor: A Process Guide to Helping* (p. 19), by L. S. Cormier and H. Hackney, 1987, Englewood Cliffs, NJ: Prentice Hall. Copyright 1987 by Prentice Hall, Inc. Reprinted with permission.

The model is also sequential in that it moves progressively from building a relationship to assessment, to goal setting, to counseling interventions, and to termination and follow-up.

The Counseling Session

Preparation

Adequate preparation is just as critical for counseling as it is for other types of interviewing, if not more so. Clinicians should begin their preparation by carefully considering the information available and the insights already gained about those involved with counseling efforts. This information includes the client's communicative disorder, any particular reactions or feelings of concern, and other areas that need attention. During the preparation stage, clinicians begin to plan how to orient the client; how to establish rapport; how to set the tone for one or more interactions; how to communicate understanding to the other party; what information to provide; and what specific attitudes, feelings, or behaviors to address. To allow for adequate preparation, appointments scheduled in advance are recommended. As a standard part of preparation, attention should also be paid to the physical environment so that the counseling space appears professional and allows for privacy and comfort.

Beginning a Session

With adequate preparation, the clinician should have a fairly clear idea of what needs to be done during a session. The clinician should begin the initial counseling session by describing the basic structure of the interaction for the client, including a description of the purpose of the meeting and the problem to be addressed. It is also helpful to describe the general results expected from the counseling session. If the clinician has initiated the session, it is a good idea to begin the meeting with a brief explanation of why the client is involved. If sessions have been initiated by counselees, it is helpful to let them begin by explaining why they have requested the session.

 "I'm glad we have this chance to talk together. I know you have been very concerned about your husband's speech. You were kind enough to share that you were frustrated with his progress. Perhaps you could describe your frustrations. Then, I think I may have a couple of suggestions for you. But first, tell me about some of your concerns."

 "I've been concerned about how you are feeling about your stuttering. It seems like you feel the whole world is listening to your every word. There are some things you may be perceiving a little incorrectly. I want to talk about several of these. A little later, I do have two things I'd like you to try. First, however, let's talk about _____."

 "I'm glad you scheduled this appointment. It's good to have a chance to talk about _____. What are some of the things on your mind?"

When participants are involved in ongoing counseling sessions, clinicians need to begin each new session by reviewing overall expectations and reassessing previous discussions and activities. Such orientations help ensure that both parties are on common ground.

The Content of Counseling

Meier and Davis (1993) point out that psychologists and other mental health counselors typically talk about three systems: affect, cognition, and behavior. *Affect* refers to feelings. The "big four" feelings are anger, sadness, fear, and joy (Hershorn, 2002; Meier & Davis, 1993). *Cognition* refers to thoughts such as, "I can't do it," "This is too difficult," "She's not getting any better," "It's all my fault that she is stuttering," and "If I had only _____." *Behavior* refers to types of actions like a dysfluency, a harsh glottal attack, changing the subject abruptly, doing or not doing home activities, wearing or not wearing the hearing aid, and so forth.

Affect
A system that focuses on feelings.

Cognition
A system that focuses on thoughts.

Behavior
A system that focuses on actions.

The topics discussed during a counseling session may be in any one, two, or even all three of these systems, depending on the needs of the client, the client's family, or other caregivers. It is important to provide counseling for parents of children with communicative impairments. Counseling can benefit such parents in at least three ways. First, it can help parents understand their own feelings and emotions that relate to the situation at hand, and this increased understanding can lead them to more effective interactions with their child. Second, counseling can provide parents with important information that increases their understanding of what needs to be done. Third, counseling can provide parents with tools to help them communicate more effectively with each other and with their child. Counseling also can bring these same benefits to spouses, adult children, and others. Any of these three benefits may occur by focusing on specific affect, cognitions, or behaviors that need addressing.

For any given counseling session, clinicians must determine which areas will be most beneficial to counselees. If the clinician's purpose is to provide the client with more information about a communicative disorder, this information will be the content of the counseling session. If the clinician needs for counselees to change their attitudes or behavior toward someone with a communicative difficulty, modifying these responses will be the primary counseling content.

In Chapter 6, we suggested that the content of information-giving interviews should be limited to three to five major points. When there are multiple areas that require attention—major points made, problems discussed, feelings expressed and understood, or behaviors or attitudes targeted for modification—counselors are advised to limit the topics to a reasonable number in one session. Introducing too many ideas for consideration at a given time can be confusing and may preclude understanding. If too many topics are addressed during a session, some or even all of them may be too superficially addressed for any good to occur. Additional topics are sometimes best introduced at different times along a counseling treatment sequence.

Closing the Interview

Interviews in which clinicians are providing information, giving instruction, or in other ways trying to promote some form of change are often closed in a fashion similar to the information-giving interviews. This includes summarizing the major points discussed; soliciting questions; expressing appreciation for clients' help, interest, and participation; and reviewing any next steps.

Sessions in which a patient or caregiver is doing most of the talking—expressing feelings, releasing and ventilating feelings, or receiving a clinician's support—usually require some advance warning when the time allotted is about to expire. Most counselors recommend preparing clients for the end of a session 5 to 10 minutes before the time is actually over. This is done with statements or questions such as "Our time is about up. Is there something else you wanted to consider?" or "We have about 10 more minutes. Are there areas you wanted to talk about further?" Cues help clients begin the process of ending a session, and are certainly preferable to ending with a blunt "Oh, our time is up. We'll talk further _____." When time does expire, these sessions are closed in the manner described in the previous paragraph.

Points to Ponder #19

You are meeting with the father of an 8-year-old boy, Drew, who has pronounced vocal nodules. You know that Drew yells a lot on the playground, and he has revealed to you that a lot of yelling goes on in his home. You need to make recommendations to Drew's father. You know from phone conversations that Drew's father is a very talkative man who tends to head off on tangents. Describe factors that can help your meeting with him to go smoothly and successfully.

Aspects of Counseling

Conditioning Attitudes and Behavior

After clinicians determine which attitudes or behaviors require attention, promoting desired change often involves providing the information that is needed and any rationales that support this information. Clinicians need to communicate to clients an understanding of what needs to be changed and why.

Clinicians then set about conditioning actual behaviors and attitudes, using appropriate shaping procedures including reinforcement or punishment. In operant terms, changes in a desired direction are reinforced while changes away from a desired direction are not reinforced or are punished. Reinforcement and punishment techniques affect the frequency of activities in that properly implemented reinforcers increase target attitudes or behaviors, whereas appropriately administered punishers decrease the frequency of these feelings or behaviors. A number of specific verbal and nonverbal methods useful for conditioning behavior are addressed in Chapter 4.

Explaining Behavioral Principles

Many counselors teach basic behavioral concepts to counselees, particularly when parents or other caregivers are involved in helping reinforce or extinguish behaviors. In these cases, it is important for the people involved to understand the elements of basic conditioning and shaping. Brown and Brown (1975) described the teaching of operant conditioning to parents and suggested the following:

> *Parents quickly grasp these principles if a common sense approach is used. Obviously, positive reinforcement might be explained as an event that increases the probability of a behavior occurring again in the future. However, parents readily understand that money and food act as rewards and are thus influential in the motivation of behavior. They also understand that individuals respond to pats on the back, smiles and caresses when the idea is put to them simply. We usually ask parents what they respond to or what makes them feel like doing something again.*

When parents begin to talk about the things that reinforce them, they begin to understand the concept more clearly. Once positive reinforcement is understood, the idea of extinction can also be explained. This explanation is often prefaced by a question such as "What would happen if someone stopped paying you to go to work?" It is also important to illustrate to parents that devices often seen as punishment (e.g., threatening the child) may in fact be rewarding and reinforce behavior, since the child thus receives attention for his or her behavior. The concept of negative reinforcement can be introduced by asking parents to relate their reaction whenever they yell at a noisy child and the noise ceases. (p. 99)

As this example illustrates, descriptions of basic behavioral techniques should be tailored to the counselee's situation and worded in ways that assure understanding.

Providing Advice

Many counseling activities involve sharing information in preselected areas. Clinicians should remember that advice must be based on sound and adequate information. They should not provide advice or guidance if there is uncertainty about the information, or if the areas discussed are beyond the bounds of their knowledge and professional training.

Having Reasonable Expectations

Cozad (1974) described the notion of being reasonable regarding expectations for children with hearing impairments. The same principle applies to various activities of speech and hearing professionals, including counseling. Clinicians need to develop realistic expectations and goals. Change can be immediate, relatively quick, difficult, or slow (Shipley & Wood, 1996). It is unreasonable to assume that all counselees can or will change dramatically in short periods of time. Clinicians need to view behavioral and attitudinal changes in incremental steps toward ultimate goals, realizing that there will be differences in the speed of change across individuals.

Providing Release and Support

Counseling can help people begin to understand and deal more effectively with situations they experience. Providing support is a critical aspect of the counseling role. Patients need support, and so do family members, friends, and other caregivers. To achieve appropriate support, clinicians need to help counselees appreciate their strengths and understand their feelings and attitudes. Accomplishing this task requires empathy and an ability to relate to the needs of others (Sweetow, 1999).

As Dodge (2000) says, parents want us to "walk through the fire with them" (p. 90). Haynes and Pindzola (1998) comment that the secret of care of a client is caring *for* the client—helping the client feel understood.

The Role of Techniques

This book includes discussion about a variety of communication and interview techniques. However, the application of such techniques is no substitute for appropriate attitudes toward others. Counselors should never become so concerned about techniques and procedures that they lose perspective of sincere care for the people with whom they work.

Working with Families

Working with families is an established part of effective clinical practice in communicative disorders (see Hegde, 1993; Luterman, 2001; Paul, 2001; Rollin, 2000). Family-centered services place emphasis on a partnership between the family and the professional rather than a more passive role for the family. Chapter 9 discusses working with families in greater depth.

Groups

Some clinicians use a group model to provide counseling functions. This can be effective, useful, and a good use of time. It is also possible to accomplish certain things that are simply not possible in one-on-one interactions. Success in groups is related to several factors, including the specific needs of individuals in the group, the group's purposes, the members who make up the group, the cultural and linguistic backgrounds of the group members, and the abilities of the clinician who is leading the group. Leith (1993) discusses three types of groups he has seen in speech therapy: the mob, therapy in groups, and group therapy. These categories are also applicable to counseling activities.

- The *mob* is characterized by chaos. The purpose is unclear and participants may be going in their own directions, often to the dismay of the clinician.
- *Therapy in groups* occurs when individuals work on different things but in a group setting, often waiting their turn to work on something specific to them. Essentially, individual work is being done but within a group of individuals.
- *Group therapy* implies interaction between members of a group. In effect, the group is involved with the treatment and progress that occurs.

Clearly, the mob is unproductive and often frustrating to many participants. Such a group is out of control and accomplishes little, if anything. Therapy in a group can be effective in some settings because individuals work on particular areas of need. True group therapy, with the possibility of some individualized work, is probably most beneficial with respect to counseling activities.

Goldberg (1993) suggests that groups in general have the following four basic functions:

1. To change speech and language behaviors
2. To provide a safe environment for practicing new speech and language behaviors
3. To provide opportunities for clients and caregivers to discuss the effects of a communicative disorder on their lives
4. To allow clinicians opportunities to observe, without interference, individuals' communicative behaviors

These are important functions that occur within well-designed group situations. Each of these functions has multiple possibilities. For example, communicative behavior can be changed in a number of ways, from helping a participant practice fluent speech to having a new member observe what is possible. Those with similar communicative problems can communicate, release frustrations, express grief, or view techniques that work well for others. Clients or caregivers can discuss their situations, share concerns, and learn from the successes of others (Rollin, 2000). These are only a few of numerous possibilities.

The basic principles discussed for sharing information and providing counseling functions can be adapted to work in groups. Absolute prerequisites for effective group work are the same fundamentals of interviewing and counseling discussed in Chapter 1: having a purpose, a plan of action, and communicating clearly. Knowing what to address, and why, is important for effective group practice. A group is approached a little differently, for example, when the purpose is to transmit information rather than to help clients share their feelings and concerns about a communicative disorder.

Often, groups are assembled by age (elementary, junior high, senior high, adult, and perhaps even older adult) or disorder type (aphasia, laryngectomy, fluency). Groupings help expedite feelings of camaraderie and similarity among individuals. This is also helpful because, unlike the "therapy in groups" model noted earlier, members have a commonality of interest.

If there are group members from diverse cultural backgrounds, this variable needs to be considered. For example, it is recommended that with Arabs, groups be composed of single-gender members. Also, Arabs may be reluctant to discuss personal issues with unfamiliar persons (Dwairy, 1998). Clinicians must always take clients' cultural backgrounds into account when planning for group activities or sessions.

Support groups exist for individuals with many speech and hearing problems—aphasia and post-stroke, stuttering, mental impairment, laryngectomy, to name just a few. Support groups may be formally organized, or unorganized to allow members to get together for coffee from time to time. These groups are important and help serve several functions for individuals or caregivers involved with communicative disorders (Atkins, 1994; Luterman, 2001; Rollin, 2000). They help members cope with their situations better, provide valuable interpersonal insights, help provide feedback about their "plights," and generally help reinforce and encourage members of the group (Goldberg, 1993).

Support groups are not counseling per se, but important activities occur in groups. Among these, members meet others with similar circumstances, learn more about their own situations as well as those of others, acquire additional information about disorders, hear about the trials and tribulations of others, find out about possibilities, and release frustrations and feelings with others who can relate directly to their experiences.

Some groups are established (or assisted) by clinicians; others are completely independent of any professional services. Thus, different groups function in a variety of ways. The points here are that support groups (a) meet important needs for many clients and they are frequently recommended for patients and caregivers; (b) assist clients and families in ways that clinicians often cannot; (c) are not counseling per se, and are not intended to replace the services clinicians need to provide; and (d) are a valuable part of serving many patients' overall needs. They are not a threat or something that can or should be replaced, no matter how extensive and effective the counseling services are. The role and nature of groups are described in more detail in Chapter 11.

Role-Playing as a Technique

Role-playing
The structured acting out or demonstrating of some behavior, or the roles specific behaviors play in the creation of problematic situations.

Role-playing, which involves the structured acting out or demonstrating of some behavior, or the roles specific behaviors play in the creation of problematic situations, is used in some clinical activities. For example, the patient who stutters may practice fluent speech as if speaking with an employer, a loved one, or someone in a store. Role-playing is also one method by which speech–language pathologists can work with parent groups.

One goal in role-playing is to help people understand how feelings, attitudes, and behaviors operate and then identify alternative approaches for handling these problematic situations. The three basic components to role-playing are a leader who provides direction to the interaction, the situation that is acted out, and the follow-up discussion.

Role-playing can help clients or caregivers explore and clarify their ideas and behavior, or gain valuable practice in a new skill. Although role-playing can be useful in certain circumstances, it also can have disadvantages, particularly when focusing on feelings in groups. Role-playing can generate great fear or distress for individuals who have reservations or inhibitions about acting out their feelings. It can be difficult for some participants to reveal negative attitudes in front of a group, and some participants may experience discomfort and separation when they find that their feelings differ dramatically from those of the rest of the group.

Points to Ponder #20

You are working in a hospital where there are many patients who have undergone laryngectomies. You see that these patients and their spouses are often very depressed, bewildered, and uninformed about "what's next" after surgery. You decide that a support group would provide a real service to these patients and their spouses. What goals would you have for the group? What would happen during group time? Describe factors that would help this group run smoothly and successfully.

Examining Personal Abilities and the Effects of Counseling

Evaluating Personal Effectiveness

Stewart and Cash (1978) suggest that counselors can determine their general effectiveness by self-evaluation. These authors list six basic questions all counselors can ask themselves:

1. Are you a good listener?
2. Do you have the patience necessary to deal with trying, time-consuming situations?
3. Are you involved with a client or the client's problem?
4. Do you have a realistic view of your counseling skills, training and experiences?
5. Do you have a realistic view of what can and cannot be accomplished?
6. Do you have a sincere desire to help people without trying to play God? (p. 184)

These questions may be general and somewhat difficult to answer objectively, but they certainly are worth considering before and after any counseling interaction. Hackney and Cormier's (1994) Counseling Strategies Checklist is another useful method for self-evaluation (see Appendix 7.A). Of course, the ultimate test of a clinician's effectiveness lies in whether the desired changes in feelings, attitudes, and behaviors occur with his or her counselees.

Evaluating Effects on Others

The observable effects of counseling efforts are the behavior and attitude changes that occur with counselees. Clinicians can evaluate the success of their efforts by asking whether a counselee followed specific suggestions, by counting the number of positive statements a counselee makes about a child or a spouse, by counting the number of "throat clears" in a prescribed time, or in many other ways. Charting the frequency and consistency of targeted attitudes or behaviors is an excellent method of examining treatment effects. A counselor should take care to select evaluation methods that fit the goals of the treatment and that involve clearly defined, observable behaviors or activities. If caregivers are being asked to apply behavioral principles, clinicians should carefully monitor their use of the evaluation methods.

Signs of Difficulties

The idea of boundaries was addressed earlier in this chapter; the idea also applies to personal effectiveness. Stone and Olswang (1989) comment that clinicians do not have to know precisely *why* something is a problem to know that a problem exists. There are some red flags clinicians recognize when there are boundary problems, or when they are in "over their heads." The following are signs of difficulties (Stone & Olswang, 1989):

- Interaction patterns are not satisfactory despite repeated attempts to correct problems.
- Counseling efforts fail to achieve desired results, or clients get worse.
- Clients become increasingly resistant to clinicians' efforts to help them.
- Clinicians get pulled in deeper to a client's problems or sense that they may not be able to resolve the problems.
- Patients respond in ways that differ from what clinicians intend.
  - Clinicians begin to develop feelings that are similar to, or more appropriate to, the client (e.g., anger, sadness, distress, remorse). This is a psychological phenomenon called *countertransference,* as clinicians begin to adopt the feelings of a client.
  - Clinicians become excessively worried or preoccupied with a case.
  - Clinicians have persistent, uncomfortable feelings about what is happening, even if these feelings or their sources cannot be readily articulated. (Adapted from p. 29)

Countertransference

A boundary problem wherein the clinician adopts the feelings of a client.

Appendix 7.B gives guidelines that are useful for helping to determine when there are problems in a counseling relationship. Note that any of these items is a signal of potential difficulties. This is not the type of list where a specified number of items checked "yes" indicates a problem, nor can this list suggest the severity of a problem. Conscientious clinicians recognize such problems as early as possible so that appropriate actions can be initiated. There are a number of possible ways to identify a problem, including evaluating interactive methods, considering the topics of discussion and recommendations, consulting a peer or supervisor, discussing the problem with the client or caregiver, or referring the client for more appropriate types of service. Exactly what is to be done will depend on the case, the extent of the problems, the relationship between the parties, the resources available, and the attitudes of people involved.

Concluding Comments

Clinicians frequently use the interviewing and counseling techniques described in this chapter and elsewhere in this book to bring about positive changes in the behavior, feelings, or attitudes of their clients. Behavioral counseling is a practical approach for speech–language pathologists and audiologists to use because it involves promoting change, uses skills in conditioning they already possess, and focuses on behavioral or attitudinal manifestations directly related to communicative disorders. Behavioral counseling is an effective approach for communicative disorders professionals because it allows for the close study of the effects of feelings and behaviors and the objective measurement of efforts to modify those attitudes or behaviors.

Cognitive approaches also are useful in speech–language pathology and audiology. These approaches provide the introduction and learning of new cognitive sets, which can promote tremendous progress and change within individuals. Often, clinicians use the best of both worlds, integrating behavioral and cognitive approaches together to promote optimal progress.

APPENDIX 7.A
Counseling Strategies Checklist

How To Use the Counseling Strategies Checklist (CSC)

Each item in the CSC is scored by circling the most appropriate response, either "Yes," "No," or "N.A." (not applicable). The items are worded so that desirable responses are "Yes" or "N.A." "No" is an undesirable response.

After the supervisor has observed and rated the interview, the two of you should sit down and review the ratings. Where noticeable deficiencies exist, you and the supervisor should identify a goal or goals that will remedy the problem. Beyond this, you should list two or three action steps that permit you to achieve the goal. After three or four more interviews, have the supervisor determine whether or not progress was evident.

≈ PART I: Counselor Reinforcing Behavior (Nonverbal)

1. The counselor maintained eye contact with the client.

    Yes   No   N.A.

2. The counselor displayed several different facial expressions during the interview.

    Yes   No   N.A.

3. The counselor's facial expressions reflected the mood of the client.

    Yes   No   N.A.

4. The counselor often responded to the client with facial animation and alertness.

    Yes   No   N.A.

5. The counselor displayed intermittent head movements (up–down, side-to-side).

    Yes   No   N.A.

6. The counselor refrained from head nodding when the client did not pursue goal-directed topics.

      Yes   No   N.A.

7. The counselor demonstrated a relaxed body position.

      Yes   No   N.A.

8. The counselor leaned forward as a means of encouraging the client to engage in some goal-directed behavior.

      Yes   No   N.A.

9. The counselor demonstrated some variation in voice pitch when talking.

      Yes   No   N.A.

10. The counselor's voice was easily heard by the client.

      Yes   No   N.A.

11. The counselor used intermittent one-word vocalizations ("mm-hmm") to reinforce the client's demonstration of goal-directed topics or behaviors.

      Yes   No   N.A.

Counselor Reinforcing Behavior (Verbal)

12. The counselor usually spoke slowly enough so that each word was easily understood.

      Yes   No   ·N.A.

13. A majority (60 percent or more) of the counselor's responses could be categorized as complete sentences rather than monosyllabic phrases.

      Yes   No   N.A.

14. The counselor's verbal statements were concise and to the point.

      Yes   No   N.A.

15. The counselor refrained from repetition in verbal statements.

      Yes   No   N.A.

16. The counselor made verbal comments that pursued the topic introduced by the client.

      Yes   No   N.A.

17. The subject of the counselor's verbal statements usually referred to the client, either by name or the second-person pronoun, "you."

     Yes   No   N.A.

18. A clear and sensible progression of topics was evident in the counselor's verbal behavior; the counselor avoided rambling.

     Yes   No   N.A.

≈ PART II: Opening Interview

1. In the first part of the interview, the counselor used several different nonverbal gestures (smiling, head nodding, hand movement, etc.) to help put the client at ease.

     Yes   No   N.A.

2. In starting the interview, the counselor remained silent or invited the client to talk about whatever he or she wanted, thus leaving the selection of initial topic up to the client.

     Yes   No   N.A.

3. After the first five minutes of the interview, the counselor refrained from encouraging social conversation.

     Yes   No   N.A.

4. After the first topic of discussion was exhausted, the counselor remained silent until the client identified a new topic.

     Yes   No   N.A.

5. The counselor provided structure (information about nature, purposes of counseling, time limits, etc.) when the client indicated uncertainty about the interview.

     Yes   No   N.A.

6. In beginning the initial interview, the counselor used at least one of the following structuring procedures:

   a. Provided information about taping and/or observation
   b. Commented on confidentiality
   c. Made remarks about the counselor's role and purpose of the interview
   d. Discussed with the client his or her expectations about counseling

     Yes   No   N.A.

≋ PART III: Termination of the Interview

1. The counselor informed the client before terminating that the interview was almost over.

   Yes   No   N.A.

2. The counselor refrained from introducing new material (a different topic) at the termination phase of the interview.

   Yes   No   N.A.

3. The counselor discouraged the client from pursuing new topics within the last five minutes of the interview by avoiding asking for further information about it.

   Yes   No   N.A.

4. Only one attempt to terminate the interview was required before the termination was actually completed.

   Yes   No   N.A.

5. The counselor initiated the termination of the interview through use of some closing strategy such as acknowledgment of time limits and/or summarization (by self or client).

   Yes   No   N.A.

6. At the end of the interview, the counselor offered the client an opportunity to return for another interview.

   Yes   No   N.A.

≋ PART IV: Goal Setting

1. The counselor asked the client to identify some of the conditions surrounding the occurrence of the client's problem ("when do you feel _____?").

   Yes   No   N.A.

2. The counselor asked the client to identify some of the consequences resulting from the client's behavior ("What happens when you _____?").

   Yes   No   N.A.

3. The counselor asked the client to state how he or she would like to change his or her behavior ("How would you like for things to be different?").

   Yes   No   N.A.

4. The counselor and client decided together on counseling goals.

   Yes   No   N.A.

5. The goals set in the interview were specific and observable.

     Yes   No   N.A.

6. The counselor asked the client to orally state a commitment to work for goal achievement.

     Yes   No   N.A.

7. If the client appeared resistant or unconcerned about achieving change, the counselor discussed this with the client.

     Yes   No   N.A.

8. The counselor asked the client to specify at least one action step he or she might take toward his or her goal.

     Yes   No   N.A.

9. The counselor suggested alternatives available to the client.

     Yes   No   N.A.

10. The counselor helped the client to develop action steps for goal attainment.

     Yes   No   N.A.

11. Action steps designated by counselor and client were specific and realistic in scope.

     Yes   No   N.A.

12. The counselor provided an opportunity within the interview for the client to practice or rehearse the action step.

     Yes   No   N.A.

13. The counselor provided feedback to the client concerning the execution of the action step.

     Yes   No   N.A.

14. The counselor encouraged the client to observe and evaluate the progress and outcomes of action steps taken outside the interview.

     Yes   No   N.A.

≈ PART V: Counselor Discrimination

1. The counselor's responses were usually directed toward the most important component of each of the client's communications.

     Yes   No   N.A.

2. The counselor followed client topic changes by responding to the primary cognitive or affective idea, reflecting a common theme in each communication.

   Yes   No   N.A.

3. The counselor usually identified and responded to the feelings of the client.

   Yes   No   N.A.

4. The counselor usually identified and responded to the behaviors of the client.

   Yes   No   N.A.

5. The counselor verbally acknowledged several (at least two) nonverbal affect cues.

   Yes   No   N.A.

6. The counselor encouraged the client to talk about his or her feelings.

   Yes   No   N.A.

7. The counselor encouraged the client to identify and evaluate his or her actions.

   Yes   No   N.A.

8. The counselor discouraged the client from making and accepting excuses (rationalization) for his or her behavior.

   Yes   No   N.A.

9. The counselor asked questions that the client could not answer in a "yes" or "no" fashion (typically beginning with words such as how, what, when, where, who, etc.).

   Yes   No   N.A.

10. Several times (at least two) the counselor confronted the client with a discrepancy present in the client's communication and/ or behavior.

    Yes   No   N.A.

11. Several times (at least two) the counselor used responses that supported or reinforced something the client said or did.

    Yes   No   N.A.

12. The counselor used several (at least two) responses that suggested a course of action the client had the potential for completing in the future.

    Yes   No   N.A.

13. Sometimes the counselor restated or clarified the client's previous communication.

       Yes   No   N.A.

14. The counselor used several (at least two) responses that summarized ambivalent and conflicting feelings of the client.

       Yes   No   N.A.

15. The counselor encouraged discussion of negative feelings (anger, fear) expressed by the client.

       Yes   No   N.A.

16. Several times (at least two) the counselor suggested how the client might feel about a particular topic.

       Yes   No   N.A.

≋ PART VI: The Process of Relating

1. The counselor made statements that reflected the client's feelings.

       Yes   No   N.A.

2. The counselor responded to the core of a long and ambivalent client statement.

       Yes   No   N.A.

3. The counselor verbally stated his or her desire and/or intent to understand.

       Yes   No   N.A.

4. The counselor made verbal statements that the client reaffirmed without qualifying or changing the counselor's previous response.

       Yes   No   N.A.

5. The counselor made attempts to verbally communicate his or her understanding of the client that elicited an affirmative client response ("Yes, that's exactly right," and so forth).

       Yes   No   N.A.

6. The counselor reflected the client's feelings at the same or a greater level of intensity than originally expressed by the client.

       Yes   No   N.A.

7. In communicating understanding of the client's feelings, the counselor verbalized the anticipation present in the client's communication (i.e., what the client would like to do or how the client would like to be).

     Yes   No   N.A.

8. The counselor frowned when failing to understand what the client was saying.

     Yes   No   N.A.

9. The counselor verbalized personal confusion or misunderstanding to the client.

     Yes   No   N.A.

10. The counselor nodded when agreeing with or encouraging the client.

     Yes   No   N.A.

11. When the counselor's nonverbal behavior suggested that he or she was uncertain or disagreeing, the counselor verbally acknowledged this to the client.

     Yes   No   N.A.

12. The counselor answered directly when the client asked about his or her opinion or reaction.

     Yes   No   N.A.

13. The counselor encouraged discussion of statements made by the client that challenged the counselor's knowledge and beliefs.

     Yes   No   N.A.

14. Several times (at least twice) the counselor shared his or her own feelings with the client.

     Yes   No   N.A.

15. At least one time during the interview the counselor provided specific feedback to the client.

     Yes   No   N.A.

16. The counselor encouraged the client to identify and discuss his or her feelings concerning the counselor and the interview.

     Yes   No   N.A.

17. The counselor voluntarily shared his or her feelings about the client and the counseling relationship.

     Yes   No   N.A.

18. The counselor expressed reactions about the client's strengths and/or potential.

       Yes   No   N.A.

19. The counselor made responses that reflected his or her liking and appreciation of the client.

       Yes   No   N.A.

Note. From *Counseling Strategies and Interventions* (4th ed., pp. 192–200), by H. Hackney and L. S. Cormier, 1994, Boston: Allyn & Bacon. Copyright 1994 by Allyn & Bacon. Reprinted with permission.

APPENDIX 7.B
Evaluating Interviewing and Counseling Sessions (Checklist Format)

Check each item that applies.

1. *Length*
   - ☐ Adequate
   - ☐ Too short
   - ☐ Too long

2. *Amount of talking*
   - ☐ Counselor talked too much
   - ☐ Time well proportioned
   - ☐ Counselee talked too much

3. *Direction*
   - ☐ Counselee given every opportunity to express himself or herself
   - ☐ Counselee given some opportunity to express himself or herself
   - ☐ Counselee seldom given an opportunity to express himself or herself

4. *Amount of interest*
   - ☐ Monotonous, aimless, poor continuity
   - ☐ Some interesting spots
   - ☐ Interesting, well-directed, good continuity

5. *Semantics*
   - ☐ Adapted to counselee
   - ☐ Sometimes inappropriate
   - ☐ Very inappropriate

6. *Responsibility*
   - ☐ Counselor assumed most of the responsibility
   - ☐ Counselor assumed some responsibility
   - ☐ Counselor gave full responsibility to counselee

7. *Depth*
   - ☐ Superficial
   - ☐ Some real problems discussed
   - ☐ Very adequate

8. *Interview controlled by*
   - ☐ Counselor
   - ☐ Counselee
   - ☐ Neither
   - ☐ Both

9. *Response to counselor*
   - ☐ Counselee responded easily
   - ☐ Counselee sometimes responded
   - ☐ Counselee resisted, would not respond

10. *Rapport*
    - ☐ High level of rapport maintained throughout
    - ☐ Rapport varied
    - ☐ Poor rapport

11. *Interaction and discussion between counselor and counselee*
    - ☐ A great deal
    - ☐ Some
    - ☐ Very little or none

12. *Did the counselor define the relationship between himself or
    herself and the counselee?*
    - ☐ Adequately
    - ☐ Somewhat
    - ☐ Poorly

13. *Did the counselor pave the way for follow-up?*
    - ☐ Adequately
    - ☐ Somewhat
    - ☐ Poorly

14. *Comments:*

EIGHT

Working with Linguistically and Culturally Diverse Clients

CHAPTER OUTLINE

- Variables That Influence Individuals from Different Cultures
- Impact of Immigrant or Refugee Status on Linguistically and Culturally Diverse Clients
- Values, Assumptions, and Linguistically and Culturally Diverse Clients
- Communicating Effectively When Interviewing and Counseling
- Suggestions for Increasing Personal Sensitivity
- Concluding Comments

Like a kaleidoscope that is constantly changing colors, the cultural and linguistic composition of the United States and the world population is becoming more richly diverse. Our globe has had demographic shifts in the last decades. In 1997, about 17% of the world's population was White; by the year 2010, only 9% of the world's population will be White (Hodgkinson, 1998). Ninety-three out of 100 children born in our world today are born in Latin America, Asia, and Africa. These trends are reflected in the United States. At the beginning of the 20th century, 97% of immigrants to the United States were from Europe; at the end of the 20th century, 85% of U.S. immigrants were from Asia and Latin America (Banks, 1999). The percentage of children in the United States who are White, non-Hispanic decreased from 74% in 1980 to 65% in 1998 (Moore-Brown & Montgomery, 2001). By the year 2020, an estimated 48% of American public school students will be persons of color (Banks, 1999).

The U.S. Bureau of the Census (2000) reported that racial and ethnic minorities accounted for up to 80% of the nation's population growth in the 1990s. In the year 2000, there were nearly 87 million persons from minority backgrounds living in the United States, up 43% from the 1990s. From 1980 to 2000, the population of individuals in the United States from racial minority backgrounds grew by over 90%, while the non-Hispanic White population grew by 7.6%. The number of immigrants living in the United States has more than tripled, from 9.6 million in 1970 to 28.4 million in 2000. According to Hudson Institute's Workforce 2000, it is projected that 800,000 legal and illegal immigrants will enter the United States annually throughout the rest of this century (Holliday, 2001).

According to the American Speech-Language-Hearing Association (1992), only 3.7% of its members and certificate holders identified themselves as Black, Hispanic, Asian, or Native American. Thankfully, this is changing, but changes are slow. In 1999 and 2000, in a survey of communication sciences and disorders programs across the United States, 416 master-degree and doctoral graduates were reported to be fluent in a language other than English (Shinn, Goldberg, Kimelman, & Messick, 2001). The reality is that predominantly White speech pathologists and audiologists serve increasing numbers of linguistically and culturally diverse (LCD) clients, and it is imperative that clinicians become culturally competent in their services to these clients and their families.

Part of becoming culturally competent is learning to avoid ethnocentrism—the belief that one's own culture is superior to other cultures, and that one's own way of doing things is the norm. Owens (2001) states, "It is easy for many middle-class, English-speaking white Americans to assume that the manner

in which they function is the only way or the right way" (p. 435).
Clinicians must become more self-aware as well as more
knowledgeable about other cultures and their value systems
and lifestyles. As clinicians hone their skills in interviewing
and counseling, these skills must necessarily include the ability to relate to clients and families from LCD backgrounds
whose needs and experiences differ from those of the dominant U.S. culture. It is critical that professionals who work
with culturally diverse families and clients recognize cultural
influences that impact their communication behaviors (Brice,
2002; Roseberry-McKibbin, 2001). Accordingly, the overall
purpose of this chapter is to alert readers to ideas that will increase their cultural competence when working with clients
and their families from LCD backgrounds. Readers are strongly
encouraged to read other sources in greater depth to enhance
and expand on the points that are introduced and summarized
in this chapter.

Variables That Influence Individuals from Different Cultures

Most clinicians are aware of the importance of not stereotyping individuals from cultural groups. Instead of viewing various cultural groups as homogeneous and monolithic, Hanson
(1998) recommends that clinicians take a situational and trans-
actional approach in which individual clients and families are
recognized as having unique characteristics and needs. Culture
is dynamic, and clinicians will relate to their clients more skillfully if they realize that each individual within a cultural group
is influenced by a number of variables (Langdon & Cheng,
2002; Roseberry-McKibbin, 2002). Linguistically and culturally diverse values, behavior, and utilization of services are
all heavily impacted by characteristics that make each client
unique. Clinicians who serve diverse clients must take these
characteristics into account so that clients will be treated as
individuals and valued as such, and not just seen as members
of a certain homogeneous group. Some of the variables to consider are addressed in the following sections.

Generational Membership

Clinicians should ascertain whether clients are first-, second-,
or third-generation members of the country of current residence, or whether their family has resided in the country even
longer. Generational membership may make a difference in
clients' openness to and belief in the efficacy of and necessity
for services. For example, Salas-Provance, Erickson, and Reed

(2002) found that in one Hispanic family they studied, the younger generation ascribed less importance to folk beliefs than the older generation and was somewhat more open to modern medical care.

Length of Residence

Clients may be long-term residents of an area with concomitant support systems, or they may be new residents with little or no support. The latter clients will need greater assistance from professionals.

Degree of Adaptation to Mainstream Culture

There are different ways in which diverse clients, especially refugees and immigrants, may adapt to U.S. culture. Some groups may adapt by integrating into mainstream cultural life more fully than others who desire to maintain separateness. Professionals should attempt to discover how individual clients and families have chosen to adapt to mainstream culture, because the degree of adaptation can affect clients' receptivity of speech, language, and hearing services. Cheng and Butler (1993) describe the following various degrees of adaptation:

- *Reaffirmation*—There are efforts to revive native cultural traditions. Persons may reject the majority culture.
- *Synthesis*—There is a selective combination of cultural aspects of both cultures.
- *Withdrawal*—There is a rejection of both cultures because they conflict; persons do not commit to either culture.
- *Compensatory adaptation*—Individuals thoroughly mainstream into the new culture; they reject and avoid identifying with their home culture.
- *Biculturalism*—There is full involvement with both cultures; persons must be able to make smooth transitions between both cultures.
- *Constructive marginality*—There is a tentative acceptance of two cultures; individuals do not fully integrate into either one.

Again, clients' degree of adaptation may impact on the provision of services for communicative disorders.

Socioeconomic Status and Upward Mobility

Increasingly, on our shrinking globe, individuals are viewed not so much on the basis of homogeneous cultural categories, but along lines of social class (Walton, 1995). Socioeconomic status has considerable impact on who LCD clients are, and it can affect issues like clients' acceptance of Western medicine, understanding of the need for and nature of special education or rehabilitation, and so forth. Socioeconomic status also greatly impacts clients' ability to afford therapy in settings where patients are charged for services.

Educational Level

Highly educated clients of any cultural background may respond differently in counseling and interviewing situations than clients who have not had the benefit of formal education. For less educated clients, interviewing or counseling may be unfamiliar concepts and thus discomforting events. Clients who have little or no formal education may also have difficulty with written documentation, meetings with groups of professionals, and carrying out written instructions.

Urban or Rural Background

Clients (especially immigrants or refugees) from rural backgrounds may feel more intimidated by large or formal settings, paperwork, and technology than clients from urban backgrounds (Arambula, 1992). This may impact clients' willingness to participate in rehabilitation involving surgery, therapy, medicine, or assistive devices such as motorized wheelchairs. It may also cause them to feel uncomfortable with (and thus avoid) large, complicated buildings such as medical centers.

Age and Gender

Among many cultures, there are strong social and role expectation lines between men and women, and the old and young. Each group has its roles and accompanying expectations.

Languages Spoken

Speech, language, and hearing services will be impacted by clients' language status (Roseberry-McKibbin, Brice, & O'Hanlon, 2005). For example, clients may be monolingual speakers of their primary language, be fluent speakers of English, or demonstrate language skills on a continuum of proficiency between these two points.

Impact of Immigrant or Refugee Status on Linguistically and Culturally Diverse Clients

Clinicians are working more frequently with multicultural clients who are of immigrant or refugee status. It is important to understand the impact of immigrant or refugee status on clients and their families and the possible effects on interviewing, counseling, and accompanying assessment and treatment efforts (Sue & Sue, 2003).

Immigrant

A person who goes to a new country to take up permanent residence.

Refugee

A person who goes to a new country to escape danger or persecution.

An *immigrant* is defined as a person who comes to a country to take up permanent residence; a *refugee* is someone who flees to a new country or power for safety or to escape danger or persecution (*Merriam-Webster Collegiate Dictionary,* 1993). There is enormous diversity among immigrants and refugees; they represent every echelon of society, from great wealth and privilege to poverty and illiteracy. They speak English in varying degrees, and experience varying levels of acculturation to U.S. life.

Clinicians must look at factors that result in a higher level of acculturation. Immigrants and refugees who have achieved a high level of acculturation are frequently more comfortable with speech-language-hearing services than those who have a lower level of acculturation. Factors that tend to result in higher levels of acculturation are urban (as opposed to rural) origin, higher socioeconomic status, a relatively high level of formal education, immigration to the United States at an early age, birth into a family that has been in the new country for at least several years, limited migration back and forth to the country of origin, and extensive contact with people outside the family or ethnic network. Immigrants and refugees with lower levels of acculturation may experience challenges that clinicians need to consider because these challenges affect service delivery.

Many refugees have witnessed or endured oppressive and traumatic experiences—persecution, disease, atrocities, forced labor, death of or separation from family members, starvation, and being uprooted. These problems can result in post-traumatic stress disorders, health problems, and many other negative sequelae, and clients who have undergone these types of experiences may need additional emotional support and counseling activities. A psychologist or other support personnel may be necessary for some clients.

Family life in the United States is often very different from that experienced in the country of origin. Older students—especially teenagers—may experience substantial difficulties because schools are considerably different from schools in their home country. U.S. schools tend to be more liberal and less formal than schools in many other countries, and this is often associated with adjustment difficulties for students and parents. Education in the United States is compulsory for immigrant children who arrive in their teenage years; in some countries, schooling is not required beyond 12 or 13 years of age. Compulsory school attendance may cause conflict between laws and cultural traditions. Some parents may discourage their children from going to school, feeling that school attendance is selfish and that the children should be involved in helping support the family rather than "indulging" in continuing education (Cheng & Ima, 1989).

Another stressor for many immigrant and refugee families is poverty. Individuals who were well-paid, highly respected professionals in their home lands may encounter new barriers because of their heavy accents or because their professional training is not accepted in the new land (Domyancic, 2000). Some people who were dentists, lawyers, and architects in their native countries may be working as custodians or secretaries in the new country, with accompanying adjustment problems. Clinicians must be sensitive to this; the taxi driver sitting in their office today may have been a surgeon or accountant in his or her home country. Clinicians must not assume that a lack of formal education is necessarily related to a client's current job.

In comparison to U.S. natives, who represent 28.8% of the population living in poverty or near the poverty level, 41.4% of immigrants live in poverty or near the poverty level. Among children of immigrants, 53% live in or near poverty. Statistics show that immigrants have less health insurance and utilize health services less than native-born Americans. One third of immigrants have no health insurance; immigrants who arrived after 1989 and their United States–born children account for a 60% increase in the size of the uninsured population of the United States (Camarota, 2001). In 1997, the foreign-born population made up 9.7% of the total population but comprised 20.7% of the uninsured population. At the turn of the century, the foreign-born, adult, nonelderly population was twice as likely to be without health insurance as its native-born counterpart (Pol, Adidam, & Pol, 2002). Thus, clinicians who work with immigrant and refugee families may expect poverty and lack of health insurance to be challenges for clients. Poverty and lack of health insurance may also compound problems in family relationships.

Many cultures have definite lines of social status related to age, gender, and place in the family. In many countries, elders (parents and grandparents) are accorded great respect and are obeyed because they are authority figures. When families come to the United States, where youth is venerated and elders are often disrespected, families may be caught in great conflicts. Elders who have had absolute authority often find that their children no longer exhibit automatic, unquestioning obedience, and these elders feel they have lost their power and dignity. Elders may want young people to maintain the "traditional" cultural ways, and the young people want to adopt the values, customs, and lifestyles of the new culture.

Children and youth often learn English more quickly than their elders and become family spokespersons, further usurping elders' traditional roles as authority figures. Children may want to marry an individual from the new culture instead of someone from their home culture or religious groups; elders may vehemently disagree with this and look on marriage to an "outsider" as a personal tragedy for the family. For example, the second author has worked with university students who would not consider marrying outside their cultural groups because of the heartbreak it would bring to their families. However, other individuals would consider such choices.

In some families, marital relationships may become disharmonious if women who have traditionally stayed home and obeyed their husbands start working outside the home to earn money for the family. When mothers who have stayed at home begin working long hours outside the home to survive financially, children may go unsupervised and feel the loss of attention. This can lead to discipline problems, truancy, and even gang membership. Life in the United States, with its dual-income households and emphasis on independence, tends to fragment some families who have traditionally been interdependent and relied on family members to meet most needs (Sharifzadeh, 1998).

Another stressor for many immigrant and refugee families is the general public attitude that immigrants cause social and economic problems that threaten current and future mainstream culture (Hayes-Bautista, Hurtado, Valdez, & Hernandez, 1992). Considerable fear leads to legislative proposals to stem the flow of new immigrants (Leslie, 1992). Clinicians who work with immigrants and refugees must make sure they do not hold biases that could negatively impact their clinical effectiveness in interviewing and counseling activities.

Health problems may affect immigrants and refugees. For example, the second author has worked with Vietnamese clients who were born during the fall of Saigon; malnutrition was rampant and prenatal care was practically nonexistent at that time. Subsequent problems in school often stem from maternal illness and lack of nutrition in utero. In other situations, some refugees who spent considerable time in refugee camps had little or no medical care, a fact that affects children's speech and language development, adults' predisposition toward strokes, and other health conditions. Clinicians who work with immigrant and refugee clients need to be especially sensitive to these factors, and consider how they may impact interviewing and counseling activities. An increased awareness of these factors assists clinicians in being supportive, understanding, and more effective.

Points to Ponder #21

You are working in a clinic that serves both child and adult clients, many of whom are from immigrant and refugee families. You see an unfortunate trend: They rarely return to therapy after the first or second session. Describe the factors that might contribute to this situation. What action steps can you take to help these clients feel more comfortable and keep coming for treatment?

Values, Assumptions, and Linguistically and Culturally Diverse Clients

Many readers of this book are from mainstream U.S. backgrounds where values and assumptions exist, many of them unconsciously. Although clinicians recognize that their own value systems are important and intrinsic parts of their beings, they cannot optimally serve LCD populations without becoming consciously aware of their own values and assumptions, and how they unconsciously may be imposing these values onto their clients (Sue & Sue, 2003).

Clinicians who come from the mainstream background of the dominant culture must carefully examine their own assumptions and values. They must make sure they do not communicate the idea that clients are wrong or inferior for believing differently about issues such as the necessity of therapy, family participation in therapy, and so forth. As mentioned earlier, the tendency to view one's own culture as correct, natural, and superior to another culture is called *ethnocentrism*. Clinicians can work successfully with multicultural families by avoiding ethnocentrism, respecting beliefs and cultural mores, and working to find methods that are culturally acceptable and are best for individual clients' welfare.

The following sections summarize some commonly held values and assumptions among persons of mainstream backgrounds. Awareness of these values and assumptions helps clinicians to work effectively with diverse clients.

Ethnocentrism

Tendency to view one's own culture as correct, natural, and superior to another culture.

Monochronic

Describes a cultural attitude toward time that emphasizes punctuality.

Polychronic

Describes a cultural attitude toward time that emphasizes completion of transactions and involvement of people rather than strict adherence to schedules.

Punctuality

 Assumption: "Punctuality is an important and intrinsic part of a professional relationship based on mutual respect."

U.S. culture is *monochronic*: Adherence to schedules and timeliness is very important. Punctuality is essential. Some cultures are *polychronic,* however, and members of those cultures stress completion of transactions and involvement of people rather than strict adherence to schedules (Reyes, 1994); time is very "elastic" and punctuality is not particularly important. For example, in Micronesia, families might arrive 15 to 30 minutes after appointments are scheduled to begin (Hammer, 1994). In the Philippines, if an event is scheduled for 11:00, it might not actually begin until 11:45 or 12:00. Among some Native American tribes, human relationships are considered more important than the clock, and punctuality is deemphasized. Promptness in some cultures is rarely a priority. Clinicians must be understanding of this; on the other hand, clinicians should also communicate to clients that if they are late and the clinician's schedule is full, clients may miss their appointment completely. Clear communication is imperative, as families may be offended if they arrive 30 minutes late and find that they must be rescheduled because the next meeting has already started.

Beginning an Interaction

Assumption: "In professional situations such as meetings, it is important to 'get down to business' as quickly and efficiently as possible."

In mainstream U.S. culture, getting to the point quickly is valued. However, this may offend some culturally diverse families. In the Hispanic culture, for example, business conversations are often preceded by lengthy chatting about topics unrelated to the purpose of the meeting (Brice, 2002). Zuniga (1998) states that professionals who work with Hispanic families should engage in *platicando*, which is the leisurely and friendly interaction that sets the stage for work to occur. Among many Japanese, informal socializing precedes "cutting to the chase"; those who get right down to business are perceived as rude and abrupt. Clinicians must determine what style is most comfortable for each client.

Platicando
The leisurely and friendly interaction that sets the stage for work to occur.

Formality Versus Informality

> *Assumption:* "Informality and social equality are the ultimate goals in all interactions between professionals and clients."

In some cultures, social status and hierarchy are very important. For example, many Japanese find it awkward and unbecoming if people do not interact according to status expectations. Social roles are clearly delineated along the lines of relative status, and people are expected to behave accordingly with appropriate courtesy and deference. In the Japanese language, there are approximately 100 words for "I" and "me." The form used depends on many variables such as the speaker's age and gender, the formality of the occasion, and the interlocutors' relative status.

In many cultures, such as the African American and Asian cultures, politeness and the use of titles are considered common courtesy (Terrell & Jackson, 2002). Among Hispanics, respect for individuals with advanced age and experience is commonly connoted by using *usted* (formal *you*) rather than *tu* (informal or familiar *you*). Persons from some cultures might be offended if clinicians call them by their first names, and they would consider it highly inappropriate to call clinicians by their first names. While maintaining confidentiality, clinicians can ask interpreters or others who know a family what is most appropriate in the situation. If clinicians are unsure, it is best to err on the side of being more formal.

Directness

> *Assumption:* "Frankness, openness, and honest discussion of situations and feelings are norms."

Although many mainstream Americans believe that speaking indirectly shows powerlessness and insecurity, indirectness is common in many cultures. Among many Asians, indirect communication styles are the norm (Chan, 1998a). In Malaysia, for example, being polite and respectful is of utmost importance. Malaysians consider direct requests to be rude, so they use indirect approaches filled with subtle hints instead (Lian & Abdullah, 2001). Filipinos prize *pakikisama,* or the maintenance of harmony and good feelings, so Filipino clients may be indirect, especially in sensitive matters (Roseberry-McKibbin, 1997). Clinicians must be careful, because what they consider direct and open communication may be perceived as offensively blunt by some clients.

Pakikisama
Maintenance of harmony and good feelings.

Gender

 Assumption: "The gender of the clinician and the client is not an important consideration; the clinician's competence is the most important variable."

Ideally this assumption is true, but for some ethnic groups, the clinician's gender is an important variable. For example, among some cultures and religious groups, it is considered highly offensive for a female clinician to ask direct questions of a male client. Likewise, in other groups, a male clinician would never be allowed alone in a room, unsupervised, with a female client. As another example, most Middle Eastern women would feel deep discomfort discussing, in an information-getting interview, personal issues such as childbirth with a male clinician. Opposite-sex clinicians would not be allowed to work with some Hindus (Nellum-Davis, Gentry, & Hubbard-Wiley, 2002). In some Iraqi families, women cannot leave the house without permission of their husbands (Buell, 1985), and it may be difficult for Iraqi men to work with "liberated" female professionals. These gender lines are difficult for clinicians who have been taught that gender should not matter in professional situations. To be optimally effective, clinicians need to provide interactional situations for clients that are comfortable and that will elicit the most optimal cooperation and communication possible.

Age

 Assumption: "The age of a clinician, relative to the client, is unimportant as long as the clinician is competent."

In many cultures—for example, the Middle Eastern, Native American, Asian, and Hispanic cultures—age is accompanied by increased respect. The older person is the one to be respected and whose opinions are sought. Conversely, young people are seen as having less wisdom and, thus, are less deserving of respect. Young clinicians may want to work in concert with an older professional or interpreter in situations where youth is a barrier to effective service.

Written Documentation

 Assumption: "Written documentation is a necessary and intrinsic part of professionals' interactions with clients and families."

Some limited– or non–English-proficient families may feel intimidated by written forms. Paperwork is not a part of interactions in many cultures, and in some cultures, signatures are required only for significant life events such as births or deaths (Cheng & Hammer, 1992). In other cultures, there is an oral tradition with no tradition of literacy. The Southeast Asian Hmong, for example, had no written language until recent years. Some Native American groups have only recently created systems for writing down information. Professionals working with certain clientele should rely more on oral than written communication. In situations where paperwork is necessary, it is sometimes best if an interpreter is present to thoroughly explain the nature of and the need for documentation.

Nature of Disabilities

 Assumption: "Speech and language therapies are usually necessary even if the client does not have an overt physical disability."

In the United States, clinicians frequently treat clients for "invisible handicaps"—language and cognitive impairments, learning disabilities, stuttering, or voice disorders. Some persons from cultures such as Hispanic and Asian cultures, however, believe that only physical disabilities merit treatment (Matsuda, 1989). Some Asian clients believe that persons with speech disorders and no accompanying overt physical impairment can improve if they "try hard." These clients are less apt to seek treatment for a stuttering child, for instance, because they believe the child is not trying hard enough (Bebout & Arthur, 1992).

The second author worked with two Hmong elementary-aged boys who had chronically low, hoarse voices characterized by pitch and phonation breaks. At her request, an interpreter called the home to speak with the parents about taking the boys to an ear, nose, and throat physician for an evaluation of the boys' vocal folds so that appropriate therapy could be provided. The interpreter told her later that, although the parents said they would follow through, he was not sure they would actually do this because only overt and visible physical disabilities merit intervention in the Hmong culture.

Intervention and Independence

 Assumption: "Rehabilitation is usually necessary because the goal for all individuals, including those with speech and language impairments, is to be as independent as possible."

According to Wallace (1993), some groups believe that a person who experiences a difficulty or impairment

> *needs to experience the challenges associated with the illness rather than receive treatment to overcome the illness ... for [other] cultures ... tradition indicates that the ill person is to be "taken care of" rather than rehabilitated back to independency. In such instances, requiring the patient to attend rehabilitation services to learn to function independently would be considered disrespectful and would cause great shame to the family.* (p. 248)

Among some Asians, rehabilitation for the individual brings great shame to the whole family because they believe that caring for this individual is their responsibility (Chan, 1998b). Among some Hispanics, friends and family may indulge children with impairments. These children may not be expected to actively participate in their own care and treatment (National Coalition of Hispanic Health and Human Services Organization, 1988). In cases such as these, a clinician's efforts to direct families toward rehabilitation may be viewed as being culturally insensitive and could be counterproductive.

 Assumption: "When clients display speech–language disabilities, Western forms of intervention are the most effective and appropriate."

When clients exhibit speech, language, or hearing disabilities, clinicians often recommend therapy. They may also recommend that clients seek out physicians who may then prescribe surgery, medications, physical therapy, other rehabilitative services, or assistive devices. Sometimes professionals discover to their chagrin that families of clients with communicative disorders, instead, use what are considered "nontraditional" forms of healing such as prayer, roots, herbs, massage, witch doctors, or tribal doctors. Most Buddhist Laotians, for example, believe that every human being has 32 souls; when a person is sick, a sorcerer performs the ritual of Baci to call back the souls of the sick person in order to help the person recover (Cheng, 1991). When a Native American family member has an illness or disability, traditional ceremonies are conducted before the family becomes involved in programs recommended by service providers (Joe & Malach, 1998). Members of the Hmong culture may not want surgical intervention because they believe that spirits in the patient's body may leave (Cheng & Hammer, 1992). Instead of going to a doctor, some Haitian families may practice voodoo (McEachern & Kenny, 2002).

Persons whose customs include holistic care, folk medicine, and prayer may feel they are not being treated respectfully by medical and rehabilitation personnel and, thus, may not follow their recommendations. Other groups, such as some Asians and Pacific Islanders, view severely disabling conditions with great stigma. They may believe that a child's disability represents God's punishment for sins (Mokuau & Tauili'ili, 1998), and they may thus be reluctant to seek out services because they want to "save face" (Chan, 1998b). Clinicians would do best to work with—not against—healers, forms of healing, and beliefs that are appropriate to clients' cultures (Saenz, Huer, Doan, Heise, & Fulford, 2001).

Family Participation

Assumption: "When a client receives rehabilitative services or therapy, the family must be as active as possible in collaboration with the clinician."

All clinicians recognize the importance of including families in interviewing, counseling, and assessment or treatment; many experts emphasize the need for clinician–family collaboration (Dodge, 2000; Lindeman, 2001; Paul, 2001; Tiegerman-Farber, 2002). Clinicians frequently counsel families that they need to be actively involved in the treatment or rehabilitation process. Families may be uncomfortable with or unprepared for the amount or type of participation expected of them because the families believe that the professional or agency is supposed to "take care of" the client. Families may be taken by surprise when professionals expect them to be actively involved in a child's special education or an elderly person's rehabilitation after a stroke. Weiss (2002) comments that if some LCD parents are asked to help make decisions and set priorities for treatment, they may view professionals as incompetent. Lynch and Hanson (1998) give the example of an LCD mother who was uncomfortable being asked for her thoughts about her child's service needs. To this mother, it was inappropriate to be questioned about her opinions because that was the professional's job.

Control of Destiny

 Assumption: "Individuals have control over their own destinies."

Many people are very deterministic; that is, they believe they have a great deal of personal control over their futures and experiences. In the paradigm of "self-contained individualism," which characterizes most of U.S. mainstream thought, professionals expect that clients will "aspire toward internal control and an exercise of personal responsibility in their own lives" (Dana, 1993, p. 16). In other cultures, which might be wrongly labeled "passive," individuals may believe that fate or the gods shape their destinies. For example, Cheng (1989) notes that Taoism, practiced by many Chinese,

> *promotes passivity, and those who practice it may display a sense of fatalism ... resulting in resignation and inaction. This basic principle of nonintervention may have a deleterious effect when parents are asked to approve intervention for remediation of language or learning disorders.* (p. 183)

Many Native Americans believe in accepting circumstances and taking life as it comes (Joe & Malach, 1998), and may appear passive in situations where treatment is needed for a family member. In counseling situations, clinicians need to strike a delicate balance between addressing clients' beliefs (e.g., that rehabilitation or therapy is not needed because the disability is the will of God or fate) and encouraging families to actively explore as many therapy or rehabilitation options as possible.

Points to Ponder #22

After working at a clinic for a while, you are having lunch with your colleagues. You don't know them well, but as you listen to them talk, you begin to understand why this clinic has not had success in serving multicultural clients. One colleague says, "They are *always* late, and I tell them to their face that I'm annoyed." Another colleague chimes in, "Yes, and they always want to chat first. We sure don't have time for that!" A third colleague adds, "Yes, and it's so irritating when they shrug and say 'it's God's will,' or use herbs, or call on some 'healer.' I mean, get real. This is America. They have just got to learn that God helps those who help themselves."

What information will you share to help these colleagues increase their sensitivity and, thus, their effectiveness?

Language in the Home

 Assumption: "Families who speak other languages at home need to speak English to their children so that the children will learn English."

In some interviewing and counseling situations, clinicians have been known to recommend that parents who speak "broken" English need to speak English, rather than their primary language, to their children. This pernicious and oft-given advice has deleterious impacts on children's language development and family communication in general (Gutierrez-Clellen, 1999; Madding, 2002). Family members should speak to one another in the language they are the most comfortable using. It is the quality of the interaction, not the language of the interaction, that is the key for children's development. Professionals should emphasize to parents that being bilingual is a positive ability and that speaking two or more languages is a great asset in today's world.

Counseling Individuals

 Assumption: "Counseling individuals in isolation can be quite effective."

U.S. culture has been termed a "low-context culture" because emphasis is placed on the role of the individual in contrast to cultures in which the individual is recognized primarily as a member of a group, not as an individual entity (Joe & Malach, 1998). Dana (1993) states the following:

> *The relentless focus on the self provided by most existing services may be alien and disquieting to persons with cultural values that define the self only in concert with others and perceive autonomy and individualism as undesirable or even unnecessary.* (p. 16)

In many situations, it is imperative for clinicians to involve the whole family in interviewing and counseling situations, not just individual members. Decision making, in many cultures, involves the whole family, including extended family members.

Along this line, it may be important to help families, especially newly arrived immigrants and refugees who feel isolated, get support from other members of their culture. Support groups can be highly effective (Saenz et al., 2001). Professionals can consider recommending local churches, community centers, and other resources when appropriate. For example, many African Americans have strong ties to the church (Terrell & Jackson, 2002; Willis, 1998), and it might be appropriate for clinicians to use religious organizations as allies in intervention when working with some African American clients (Randall-David, 1989). Clinicians should recommend support systems that are appropriate for each family.

Communicating Effectively When Interviewing and Counseling

Clients come into interviewing and counseling situations with varying degrees of proficiency in the English language, which presents challenges for effective communication between clinicians and clients or families. The following suggestions are useful for clinicians to implement with clients who experience difficulties communicating in English.

Loudness

Do not increase the volume of your voice. Clients (with the exception of those with hearing impairments) do not need clinicians to shout at them or speak in loud tones. It is shocking to see how many clinicians speak loudly to individuals whose English proficiency is limited. This can make clients feel they are being treated like children.

Rate of Speech

Decrease your rate of speech and pause often. Many readers have had the experience of taking a foreign language class, and then traveling to a country where that language is spoken and not understanding conversational speech because it was "too rapid." Similarly, many LCD clients benefit when clinicians use slow speech rates and pause between sentences, giving the client time to process what was just said.

Articulation in Connected Speech

Articulate each word clearly, but do not overexaggerate. Some clients relate that they do not understand because the "words run together so fast." For example, we usually coarticulate "How is it going?" as "Howzitgoing?" Clients do not know what "howzitgoing" is—it could be a type of food, a style of dress, or a cloud formation. They do understand "How is it going?" when each word is produced separately and the copula is not contracted. This is especially true for clients raised in countries where British English is taught. Some Japanese and Koreans, for example, have difficulty with spoken U.S. English because it is not pronounced as precisely as the British English taught in Japanese and Korean schools.

Language Length and Complexity

Avoid the frequent use of long, polysyllabic words, as well as the use of slang, idiomatic speech, technical jargon, and abstract terminology. Use short sentences and phrases. It is very important not to use run-on, lengthy sentences because clients have a hard time comprehending these.

Repeating Key Information

A thread running throughout this book is that clients need to hear key concepts several times. This is especially true for clients who speak English as a second, third, or fourth language. Repeating key concepts is important.

Nonverbal Cues and Body Language

Proxemics (the study of the use of distance) and *kinesics* (the study of the use of facial expressions and gestures) differ among cultures. Be aware and accepting of nonverbal cues and body language that are culturally appropriate for clients. In many cultures, people are very sensitive to nuances of facial expression and body language. For example, among some members of the African American community, it is considered aggressive and disrespectful to make direct eye contact with an authority figure. Conversely, an Arab often looks at a conversational partner with great intensity (Fast, 2002). Among some Latin Americans, kissing both cheeks in greeting is common. Most Asian children are expected to listen and speak very little when interacting with adults (Fung & Roseberry-McKibbin, 1999). Many Chinese individuals keep their faces expressionless, and Westerners may perceive Chinese people as having poor eye contact. Individuals from the Carolinian and Chamorro cultures tend to communicate extensively with their eyebrows; a speaker may raise the eyebrows to acknowledge a question, to greet another person, or to affirm or negate something that has been said (Hammer, 1994). Nonverbal cues are important, and it is helpful for clinicians to understand them and, as appropriate, to act in ways that are consistent with that family's culture.

Proxemics
Study of the use of distance.

Kinesics
Study of the use of facial expressions and gestures.

Size of Interaction Groups

As noted in Chapter 1, there are two parties to an interview—the party that is conducting an interview and the party being interviewed. Encourage families to bring people who are important to them to a meeting. This can include friends, extended family members, and clergy. Many families will feel more comfortable and supported with these persons present.

Do not, however, overwhelm clients by bringing too many professionals into an interaction. In some interviewing and counseling situations, clients are surrounded by a coterie of professionals such as a speech–language pathologist, a surgeon, a psychologist, a physical therapist, an occupational therapist, and a nurse. This may be intimidating, and it is best to keep the number of professionals in a group as small as possible.

Flexibility

Be flexible and willing to provide assistance in establishing meetings. This could include meeting families in their homes, providing child care for siblings, or arranging transportation for families. Clinicians may need to meet with families in school cafeterias or on park benches; at least one author (Kozloff,

1994) has met with parents in their cars. If clinicians insist on meeting with clients only in offices, they may not get to see certain clients or families at all.

Extra Time

Be patient and allow extra time for meetings. Meetings frequently take more time when clients do not speak English as a first language. It is important to avoid appearing hurried. Families from some backgrounds, such as the Native American culture, may not discuss their true concerns if they feel rushed. Hispanic families may feel that if clinicians are in a hurry, they are showing the family disrespect or a lack of concern (Zuniga, 1998).

Suggestions for Using Interpreters

Professionals may need to utilize the services of interpreters during interviews and counseling with clients who speak little or no English. Clinicians must be sure to use only those interpreters who have been trained properly; have good bilingual communication skills; act in a professional manner; have the ability to relate well to members of their own cultural group; and understand and carry out their ethical responsibilities, including maintaining confidentiality.

Several reports in the literature give excellent guidelines for situations in which interpreters' services are utilized (Isaac, 2001; Langdon & Cheng, 2002; Roseberry-McKibbin, 2002). These guidelines include the following:

• *Speak in short units and avoid professional jargon.* A major problem for many interpreters is that professionals speak in lengthy utterances that are technical and difficult to remember for translation.

• *Look at the client (or clients) as well as the interpreter when speaking and listening.* This is difficult for most clinicians because they tend to speak to and look at the interpreter only. This can make clients feel left out and unimportant. Clinicians must discipline themselves to make warm and caring eye contact with clients as they talk.

• *Remember that in some cultures, a man's opinions and statements are given more weight and credence than a woman's.* A female clinician will often find, in these cases, that having a male interpreter adds authority to the meeting (Hays, 2001).

• *Encourage the interpreter to translate clients' words without paraphrasing them as much as possible.* Some words or phrases have no direct translation, but clinicians need to hear exactly what clients say.

• *Explain the purpose, structure, and generally anticipated topics of discussion of an interviewing or counseling session to an interpreter beforehand.* Many interpreters report feeling "thrown into" situations for which they are completely unprepared. Although time is always at a premium, and clinicians do not usually have the luxury of long conversations with interpreters, clinicians should take some time to prepare interpreters for the situation ahead of them. Interpreters will be more effective if they are prepared, and they will be more successful in eliciting clients' cooperation when they can thoroughly explain rationales for clinicians' questions and requests. Interpreters must understand the interview questions completely and know how to record clients' responses (Roseberry-McKibbin, 2002).

- *Tape record the session,* if the family is comfortable with this. It is always helpful to have an audiotape to refer back to if questions arise.

- *Seat the interpreter as close to family members as possible.* Clients will be more comfortable if they are sitting near the interpreter.

- *Begin the meeting by introducing everyone and explaining the purpose of the meeting.* Clients should hear the names of each person and understand what each person's role is. The purpose of the meeting may need to be reiterated several times.

- *Be on hand at all times during the meeting.* Do not leave the room for coffee, phone calls, or errands. It is important to be present throughout in case questions or different topics of discussion arise.

- *Encourage family members to ask questions.* Many cultures consider it disrespectful to question professionals because they are viewed as authority figures. Clinicians need to ask interpreters to encourage family members to ask questions, if interpreters feel comfortable doing this.

- *Periodically check on the accuracy of translation and clients' understanding of what is being said.* Clinicians can ask family members to repeat instructions, but should avoid asking, "Do you understand?" (Bondurant-Utz, 1994). Family members may feel put on the spot and, to save face, say they do understand when, in fact, they do not. Having family members repeat what they have heard lets clinicians know whether or not the context of the interaction is understood.

- *Discuss the session with the interpreter afterward.* This gives both individuals the opportunity to clarify information, ask questions, make comments, and discuss the meeting.

- *Thank interpreters and pay them for their assistance.* Professionals need to treat interpreters with respect, dignity, and appreciation. Too often interpreters feel that they are spread very thin and are constantly rushing around, having their services utilized by professionals who may or may not appreciate the invaluable services provided. It behooves clinicians to remember that services to some families would be difficult, if not impossible, to provide without interpreters. Interviewing and counseling can be sensitive and highly charged, and it is especially important to have the services of competent interpreters who are well trained and who feel appreciated for the services they provide.

⚬∘ᴼ◯ Points to Ponder #23

At your clinic, you need to meet with the parents of Alexi and discuss your recommendations for treatment. Alexi has been diagnosed with a language-learning disability; Alexi's dominant language is English, but his parents speak only Russian. You don't know much about the Russian culture or language, and feel intimidated by this situation. Thankfully, though, there will be an interpreter present at the meeting. How can you prepare to handle this situation? What will you do to help this meeting be successful and productive?

Suggestions for Increasing Personal Sensitivity

Many professionals truly desire to increase their sensitivity to and consequent effectiveness with clients from diverse backgrounds. Ivey, Pedersen, and Ivey (2001) suggest that the clinician develop "multicultural intentionality," which is composed of awareness, knowledge, skills, humility, and the ability to recover when mistakes are made.

The suggestions in the following sections, based in part on Lynch and Hanson (1998) and Roseberry-McKibbin (2002), will assist individuals in developing their multicultural intentionality to provide more effective services to LCD populations.

Use of Terminology

Do not use terms that have negative connotations. For example, terms such as "at risk," "culturally deprived," and "culturally disadvantaged" imply that clients are being judged by an Anglo-European standard. This is ethnocentric and racist.

Study of Cultures

Study the culture or cultures that are common to your geographic area. As one frustrated student said several years ago, "There's no way I can learn about all these different cultures and remember everything about them!" This legitimate feeling is shared by many professionals, who feel overwhelmed as they face what can seem like a huge and endless task of learning details about cultural groups. It is most efficacious to learn about the group or groups that clinicians see most commonly in their geographic work areas.

Names of Cultural Groups

Learn and use the names of cultural groups as assigned by the group members. This will save many misunderstandings; however, each client and family must be taken on individual terms. For example, the second author has always used the term "Native American," but, several years ago, a Native American student stated emphatically that she wished to be referred to as "American Indian." Another student, who was from Mexico, said he did not like the term "Latino." It is best to ascertain the preferences of each individual and family.

Common Words and Phrases

Learn and use some common words and greetings in the language(s) of the limited–English-proficient families and clients served. Clients generally appreciate a clinician's efforts to relate to them, even if it is only by using a few simple words or phrases in their language.

Multicultural Contacts

Establish relationships with persons from the local community who can serve as cultural informants and mediators. Such relationships are an invaluable part of working effectively with diverse clients and their families (Corey, 2001). Cultural mediators, informants, or interpreters from clients' backgrounds frequently can make more headway with individuals than professionals working alone can. Some LCD clients feel more trust in and comfort with persons from their own communities.

Reading

Read what you can about the cultures and languages within the community. This information can be obtained from university and local libraries, as well as from individuals. Several excellent sources of information about cultural groups include Battle (2002), Brice (2002), Cheng (1991), Dwairy (1998), Hays (2001), Lynch and Hanson (1998), Paniagua (1998), Roseberry-McKibbin (2002), and Sue and Sue (2003). Also, look for and read publications and information from the cultural communities themselves. Read their magazines, newspapers, and books (Hays, 2001).

Interaction with Other Cultures

Interact, both during and outside of work, with members of the cultural communities being served. Professionals can take time to do simple things such as going to an ethnic grocery store, attending church services or community cultural functions, going to centers for minority groups, and participating in various LCD holiday celebrations. Participating in these events provides opportunities to learn about other cultures in a broader manner than that provided by just seeing clients in one's office.

Ethnographic Interviews

Ethnographic interviewing is used to gather information about a culture or individuals from that culture from a LCD informant's point of view. Conduct ethnographic interviews with members of the culture being served; do not interview just one member of that culture and base assumptions on that one person's viewpoints and perspectives. Questions can include, but should not be limited to, the following, which are based on and adapted from various authors (Bondurant-Utz, 1994; Mattes & Omark, 1991; Roseberry-McKibbin, 2002):

- What is the typical family size and constellation in this community?
- What is the typical family authority hierarchy?
- What are the roles of extended family members and siblings?
- What are the culture's parenting practices?
- What behaviors are expected for showing courtesy (e.g., avoiding eye contact with authority figures, not questioning professionals' decisions)?
- How does this cultural group view the role of special education? Of rehabilitation?

- How does the cultural group view the role of the impaired individual and the causes of handicapping conditions?
- What healing systems are used by group members? Would nonmedical or medical intervention violate beliefs in these systems?
- What role is played by factors such as poverty or immigrant/refugee status?
- What are the primary family or community concerns (e.g., health care, food, jobs)?
- What kind of community support is available for the family?
- What are the philosophical or religious influences on members of this culture?
- Do members of the culture perceive racism or discrimination from the mainstream culture? If so, how might this affect attitudes toward intervention?

Home Visits and Inquiring About Cultures

Visit families' homes if they are comfortable with this idea. Home visits, when appropriate, provide unique insight into individual families' ways of living and interacting. Ask clients to share important aspects of their culture with you. Many times, professionals are afraid to ask clients about their cultural backgrounds. Although professionals must be careful not to pry or make clients uncomfortable, clients may be delighted to be asked to share information about their culture. Some of the best information about various LCD groups comes from asking clients to share about themselves and their cultures.

Diversity Within Cultures

Recognize the tremendous diversity that exists within each culture. Learning about other cultures is an exciting, dynamic, and ongoing process. Clinicians can never assume that, because they have read a chapter in a book about Asians or attended one or two workshops about Hispanics, they can settle comfortably into, or operate effectively, from that small knowledge base, as though all Asian or Hispanic clients possess the characteristics learned from those sources. Students and professionals must constantly respect and be aware of the great diversity that exists within each culture, and not stereotype individuals or try to put them into rigid, preexisting frameworks into which they may or may not fit. Each client and each family is unique.

Diversity in Languages

Recognize the diversity within languages. For example, people can go to any part of the United States or Canada and understand the English used. In many other countries, however, there is a great variety of languages and dialects. The second author was raised on the small island of Tablas in the Philippines. Residents of Odiongan spoke Odionganon as the local vernacular; on the other side of Tablas, in the town of Looc, residents spoke Loocnon. Both were distinctively different languages.

More than 1,200 indigenous languages are spoken in the Pacific Islands, and many of these languages are mutually unintelligible. There are more than 87 dialects in China. Clinicians must be aware that people from the same general language group may speak mutually unintelligible dialects. When clinicians use interpreters, they need to make sure the interpreter and client have at least one dialect in common so that they can understand each other.

Religious Influence

The influence of religion and religious beliefs was addressed in Chapter 3. Be sensitive to the role that religion plays in clients' lives. Religions affect services to and interactions with clients. For example, during the month of Ramadan, most Muslims do not have food or drink between sunrise and sundown; thus, clinicians might not want to offer food or drink to Muslim clients during Ramadan. Buddhists have a special 3-day holiday in August (Nellum-Davis et al., 2002); therefore, Buddhist families may not be available for sessions during these days. It also may be difficult for some Buddhist families to accept certain forms of medical intervention, such as cleft palate surgery, because they believe that children with disabilities will be reincarnated to a whole form (Anderson & Fenichel, 1989). There are many other possible influences of religion and religious beliefs.

Sharing Information

As clinicians learn about LCD clients and their backgrounds, the information should be shared with other professionals. This is helpful for everyone because personal and professional experiences benefit other clinicians and the clients they serve.

≫ Concluding Comments

As we continue into the 21st century, exciting challenges await our profession. One of these major challenges is to effectively serve an increasingly LCD population whose members have unique characteristics, needs, and expectations. There are a number of areas clinicians need to consider when working with LCD clients and families. Learning about other cultures, languages, and values of clients is a continual journey—always interesting, sometimes challenging, and most of all, deeply rewarding. Our diverse clients always serve as a reminder of one of life's great truths: We must never stop growing and learning to live well together.

NINE

Working with Difficult Situations

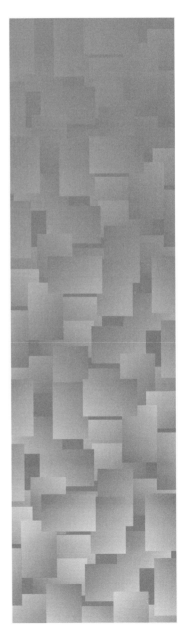

CHAPTER OUTLINE

- Potentially Difficult Communication Behaviors
- Emotions, Attitudes, and Behaviors
- Other Factors, Conditions, and Situations
- Concluding Comments

n a helping profession, most of a clinician's work is with people—patients, family members, or other caregivers—who are concerned about the problems being experienced and are eager to assist. These people are typically cooperative and often appreciative of a clinician's efforts. Working with this majority of clients and their families is a true source of personal pleasure and professional gratification. There are, however, some situations that are not as pleasant, at least initially, and some individuals who are simply less cooperative than others.

This chapter addresses situations and events in interviewing and counseling sessions that are sometimes confusing or frustrating to clinicians. It is important to note, however, that, like beauty, "difficulty" or what is perceived as a "difficult situation" is often in the eyes of the beholder. What is a very difficult situation for one person may not be for another. This often relates to the clinician's level of knowledge of self and others, experience, outlook, and approaches to people and clinical work. It is important to realize that there is no magical formula for working with difficult situations or people. Rather, clinical workers need to react (or not react) to situations at hand and develop steps for working with circumstances on a case-by-case basis. There are, however, some basic principles that help clinicians understand difficult situations and, often, react appropriately. Several general, introductory suggestions include the following:

- Make yourself stay calm, cool, and in control while minimizing your own levels of emotional involvement.
- Try to understand as fully as possible what might be motivating or happening with the other party.
- Identify the specific behaviors, attitudes, or other factors that are of concern to you.
- Do not allow yourself to overreact negatively to anything that is said, at least not visually. Your heart may be pounding and stomach churning, but do not let the other person see this.
- When dealing with individuals who are culturally or linguistically different, and who demonstrate values or attitudes of concern, try to understand their viewpoints or actions in a cultural perspective.

The application of these suggestions should be reconsidered while reading this chapter. It is also worth remembering that clinicians typically deal with "crazy-making circumstances, not crazy people" (Moses, 1985, p. 84). People with communicative disorders sometimes come into clinical settings frustrated, bewildered, confused, depressed, angry, or filled with fears about what today and the future will bring. Clients and their caregivers may be cooperative, concerned, and caring, or they may be what clinicians perceive as uncooperative, apathetic, or counterproductive in their attitudes and behaviors. Dealing with a communicative difficulty can indeed be a "crazy-making circumstance" for clients, families, friends, and others. The clinician's task is to help these people deal effectively and productively with their disorders.

Potentially Difficult Communication Behaviors

There are several types of behaviors that, although they may not occur every day, are seen in clinical settings. These behaviors include resistance, denial, questioning, discrepancies, shifts of conversational focus, "recurrent themes," and gaps of information. Some of these—types of resistance, denial, and some forms of questioning—are similar to or related to active defense mechanisms, which were discussed in Chapter 3. Other aspects of client behavior—discrepancies, conversational shifts, recurrent references, and information gaps—have more to do with the flow of conversation and information between a clinician and a client, and may result from defensive reactions or lapses of memory, or are just inadvertent actions. Clinicians try to assess why they occur and work with these areas. Of course, sometimes clinicians are fully successful doing this; other times they are less successful than desired. A good deal of a clinician's success in this area begins by identifying what is really happening.

Resistance

Resistance is a natural phenomenon that occurs to some degree in many, if not most, relationships. Resistance usually occurs when individuals fear change, are uncertain about the situation, or do not want to take a deeper and more truthful look at themselves (Kennedy & Charles, 2001; Okun, 2002). In a clinical setting, resistance can be expressed by behaviors such as tardiness, an abrupt change of topic, "forgetfulness," subtle or overt forms of inattention, silence, disagreement with something shared, or the failure to follow through on suggestions (i.e., the hearing aid not worn, the homework assignments not practiced, the appointment with the physician not made).

Resistance tends to occur early in a clinical relationship during assessment activities or in the treatment process. Brammer (1993) lists several of what he calls the "realities" of a new relationship, each of which can result in resistance:

- It is not easy to receive help.
- It is difficult to commit oneself to change.

- It is difficult to submit to the influence of a helper; help is a threat to esteem, integrity, and independence.
- It is not easy to trust strangers and to be open with them.
- It is not easy to see one's problems clearly at first.
- Sometimes problems seem too large, too overwhelming or too unique to share them easily.
- Some cultural traditions deprecate giving and receiving help outside the family. (p. 56)

Resistance also occurs when there is disagreement about something said or done, or when something has been misunderstood. The patient who disagrees with a clinician's comments or recommendations is likely to resist, in one way or another, the clinician's findings, conclusions, or suggestions. Also, patients who develop ill feelings toward a clinician tend to be resistant. The ill feelings may be a reaction to a clinician's attitude, something said, a gesture, or another form of body language. It is important for clinicians to evaluate whether they are doing something that is engendering resistance, or whether the resistance has other causes. For example, if a parent does not really believe a child needs treatment, but allows the youngster to be enrolled for services anyway, ambivalence or resistance may occur. The parent might not even be conscious of such feelings. In such a case, clinicians try to overcome the ambivalence or resistance by working with the parent's feelings about the need for services because these feelings are the source of the problem.

Another source of resistance is change itself (Brammer, 1993). Consider the following explanation, from MacLean and Gould (1988), of how change and risk apply to the experience of resistance:

> *Change implies the giving up of something old, and learning, doing, being something new. There is a sense in which the old has to be unlearned, and new ways relearned. It is not surprising that clients (and all of us) tend to stick with what is known—the habitual, familiar way of behaving. Giving up these old ways like giving up familiar friends, there are risks involved.* (p. 33)

Often a client's resistance can be overcome in time, as the two parties accumulate experiences together and trust and faith grow. Lavorato and McFarlane (1988) describe resistance and one approach used in the beginning with a voice case:

> *For some individuals, whether to engage in voice therapy or not is a major decision. Perhaps they do not under-*

stand the reason for it, or do not want to change their voice, or spend the time and money required, or just feel silly engaging in therapy. Advising and explaining the rationale for therapy is sufficient for most clients. Playing audiotapes or videotapes of previous successes can be an inducement for others. The case that follows required a different approach. The client was a nurse who was "sprawled out" in the waiting room and stood reluctantly, looking angry, when greeted.

CLINICIAN: And what is your concern about your speech?

CLIENT: I have none. I just went to the doctor with an ear problem, that's all. There's nothing wrong with my throat.

CLINICIAN: What did he say was wrong with your throat?

CLIENT: He said my vocal cords look irritated and that I was talking wrong. Hell, I know how I talk! I've been husky all my life. So is the rest of my family. We all talk like this. We talk loudly, and all the women have deep voices. He has followed me for my ear problem for two weeks, and all he talks about is my throat. I don't have the time or interest to work on my voice.

CLINICIAN: That's kind of irritating. You don't need another problem in your life.

CLIENT: You'd better believe it. I'm divorced and have complete responsibility for my children. I'm busy.

CLINICIAN: Look. I'm concerned about your not wanting to be here. I respect your feelings about this and feel that you should not be forced into anything. At this point, what would you like me to do? If you want me to cancel this session, I will do it right now.

CLIENT: (*Less abrupt, more receptive in posture, tone of voice, choice of words, rate of speech.*) Well, what will happen if I don't follow through with his recommendation to see you?

CLINICIAN: (*Explains the possible outcomes of her problem if left untreated.*)

CLIENT: I do talk a lot. I lecture—and wish that I didn't have to do that. A lot of times, my voice is almost gone by the time I finish a lecture. I don't really like my voice—it distracts from my message.

CLINICIAN: Some of my clients say they begin to get nervous when the voice begins to go and they have more talking to do.

CLIENT: It is very distracting. Not only that, but my throat occasionally gets an irritated feeling and it is uncomfortable talking.

CLINICIAN: I know what you mean.

CLIENT: What is involved in voice therapy? How many times would I have to come in?

The client agreed to an evaluation and to initiate therapy. Giving her the option to do so was critical. It put her back in control and indicated the clinician's respect for her feelings and situation. It also led her to be more open about her problem. (pp. 246–247)

A more emphatic form of resistance is *rejection*—the conscious, active unwillingness to agree with the clinician's descriptions, interpretations, conclusions, or recommendations. When rejection occurs, clinicians need to consider carefully a client's underlying feelings. This can be done by pleasantly, but directly, reflecting a client's messages.

 "You feel differently about it. Tell me about how you are feeling about _____."

 "You don't fully agree with that, do you?"

 "Tell me about your concerns with this recommendation."

Sometimes clinicians need to use a more direct comment to get at the source of the rejection.

 "You are very quiet today. Tell me about it."

 "You seem uncomfortable talking about _____."

 "I sense that you would rather talk about _____ than _____ today."

 "This is the third time you've been late this week. This seems to be a pattern. I'd like to know what's really bothering you?"

Resistance from clients from diverse backgrounds may occur for several reasons, including trust issues (Sue & Sue, 2003). Certain cultures are also less direct than the mainstream culture, so a highly direct clinician can engender resistance when working with clients from such a background. Resistance may relate to how a culture views communicative problems or deals with problems. In some Native American tribes, the extended family is responsible for taking care of problems—outside intervention is less acceptable. Many devout Muslims believe that only Allah knows the future, so planning more than a few weeks ahead does not make much sense. Discussing long-term plans and strategies may not seem as important to these individuals as clinicians would like (Nellum-Davis, Gentry, & Hubbard-Wiley, 2002). Therefore, what might appear as resistance is reflective of cultural outlook and beliefs.

Denial

Denial is a response that clinicians see with some frequency with communicative disorders. For example, audiologists often see patients whose hearing has been impaired for long periods of time (Hansen, 2001). As a frustrated spouse might complain,

 "I've told him for years to go get his hearing tested. But, oh no, not him and his pride! He always said his hearing was as sharp as a tack. Trouble is, he couldn't hear me tell him he was wrong."

There are parents who deny, sometimes for long periods of time, that their child actually has a speech, language, or hearing problem (Paul, 2001). A number of clinicians have been told on more than one occasion that "I am not concerned about it; he'll outgrow it," or "He'll start talking. His father didn't talk until he was 4 years old!" Failure to recognize a problem and the use of rationalization are forms of denial. *Denial* is a defense mechanism people employ when they are not ready to admit that a problem exists and begin remedying the situation. This is sometimes seen in patients who are "just not ready" (see Brammer, Abrego, & Shostrom, 1993). Like resistance, it is a response that people may not be conscious of using.

Denial is a very common characteristic of chemically dependent persons and their families. Sometimes no one—the chemically dependent person, family members, friends, coworkers, superiors—is ready to fully acknowledge the problem, its ramifications, or its solutions. A form of denial is *minimizing,* or making some problem out to be less than it actually is. In the field of chemical dependence, minimization is encountered frequently. For example, when asking a practicing alcoholic or drug addict the quantity of alcohol or drugs being used, it is common for respondents to report a figure that is considerably

Denial
A defense mechanism that people employ when they are not ready to admit that a problem exists and begin remedying the situation.

Minimizing
Making a problem out to be less than it actually is.

less than what is really being used. The same person may also vehemently convey that the drinking or using has little effect on self, family, friends, school, or job. This person is minimizing the problem and its effects.

Patients and families who deny the existence of a condition or minimize a problem and its consequences need time, knowledge, and support to help them acknowledge and cope with what is actually happening and begin to accept what needs to be done. This process takes time, and it certainly takes the understanding, support, and often the caring and persistent direct assistance of a clinician.

For some individuals, denial is a temporary solution along the road to understanding and agreement. Denial acts to help them "buy time" while evaluating if what they feel is true and what is in their best interests or in the best interests of the family member with a communicative disorder. Clinicians need to realize that even if clients or loved ones deny something outwardly, they may still—behind the cover of the denial—be contemplating whether the information is true and the clinician's feelings or descriptions are accurate. Thus, clinicians have heard comments like the following:

 "When you first told me my daughter would not improve without therapy, I really didn't believe it. But the more we thought about how she's doing and what you told us, the more we began to think you were right."

 "I know I said I can hear fine and don't need a hearing aid. But I've been noticing that it is sometimes a little hard to hear everything. Can we talk about it again? I'm still not going to get a hearing aid, but I want to talk about it and make sure I understand what you said."

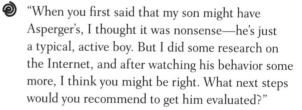 "When you first said that my son might have Asperger's, I thought it was nonsense—he's just a typical, active boy. But I did some research on the Internet, and after watching his behavior some more, I think you might be right. What next steps would you recommend to get him evaluated?"

These examples illustrate how the person who denied something thought about the information that was conveyed and altered the previous stance of complete denial.

In some cases, clinicians need to be very candid about the denial:

 "I have worked intensively with your father for a month now and he's made very little progress. All of the medical reports indicate that he has severe brain damage. The brain is just not working like it once did. But you still seem to feel that he will be fine again in time. I know you would like to see major improvement, but it seems like it's difficult for you to come to grips with the fact that he is not going to be the same as he was before."

"I know you have felt that Jason was going to start speaking at any time. But he's almost 4 now, and he's still not talking. I'm feeling like we may have two problems. One is Jason's inability to talk. The other is that you are having a hard time dealing with this problem. I think this is difficult for you to accept. Let's talk about how you are feeling."

Neither of these examples is necessarily typical of most clinical discussions with patients or family members. However, the examples do illustrate the types of conversations clinicians need to conduct in certain situations of denial.

There are degrees of candor, however, that are not appropriate with clients from linguistically or culturally diverse backgrounds, particularly from cultures that place a greater value on indirectness. It is also important to consider whether an individual is denying a problem in the traditional Anglo-European sense; it is possible that the difficulty is not necessarily viewed as being a problem within this group, or that the notion of intervention is inconsistent with cultural or even religious values (Salas-Provance, Erickson, & Reed, 2002). O. L. Taylor and Clarke (1994) remark that "societies seem to have different perceptions of what aspects of communication, if any, they consider pathologic and what to do about it, if anything" (p. 109).

There are instances in which identifying someone as disabled or impaired stigmatizes the individual. In the Philippines or China, for example, the idea of "deformity" may be viewed as a curse that ostracizes an individual from society. In other cultures, it is particularly difficult for fathers to accept that there may be anything wrong with their sons. Such views can be seen as denial or resistance, but they also reflect cultural values.

Points to Ponder #24

You have a new patient: a 59-year-old man named Jim who has been diagnosed with Parkinson's disease. Jim, a vocal and outgoing salesman, has always been an avid outdoorsman who loves camping. In addition, he makes presentations in states to which he travels. Jim's doctor has sent him and his wife, Carolyn, to you because Jim is beginning to experience some signs of dysarthria of speech. Carolyn appears very impatient during the meeting, and Jim says, "I have no idea why I'm really here. I'm going to be fine. I don't need help. I mean, look at Michael J. Fox. They could find a cure for this thing tomorrow. We really feel like we're wasting your time, but the doc insisted that we come." How will you handle this situation?

Questioning

There can be many reasons why clients question a clinician's assessment conclusions or treatment suggestions. The clinician might be wrong. In one case, a clinician told a client's parents that she would outgrow her articulation problems. Unfortunately, an oral examination had not been performed adequately; the presence of a severe ankyloglossia (tongue-tie) was undetected. This child could not have outgrown the speech problem nor would therapy have remedied speech difficulties; rather, surgical intervention was needed. Fortunately the parents had questioned the first diagnosis and sought a second opinion.

Clients may also question a diagnosis or prognosis because they are simply unable, at that point, to fully accept what the clinician found. They cannot accept the findings because the ramifications may be quite painful and life-changing. For example, if an audiologist obtains hearing test results that are consistent with the presence of an 8th cranial nerve tumor, the audiologist will refer the client to an otolaryngologist who may recommend magnetic resonance imaging to ascertain whether or not a brain tumor (8th cranial nerve neuropathy) is present. The client, overwhelmed by the possibility of having a "brain tumor," may question the audiogram extensively, hoping, of course, that the results are wrong or that there has been a mistake. We sometimes see this with parents of children with disabilities upon initial diagnosis. One father said angrily to the second author, "Hey, I don't like the term 'learning disability!' And how do you know that? Where else can we go to find out if that's really true?"

This is not an uncommon reaction to events in life. Denying a diagnosis provides a temporary solution to the inability to understand and cope with what is happening. Likewise, questioning a diagnosis or asking for a second opinion should not necessarily be interpreted as an attack on the professional, but may be an important step toward understanding and acknowledgment (Cunningham & Davis, 1985).

Sometimes clinicians see patients and families who do not ask questions, such as the passive nonlisteners described in Chapter 2 (see "Listening and Activity Levels"). Also, individuals from some cultures (e.g., Hispanic or Japanese) tend not to openly disagree or question clinicians in areas of disagreement or confusion out of respect for the clinician.

As with resistance and denial, then, it is important to realize that there are many possible sources for questioning behavior—or the lack of questioning. Resistance, denial, and questioning a clinician can all act as hesitations or interruptions of the diagnostic or therapeutic process. They can be engendered by the clinician, or they can have causes independent of the professional services provided. In any case, clinicians are obligated to help clients understand the situation as thoroughly as possible. This is most easily accomplished by providing accurate information, genuine support, and appropriate summaries of findings and conclusions.

Discrepancies

Ivey (1994) describes several types of discrepancies and mixed messages that can occur in clinical situations.

- *Discrepancy between nonverbal behaviors.* The individual displays a pleasant, "no problem" smile accompanied by a tightly clenched fist.
- *Discrepancy between two or more statements.* "My son is perfect, but he just doesn't respect me." "I agree with what you are saying but still think an in-the-ear aid would be better."
- *Discrepancy between what one says and what one does.* Individuals say they "agree with the diagnosis 100%" and promise to do everything possible to help, but consistently fail to complete the homework requested.
- *Discrepancy between a statement and nonverbal behavior.* The client states that the stuttering does not bother him; meanwhile, tears swell in his eyes and his fists are tightly clenched.
- *Discrepancy between the views of different people.* A father and mother disagree about the impact of a communicative disorder on their child. Brother and sister

tell conflicting versions of how much their father's loss of hearing is affecting their everyday lives. (Adapted from pp. 78–80)

Often, clinicians can clear up a discrepancy or mixed message by probing, which is usually sufficient to resolve accidental or inadvertent discrepancies. For example, suppose a client indicated at one point that her hearing seemed better in her right ear, but later said the hearing was better in the left ear. Rather unobtrusively, a clinician could say, "Let me make sure I have it straight. Tell me again which one is your better ear." The patient's response could then be summarized back to the client for reconfirmation; for example, "So it is the hearing in your left ear that does not seem as good." The clinician may want to probe this again at a later time for further confirmation that the left ear is of primary concern.

At other times, clinicians need to explicitly identify a discrepancy for the patient, as in the following examples:

 "Mr. Smith, you mentioned that Johnny started talking at about 2 years of age. Mrs. Smith, you seem to recall that it may have been as late as age 4. Let's talk about this."

 "Sandy, you said your stuttering is not really a problem and that it doesn't really bother you. But it looked like you were about to cry when you said that. Tell me how you're feeling about your stuttering."

 "Robert, you say you like your hearing aid and that it helps you hear better. But your teacher says you are not wearing it in class. I'm confused. You say you like it and it helps, but you aren't using it. Can you help me make sense of this?"

Most discrepancies and mixed messages can be resolved, or at least understood better, with such confronting techniques. An even more direct form of confrontation is reserved for extreme cases.

 "On one hand, you tell me how concerned you are about Tom and his problems, and that you will help in any way possible. On the other hand, his home practice is not getting done. What you say does not seem to mesh with what is actually happening. Help me with this inconsistency."

 "You say that your stuttering is no big deal and it doesn't really bother you. But you almost cry every time I ask you about it. It seems like you are really hurting. Your words are saying 'no big deal,' but everything else is saying that it is a big deal. Tell me about these inconsistencies."

Certain disorders can also present a form of discrepancy. For example, many individuals with aphasia exhibit "yes–no" confusions in their speech: "yes" sometimes means "no," or vice versa, or the two terms are used inconsistently.

Clinicians also need to be sensitive when working with members of linguistically and culturally different populations because language barriers and cultural differences can cause confusing or seemingly discrepant responses, or perceived discrepancies between what someone agrees to do and the lack of follow-up that occurs. Chan (1998b) notes the following:

> *While apparently concurring in some manner (through failure to express or defend an alternative point of view) or ostensibly indicating agreement, Filipinos may actually be privately opposed to the issue at hand. Thus ... mistakes will go unmentioned, questions unasked, and issues unsettled.* (pp. 392–393)

Out of respect, some parents from the Hispanic culture also may not openly disagree with clinicians; thus, they may give the appearance of following directions or agreeing to something without fully intending to follow up (Brice, 2002). Discrepancies also occur among family members, particularly when some within the family acknowledge a difficulty but others do not.

Conversational Shifts

A shift in the conversation may mean that a given subject has been discussed fully and that it is now time to move on. A conversational shift that is distinctly abrupt, however, can indicate that interviewees or counselees feel that they are revealing too much about themselves (or their parents, children, or significant others). An abrupt shift in conversation is also an indication that the topic is too painful or too sensitive to discuss (Shertzer & Stone, 1980). Thus, abrupt conversational shifts can be unstated comments that "I do not want to discuss that," "I am not ready to talk about that now," or "That's none of your business."

During a first meeting, it is sometimes best not to force an issue that is sensitive for a patient; rather, it may be better to wait until a more secure and trusting relationship has been developed. Clinicians should make a mental note of the conversational shift, because stopping to write a note tends to engender suspicion, distrust, or fear. It may be helpful to return briefly to the topic at least once more during the session; if the same reaction (i.e., another abrupt conversational shift) occurs, clinicians can be fairly sure the topic is a sensitive one. If necessary, this topic can be pursued more directly at a later time.

The mother of a client provided a good example of an abrupt conversational shift away from a sensitive area. During the first meeting, the clinician asked the mother when she first noticed her son's speech problem. She quickly changed the topic with the question, "Can you help my son or not?" The clinician gently moved back into the sensitive area twice more later during the first session, and each time she abruptly changed the subject. It was obvious that, for whatever reason, she felt very sensitive about the question.

The child was subsequently enrolled for therapy and the relationship as professional and parent developed well. After the child's third therapy session, the clinician asked the mother to join him in his office for a brief chat. There was a brief discussion about the progress seen to that point. Then the clinician commented,

> "The first time we met, I asked you about when you first noticed your son's speech problem. This was not an area you were ready to discuss at that time. If you are still not ready to talk about it, that's okay. If it is an area of importance to either you or your son, please feel free to talk about it. Either way is okay."

The mother thought about those comments for a couple of moments and then shared the following:

> "I knew immediately that you knew there was a problem, but thank you for not pushing me. I just couldn't talk about it then! Kevin, my mother, Kevin's parents, and my sisters all said Darrell had a speech problem and that I needed to get it taken care of. I guess I just couldn't face Darrell being anything but normal. Now I know I was wrong. I've really messed him up by waiting so long. He'll never catch up, will he? It's all my fault for being so stupid!"

It was important for her to express what was really bothering her. This provided us with an opportunity to deal with her guilt, to look again at the prognosis for her son, and to establish an even more positive and trusting relationship. As she and her son left that day, her final comments were,

🌀 "Thank you again for not pushing me when I couldn't
have told you, and thank you for asking me again
when I could. I needed to tell someone who could
understand. Thank you again."

Conversational shifts can occur at any time during diagnostic or treatment sequences. The point that needs to be
emphasized is that conversational shifts are often meaningful
and important. Clinicians need to develop the habit of men-
tally tucking away sensitive topics that are revealed by conversational shifts. Such shifts need to be addressed at some point,
but it is often unproductive to pursue or confront them too
early in a relationship.

Recurrent Themes

Clinicians sometimes find an interviewee returning several
times to one or more topics of discussion (Shertzer & Stone,
1980). For example, a patient may return to the subject of the
costs of services, to the cause of a problem, or to a prognosis.
There is no limit to the number of recurrent themes possible.
Recurrent themes represent areas of particular concern to interviewees. At some point, clinicians need to address these
topics, which will recur until a client's concerns have been resolved, or—even worse—the client stops mentioning them al-
together out of the belief that the clinician is not listening, is
unconcerned or uncaring, or is incapable of helping. Thus, a
clinician's failure to respond can lead to having two problems:
The first problem is the area addressed by the recurrent theme
and the second is negative feelings about not "picking up on"
the area of concern.

There is another reason why clinicians should deal directly with recurrent themes. When clients and their concerns
are not resolved, it is not possible for clients to concentrate
fully on other areas of importance. For example, if patients are
preoccupied with the costs of services, they will have difficulty
staying focused on a clinician's diagnosis, treatment recommendations, or other areas of discussion.

The content of recurrent themes dictates how clinicians
deal with them. When the focuses of recurrent themes are
on past actions or events, these may need to be discussed as
springboards to the present and the future. Deep-seated feelings of guilt may need to be discussed openly, or clinicians may
need to make a referral for appropriate counseling.

The type of cognitive or behavioral counseling discussed
in Chapter 7 is helpful with many clients. Clinicians provide
a new cognitive set; reinforce thoughts and verbalizations that

are productive and appropriate; and punish or do not reinforce tangential, less important, or unproductive recurrent themes that have already been addressed.

Information Gaps

Gaps in information occur for a number of reasons. For example, a military parent may have been away from home for protracted periods of time; adoptive parents (particularly of children adopted overseas or from drug- or alcohol-dependent birth mothers) may not have information about their child's prenatal, birth, or early developmental history; or a patient may have been comatose or under heavy medication and have little, if any, recall of certain events or time periods. Other factors also influence the recall of information.

Time
Ask the parent of a 2-year-old when her child started walking and you will probably get a precise answer. Ask the same mother the identical question 15 years later and the answer is often more general or tentative. This reflects the amount of time that has passed since the event in question.

Birth Order
Ask a parent when his first child started to talk and you will usually get a quick, reliable answer. Ask the same parent when the fourth of his six children started to talk and see what happens. You may hear something like, "Well, let me think about that for a moment. Lisa came after Terry. John wasn't born yet, so …" In general, it is more difficult for parents to recall specifics about each child when they have a larger number of children.

Simultaneously Occurring Factors
Ask a stay-at-home parent of a 3-year-old when the child first developed two-word phrases. Now ask another parent of a 3-year-old the same question, but assume that this parent was involved in a career and with the ongoing care of a terminally ill parent at the same time. You can guess which parent is more likely to know the answer to the question.

The effects of multiple, simultaneously occurring factors is seen with many recent immigrants and refugees and their families. Some families have lived in several countries, in different places within these countries, and experienced a number of simultaneously occurring hardships during this time (bureaucracy, unfamiliar customs, health issues, intrafamily separations) (Roseberry-McKibbin, 2002).

Memory, Health, Environment, and Other Factors

Memory, health, environment, focus of attention, and a plethora of other factors all affect what a person remembers. An individual's personality and intellect are also significant factors. For example, some 2-year-olds are almost nonverbal, and others can put together semantically, syntactically, and morphologically correct sentences. Some 20-year-olds do not know how to use a dictionary, whereas others can fully explain nuclear fission or how television works. There are elderly people who cannot remember what they ate at a just-completed meal and others who can recall and marshal incredibly complex details from their past. Many factors can create knowledge gaps, and clinicians need to carefully interpret why an information gap is occurring before overinferring anything from it.

Other Types of Gaps

There is another potential source of information gaps. For example, as Shertzer and Stone (1980) comment,

> Gaps, particularly if they are repeated, may be significant to understanding the client. A counselee who describes the members of his or her family but omits mentioning a brother or sister leaves a gap that may have meaning fundamental to understanding the problem. (p. 299)

Clinicians working with communicative disorders sometimes find similar gaps in the presentation of information related to family interactions, the identification of a problem, or someone's attempts to work with the problem. When such information gaps occur, clinicians may need to further explore these areas.

Emotions, Attitudes, and Behaviors

Anger

Anger is often a reaction to feeling frustrated, afraid, or threatened (Hershorn, 2002). Anger is also a common reaction to feelings of discomfort, desperation, or powerlessness—for example, when everyday situations get out of control. A long line at the supermarket, poor service in a restaurant, a poor grade on a paper, a missed deadline, a rejection, and an accidental breakage of a valued possession are examples of everyday situations that potentially provoke anger.

People have different ways of showing or dealing with anger. People with "short fuses" become quickly and demonstrably angry and may openly express their hostility. Other people, meanwhile, may become angry but consciously endeavor not to show their anger. Still others who "take things in stride" seem to handle provocative situations passively, without apparent emotion, and may not even consciously experience anger in such situations. Imagine an overcrowded waiting room of a busy physician who is running several hours behind schedule. The room is filled with agitated people, all reacting differently to the situation. Some patients read quietly, others pace, some check their watches every few minutes, others ask the receptionist how much longer it will be, others ask to use the phone, and still others complain bitterly to the room at large about the delay. The point is, people experience and exhibit frustration and anger in different ways.

Illness tends to engender anger (Enelow & Swisher, 1986). The level of discomfort patients feel—as well as their fears for their health, their recovery, and their finances, or their frustration dealing with bureaucratic procedures, poor interagency cooperation, or uncooperative insurance companies—are all factors that may influence the degree and frequency of anger clinicians see, irrespective of the type of setting in which they work.

Clinicians themselves can be a source for angry feelings when they are perceived as being brusque, sarcastic, condescending, uncaring, or thoughtless (McFarlane, Fujiki, & Brinton, 1984). Thus, when evaluating the reasons for a patient's anger, professionals should always examine their own behaviors to see if they are responsible for provoking the responses. Of course, there are other times when a patient's anger has been generated elsewhere, and the clinician just happens to be the first person available for its ventilation. Consider, for example, the unfortunate clinician who is the first person to see a now-irate client who was running late and then had to drive around for 45 minutes searching for a parking place. You know who is going to hear about it!

There are also some individuals whose whole lives seem surrounded by anger. As Enelow and Swisher (1986) write,

> *The chronically angry man or woman is always a difficult problem for the interviewer. Often his difficulties are related to anger. The clinician must keep in mind that he is not the primary or sole target of this anger. Observation and the history of the patient should make clear that this is part of the patient's life style.* (p. 97)

Although it is a possibility to be considered, usually it is not the case that the clinician has engendered the client's anger. Stroke patients who have been rendered unable to communicate typically are not angry with the clinician. Rather, these patients may be angry and frustrated about what has occurred, the excruciating fears associated with newly encountered problems (Am I going to die? Will I ever be able to speak again? Or to understand others?), the horribly scary fears for the future (Am I always going to be like this? What will my spouse or children do? How can I afford this? Can I ever go back to work?), or even difficulties performing the tasks presented by the clinician.

Clinicians who work with patients with acquired neurological disorders, such as aphasia, often ask patients to identify, name, or describe the functions of common objects (a ball, pen, stamp). These are tasks that would be asked of 1- or 2-year-old children under normal circumstances. Such task presentations are needed to evaluate levels of communicative functioning, but these tasks can be perceived by adult patients as demeaning and can lead to feelings of frustration and anger.

When dealing with anger in these situations, clinicians should realize that they have not created the irritation. The professional's approach should be warm, supportive, and understanding. One 22-year-old patient who was a very talented professional musician had been in a near-fatal automobile accident. At the time he was first seen, the patient seemed to comprehend everything rather well but was barely able to phonate an "ah" on command. About halfway through the evaluative session, he had a violent temper tantrum (which is rather common among patients with injuries to the brain). Test items went flying through the air and he screamed an "ahhhh" that seemed to exceed 110 or 120 decibels. When the tantrum subsided (tantrums do subside if you wait long enough), the first author quietly asked, "Were you mad at me, mad at what I was asking you to do, or mad at what has happened to you?" The client responded by pointing to himself and forced out a vowelized approximation of the word "me." This provided an excellent opportunity for the first author to acknowledge that the man had gone through a horrible experience and to express the desire to help him learn to communicate again. After this, and again only in forced and labored vowels, he said "thank you" and reached out to touch the first author's hand. We held hands for a few moments, and then it was back to work with one very motivated, cooperative patient.

As the first author reflects on this encounter, any other response would have been less productive. Responding with anger, trying to settle him down during the tantrum, telling him that such outbursts occur commonly with brain injuries, or moralizing that 22-year-olds should not behave like that would not have been in the client's best interests. No other response would have created the warm, cooperative relationship that subsequently emerged during that session and the sessions that followed.

Many clinicians are uncomfortable dealing with anger, especially if they are new, inexperienced clinicians. What does a clinician do when a client or family member becomes angry? Burns (1999) describes a practical, four-pronged technique for disarming an angry person: (a) compliment the person on something he did right, (b) disarm the person by finding something to agree with, (c) encourage the individual to talk openly about why he is angry (keep reflecting the person's words back to him), and (d) engage in feedback and negotiation (acknowledge that you might be wrong, express your point of view). The following dialogue illustrates how a clinician might use this technique with an angry parent:

PARENT: I am really upset at you. I feel so mad!

CLINICIAN: Thank you for telling me. I appreciate your honesty in expressing your feelings to me directly. Let's talk about your anger. Tell me what's bothering you.

PARENT: You are not giving Johnny the services he needs. He isn't improving in his fluency! And this report you wrote is Greek to me.

CLINICIAN: It must be frustrating for you to feel that Johnny isn't improving and that you don't understand the report.

PARENT: Yes, I'm definitely frustrated!

CLINICIAN: Let's take this one step at a time. Tell me what it is specifically about Johnny's therapy that makes you feel angry.

PARENT: Well, he just doesn't seem to be improving very much. He still stutters a lot!

CLINICIAN: So, in your view, Johnny continues to stutter and shows only minimal improvement.

PARENT: That's right.

CLINICIAN: When does he seem to stutter the most?

PARENT: Well ... at the dinner table when we are all together.

CLINICIAN: Tell me in detail what the conversation is like at dinner.

PARENT: His two older brothers and little sister keep interrupting him. He can't get a word in edgewise. Then he stutters more.

CLINICIAN: So you're saying that when Johnny's siblings interrupt him, he is especially disfluent.

PARENT: That's it!

CLINICIAN: I'm sure you recall the booklet I gave you about stuttering, and our discussion about the

importance of the people around the stutterer
taking turns and not interrupting.

PARENT: Yes … yeah, that's right.

CLINICIAN: Sometimes it's hard to apply all that information at once. Let's review exactly what techniques your family can use.

PARENT: Thanks, I'd forgotten about that.

CLINICIAN: No problem. Will you please tape your dinner conversations for the next 3 evenings and bring them to me next time you bring Johnny to therapy? I'd like to listen to the tapes with you and, together, we can assess how effective the turn-taking techniques are. How does that sound to you?

PARENT: Great.

CLINICIAN: Now, the second thing you mentioned was the report. Which parts of it were unclear?

PARENT: Well, I don't know what a *phonatory arrest* is. And what does *frequency count* mean?

CLINICIAN: Phonatory arrest is when the word gets stuck in the child's throat. He might say, "Ah-ah-ah-ah-I want to eat." And a frequency count refers to counting the number of disfluencies, or moments of stuttering, in a conversational sample. For example, we might say that your son stuttered 15 times in 3 minutes of conversation.

PARENT: Thanks, I get it now.

CLINICIAN: Thank you again for openly expressing your feelings to me about Johnny's progress. Please feel free to set up a meeting any time so that we might continue working together to help Johnny become more fluent.

Points to Ponder #25

You are talking with the family of a 15-year-old girl, Angela, who is developmentally delayed (overall IQ of 60). The family has requested that Angela be mainstreamed into regular high school classes, and express a great deal of anger at your suggestion that she be placed in a classroom for students with special needs. They question every detail of your report, and tell you that she is bound for college (after saying earlier that she did not talk until she was 4 years old and has always been "slow"). They keep bringing up her older brother, Bob, who is on a football scholarship at Stanford University. Discuss ideas for dealing constructively with these parents. What will you say to them?

Overprotection

The instinct to protect is basic for all animals, including humans. We protect ourselves, our family and friends, and our possessions in order to prevent loss or harm and to ensure survival. We use seat belts to prevent severe injury in the event of an accident, take vitamins to maintain health and avoid illness, and lock doors to prevent uninvited intrusions. Protection is a basic human need.

Problems emerge, however, when people try to overprotect those for whom they care. An overprotected individual is shielded from opportunities to experience life, to become more independent, and to make optimal progress. Overprotection often creates a variety of strains and imbalances on basic family structures (Cunningham & Davis, 1985). A spouse, a parent, a child, a teacher, or anyone with deep feelings of love or concern for another person can be overly protective. It is not unusual to encounter overprotective attitudes in the person whose spouse is experiencing a communicative disorder or in the parents of a child exhibiting a severe speech, language, or hearing difficulty.

The notion of being overprotective is culturally relative. Mainstream society values freedom and independence; other cultures place less importance on these values. Some Pacific Island families, for example, protect children with physical impairments and do not expect them to become independent (Fitzgerald & Barker, 1993). In the Micronesian Chamorro and Carolinian cultures, parents acquiesce to their children's desires to minimize the frustration of those who have had medical problems and illnesses (Hammer, 1994). Arambula (1992) notes that some Hispanic families may feel

> *that the elderly family member (e.g., stroke victim) has "had a difficult life" and that it is the family's turn to take*

care of the patient. The philosophy of "helping patients help themselves" on which rehabilitation specialists base their effort to instill a sense of independence in the patient often conflicts with what the Hispanic patient and family desire. (p. 385)

Clearly there are cultural interpretations to what is deemed taking care of responsibilities, appropriate levels of protection, and overprotection. Excessive overprotection that interferes with appropriate progress, however, may need to be dealt with clinically. The least effective method of dealing with overprotection initially is confrontation. Even alluding to overprotectiveness often engenders the type of defensiveness that underpins the overprotection in the first place.

Frequently, an effective method to use in dealing with overprotection is to engage the person who is overprotecting in helping devise strategies and methods to develop independence and self-reliance on the part of the patient. A clinician's chances for success are much greater with the help of the overprotective person, whether or not that person is ever apprised of the overprotectiveness. This allows the person who is overprotecting to continue to be somewhat "overprotective" while helping devise and implement methods that will increase the patient's overall independence while decreasing the overprotectiveness.

The second author encountered the situation in which a mother, Ms. B, was being quite overprotective of her fourth-grade son Carlos who had a head injury. She would not let him go on field trips, play at recess, or go to other children's houses. The second author talked with Ms. B about how much she loved her son, and the fact that she clearly had worked hard in rehabilitation to get him where he was in the fourth-grade classroom. Then, the second author gently suggested some cooperative strategies between Ms. B and the school to "improve Carlos's social life." Ms. B was very amenable and began giving Carlos more freedom to be with his peers.

Entitlement

All patients are entitled to appropriate, effective, caring services. There are a number of factors that relate to people's feelings of what they are entitled to, and these feelings or expectations can influence clinicians' views toward their clients. The issues of time and patients' expectations of what a professional–client relationship should be are important considerations. As Reyes (1994) comments,

Many Western cultures place much emphasis and importance on adherence to structured schedules, whereas

other cultures may view time as a relative concept, with the quality of interpersonal relationships taking priority over schedules and punctuality. ... People who are event-oriented tend to be more concerned that an activity be completed, regardless of the length of time required, and emphasize unscheduled participation rather than carefully structured activities. (p. 165)

Clinicians do meet what has been called the "entitled client" from time to time (Edinburg, Zinberg, & Kelman, 1975). These are persons who, for whatever reason, seem to think that their own problems, concerns, or needs are paramount. In extreme cases, the fact that a clinician is working with someone else or is in some other way busy seems incidental or even surprising to these clients, who sometimes behave as if they expect everything else to be dropped because their concern needs immediate attention.

An example of the entitled person is one who insists on being seen immediately, even if the clinician is booked and has no time available. A patient illustrated this type of behavior when he telephoned the first author's office. The secretary, through no fault of her own, could not discourage this insistent (and persistent) person.

SECRETARY: Mr. Smith [name changed here] has called three times and insists that he must speak with you right this minute.

CLINICIAN: Tell him I will try to call him back this afternoon.

SECRETARY: He already told me "no way." He says he must talk with you right now.

CLINICIAN: Okay, tell him I'm with someone, but put him through ... Hello, Mr. Smith.

CLIENT: Hi. I need to talk with you.

CLINICIAN: Mr. Smith, I wish I could talk with you now, but I have two people in my office. I'll call you between 4:00 and 5:00.

CLIENT: You sound busy. Now, here's the problem...

Such people are difficult to work with because their emotional and intellectual makeup is such that they tend to believe the world revolves around them and their problems. Entitled clients seem to feel they have certain rights, and they tend to be outraged if clinicians fail to respond immediately to their wishes and desires (Edinburg et al., 1975). The clinician who acquiesces to the entitled client runs the risk of negatively affecting other people's care or inappropriately disrupting the schedule.

At one public school in the second author's district, a boy named Brandon had special challenges which included, among other things, literally quacking like a duck all day long. His father wanted his son "fully included" in the second-grade classroom. When the clinician pointed out to him that the quacking was disruptive to the teacher and the other students, this father said, "I don't care about them. All I care about is my son, and I want him in there with all the other kids." Clearly, people can have feelings of entitlement about themselves, their children, or both.

There are many possible sources for entitlement feelings, which are beyond the scope of this book. In behavioral terms, however, these clients' insistent methodology is reinforced in life often enough to maintain its continuation (i.e., it works). Clinicians may need to address the problem presented by such individuals because the problem can affect the care provided to other clients. There is no easy remedy; "entitled" individuals differ in their persistence and sensitivity. The following suggestions can be tried:

- Explain that the person cannot be seen on a "drop-in" basis because your schedule and the schedules of your other clients will not allow it.
- Just say no. You cannot talk right now, but you can call or see the client at a specified time later.
- In a setting that charges fees, offer to reserve a specific time each day for that patient. Explain that this time will be reserved and charged, whether or not it is used.
- Convey your willingness to consider helping the patient find another professional who might be more available, whenever help is needed and without advance notice.
- Suggest the option of seeking counseling to help remedy the underlying difficulties.

These alternatives are not possible in all settings nor are they necessarily appropriate with all clients. The examples do, however, illustrate the range of options available.

Another method of altering such behavior is direct counseling by a clinician. Realizing that most speech and hearing personnel are not trained in mental health counseling, there is no attempt to focus on underlying issues or etiologies of the entitled feelings. The clinician identifies and discusses with the client the types and frequencies of the intrusive behavior. Acceptable limits and appropriate goals are then established. Subsequent behavior that is within these limits is reinforced while exceptions are punished (e.g., "I will not see you now, and it disappoints me that you've violated our agreement. I'll see you on Tuesday"). In another example, the clinician could say to a client who was always "just dropping by," "This is the second time this week that you have come by without an appointment or even a phone call. Remember that we said I will not see you without an appointment. Please come back next Monday during your regular time from 10:00 to 11:00 in the morning."

Fortunately, relatively few clients feel such inappropriate or extraordinary feelings of entitlement. When such clients are encountered, however, they present some very real problems for clinicians. Clinicians must be firm and must hold to their boundaries without granting exceptions.

Insatiability

A client who appears insatiable is never really satisfied with what is occurring or what has been done. This person often demands more time, more sessions, more homework, a better hearing aid, faster progress, and longer interactions with the clinician. There are, indeed, limits to what clinicians can do. Clients who are insatiable may also feel entitled, but the two can occur independently. Consider the following advice of Edinburg et al. (1975):

> *The counselor must find a way to make explicit to the [insatiable] client that his need for immediate gratification is excessive. Because the client will require some gratification, the counselor must also find a way to preserve reasonable therapeutic boundaries without causing the client undue pain. The boundaries are necessary because the counselor also knows that these clients become more anxious and guilt-ridden if they fear that these powerful impulses are uncontrollable. The demands and fears are confirmed if the counselor does not set clear limits. The counselor's ability to maintain limits and to protect himself indicate to the client that his insatiable demands can be resisted and managed. (p. 83)*

Overly Verbal

An overtalkative patient is somewhat similar to an entitled patient in that the individual can really disrupt a clinician's work schedule and personal life. Taking a phone call from an overtalkative patient at the end of the day can result in concerned, disappointed, and perhaps even angry family members or friends. As Enelow and Swisher (1986) note,

A most difficult problem for the beginning and experienced interviewer alike is the overtalkative patient. The patient may be seen as a barrier to getting a day's work done with reasonable efficiency. He very often frustrates the clinician's efforts to get sufficient relevant information within reasonable time limits and he is usually a major source of irritation. … Such a patient, then, slows down the clinician and imposes a burden of self-restraint upon him. … There is usually an aggressive quality to such a patient's communication which has a controlling or dominating effect. One type of overtalkative patient is the obsessional individual who insists on giving an over-detailed account, omitting nothing, not even the most trivial detail. (p. 92)

When working with such patients, clinicians need to be careful that they are not encouraging them to be overly verbal. The verbal, vocal, and nonverbal communicative encouragers and inhibitors discussed in Chapter 4 need to be carefully used and controlled. For example, clinicians want to make sure they are not unknowingly using positive head nods, forward leans, or other encouragers ("I see," "Uh-huh"). It may be necessary to employ inhibiting devices such as backward leans, guggles, or interruptions. The introduction of tightly closed questions, followed by a series of follow-up closed questions, can also help keep the person "on task" and less verbal than might otherwise be the case.

Sometimes a client or family member interrupts the clinician continuously, with a resulting negative impact on the interaction. If these interruptions are quite frequent, Pachter and McGee (2000) suggest that the clinician can say,

- "I'll discuss that as soon as I'm finished."

- "I'll be happy to address that as soon as I finish my thought."

If the client keeps interrupting or pressuring the clinician, the "broken record" technique can be quite effective:

CLINICIAN:	So, as I was saying, we are recommending a community-based support group here in Townville for—
CLIENT:	Well, what about support groups in other places?
CLINICIAN:	I'll be happy to address that as soon as I finish my thought.
CLIENT:	But in River City, there's an excellent support group.

CLINICIAN: I'll be happy to address that as soon as I finish my thought.

CLIENT: I'd really like to talk about the support group in River City.

CLINICIAN: I'll be happy to address that as soon as I finish my thought.

If clinicians have seen the person before and are aware that the individual is overly verbal, they might start the interaction with closed questions, and rely predominantly on closed stimuli during the entire interaction. It is also a good idea to avoid scheduling such a person early in the day's appointment schedule.

The patient who rambles is also a potential problem. This person tends to talk in circles or move from point to point without apparent transitions or logical progression. Sometimes, topics do not appear germane to the discussion. With such individuals, clinicians can use orienting devices discussed in Chapter 4. The use of summarizing or reorienting comments ("Let's get back to our discussion of _____.") are helpful in keeping the person on task, whereas the use of reflections ("So you felt that _____.") or encouragements should be avoided.

In one case, the second author was with a highly agitated mother in an elementary school who literally rambled until the the second author had 4 pages of notes on the conversation. (This was a special situation where the school principal asked the second author to calm this mother down, so the clinician felt obligated to spend extra time carrying out the principal's request.) The second author began saying things like, "Yes, I have here at the top of page 2 that you are concerned about Marissa's pronunciation" and "You mentioned that. At the bottom of page 3, I have your comment about her attention issues." The mother began realizing that she was repeating herself, and eventually concluded the conversation.

Enelow and Swisher (1986) describe another type of overly verbal client—the individual whose oververbalizations result from excessive anxiety or stress. Enelow and Swisher suggest that friendly, reassuring, or supportive comments about the patient's fears and anxiety are often enough to reduce tendencies to oververbalize.

Points to Ponder #26

You have been asked to go to the home of Juan, a sweet, shy 17-year-old who is being home schooled at the district's expense. Your special education director has asked you to carry out a comprehensive assessment of Juan's language skills. The special education director told you the following information about Juan: His mother, Josefina, is from Nicaragua. Juan was born with substantial brain damage, the fault of a doctor who had been drinking and did not want to leave the party to deliver this "welfare baby." Josefina fought for her child, and at the age of 17, he is now completely ambulatory. He can read simple stories, write 20 to 30 words, and speak in simple sentences. However, Josefina will not let him go to regular high school classes or extracurricular events, insisting that he remain home so that the other students will not make fun of him. Although the state has a substantial budget deficit and major reduction in monies allotted to schools, Josefina hired an attorney to force the district to spend thousands of dollars on special tutoring for Juan (tutoring that turned out to be ineffective because it was substantially above his cognitive level). She calls the special education director almost every day, and is known for "talking a blue streak" during meetings. Describe how you might approach Josefina when you go to the home to assess Juan. What specific ideas might you utilize to increase your chances of successful interactions with her?

Hostility

A personal anecdote is used to introduce this section on hostility. The first author's first professional position was in a school setting. A child was referred for speech and language screening, and after he had worked with the child for a few moments, it became obvious that the child's speech and language skills were considerably behind normal expectations for her age. The first author called the parents to discuss the findings. After he identified himself and described his affiliation with the school, the parent responded, "If you're working for that (expletive) school, then you couldn't be worth a (expletive) either." The parent then hung up on one very surprised new professional.

The first author sat back and reflected on what had just happened. It was apparent there were some feelings about the school. But was it also him? Something he said? The way he said it? Fortunately, a kind coworker was able to assure this new clinician that the child's parents were irritated with the quality of services that the child's older brother had received previously in this setting. It really wasn't him. This anecdote illustrates that the person who is subjected to someone's anger or hostility may not be the person who engendered such dissatisfaction.

A client's hostility may be the result of a negative experience in the setting; previous interactions with an insensitive or less than fully competent professional; frustrations with or fears about a communicative difficulty; displacement of feelings toward a previously seen professional who first identified the communication difficulty or whose prognostic suggestions did not materialize; or any number of other, often unknown, reasons. It also may be the clinician who causes hostility. The source of irritation can be discovered by probes such as the following:

 "You seem a little angry at _____."

 "I sense that you're rather irritated about _____."

The blanks can be filled in with whatever is appropriate (e.g., a clinician, a physician, a setting or agency, parking, certain test results, a child, the child's progress). Such probes allow clients opportunities to ventilate and release emotions and feelings; providing a release is one important function of interviewing and counseling.

One thing clinicians need to watch when working with hostile patients is the timing of anything they say. Clinicians should try to get patients to express what is on their minds and give them a full hearing before responding (Moore-Brown & Montgomery, 2001). If clinicians respond too early or with a ready-made explanation, the full range of a patient's feelings may go unexpressed. Responding too early also appears defensive and may further fuel feelings of hostility.

Rather than deal with hostile feelings, some less-effective clinicians try to ignore the situation and pretend nothing is wrong. This is inappropriate because it solves nothing and can, in many cases, make matters worse. Both parties may become angry or hostile.

Intellectual

Using intelligence and reasoning abilities in a thoughtful and disciplined manner.

Intellectualization

A defense mechanism characterized by use of formal or learned language to conceal unresolved feelings or anguish.

Intellectualization

The term *intellectual* means using intelligence and reasoning abilities in a thoughtful and disciplined manner. *Intellectualization,* on the other hand, is an ego-covering defense mechanism. The person who intellectualizes is essentially talking from the head rather than from the heart. Intellectualization often conceals unresolved feelings and anguish. Consider Edinburg and associates' (1975) descriptions of an intellectualizing counseling patient:

> The intellectualizing client has generally read several books on counseling or has avidly gleaned some knowledge of counseling from movies, friends in counseling or other sources. This client, in telling the counselor about the problem, uses language and tone that resemble formulations being presented in a formal seminar. These presentations are without any affect and seem as though they might be about someone else. (p. 73)

Kennedy and Charles (2001) provide another description:

> Intellectualization refers to the manner in which some persons talk about their problems with apparent clarity and in great detail but without much emotion. They drain away their emotions by abstracting their problems. They do not sound emotional when they are speaking about serious personal subjects. They are doing it at a distance, and the most important clue is the fact that their feelings do not seem to be present. (p. 115)

These descriptions present a good picture of someone who is intellectualizing. These people often appear learned and knowledgeable, but there is often very little apparent emotion or feeling; there seem to be discrepancies between what they say and how clinicians might expect them to feel.

Persons using intellectualization may expound on certain theories or beliefs (e.g., the cause of stuttering or a specific genetic syndrome), cite and describe the works of practitioners or researchers, or even exhibit an inordinate interest in why a disorder exists rather than what needs to be done from a remediative standpoint. These behaviors should send up a red flag, signaling clinicians to investigate further. In many cases, the person's knowledge is confined to the specific works identified. Some caution is needed with this last comment, however, because there are patients and caregivers who have appropriately read a number of sources and who may even be familiar with current research in the disorder. (This is one good reason for clinicians to keep up with the literature.)

Clients who intellectualize can be difficult to deal with because they have covered their real feelings with the defense mechanism and know just enough to be biased but not fully informed. Clinicians may assume that intellectualizing clients understand more than they really do; clinicians may be intimidated by the apparent amount of knowledge, and often are thrown off by a client's apparent level of objectivity. One way of finding out how much a client actually knows is by asking questions such as the following:

 "Which stuttering theory is the most interesting for you?"

 "Schwartz discussed a number of ideas. Which ones are of particular interest to you?"

 "There are a number of language arts programs. Which ones are you thinking about?"

Clients who intellectualize or who are well-read or intellectual may ask clinicians if they have read a particular book or article or have seen a particular Web site. The client may refer to a wide range of sources: *Reader's Digest, Psychology Today, Modern Maturity, The New England Journal of Medicine,* or highly specialized journals in speech, hearing, and related fields. It is virtually impossible to keep up with all published information. If you have not seen a particular item, say so. Sometimes it is useful to ask patients if they would care to share an article. When both clinician and client have read the same information, they have a common basis for discussion.

It is important to consider the potential true feelings of persons who may be intellectualizing. Intellectualization is an ego-saving reaction that helps individuals remain distant from the need to face and deal with true feelings or the realities of circumstances. This often occurs at subconscious levels; these individuals may be unaware that this is occurring.

Paranoia

Everyone has fears and concerns, and many of these are normal. Occasionally, however, clinicians encounter a patient who exhibits *paranoia.* The characteristics of paranoia include unhealthy fears, suspicions, and feelings of persecution. Individuals exhibiting paranoia may be chronically angry, suspicious, and distrustful. They are convinced that other people, agencies, or institutions are against them or are out to get them. Some paranoid individuals brood, are moody, carry grudges, and are overconcerned about comments and circumstances made recently or in the past. It is common for paranoid patients to dis-

Paranoia
A psychological disorder characterized by unhealthy fears, suspicions, and feelings of persecution.

trust the motives and intentions of clinicians and others who work with them (Enelow & Swisher, 1986).

The truly paranoid patient is easy to identify; such a person appears defensive when asked certain questions. Responses like "Why do you need that?" or "I don't see why that's important" are rather common. These patients may make negative comments about others in the family, other agencies, or other professionals. With a patient exhibiting paranoia, a good approach is to be consistent, low key, tactfully firm, and sensitive to topics that arouse the patient's suspicions and anger. This approach allows time for some trust to be built.

The clinician will also want to limit, or at least carefully use, warm and reassuring verbalizations and nonverbal behaviors because these reassurances tend to threaten some paranoid patients (Enelow & Swisher, 1986). There is the temptation to provide calm, rational explanations of reality that contradict the paranoid feelings, but this often can be counterproductive, at least initially, because of the strength of the ego defense. The patient's paranoia is not rationally based in the first place, so using rational arguments essentially deals on a different "wavelength."

Other Factors, Conditions, and Situations

Chemical Dependence

Chemical dependence and alcohol and drug abuse are pervasive problems in society. In 1991, it was estimated that 20.4 million people in the United States had a drinking problem and that 81.6 million family members were touched by alcohol problems (Kinney & Leaton, 1991). These figures do not include illegal or prescription drug abuse. Substance use is associated with a number of communicative disorders, most commonly the effects of fetal alcohol syndrome (FAS), laryngectomy, and certain neurological disorders.

Because of greater public awareness of the problems associated with chemical use (e.g., stringent legal definitions of drunkenness, greater penalties for substance use when driving, and "don't drink and drive" and "sober graduation" campaigns), the percentage of motor vehicle deaths resulting from use of alcohol dropped from 50% in 1980 to 38% in 1989. However, alcohol continues to be a major contributor to automobile accidents, falls, drowning, burns, suicide, domestic violence, and crime in general (Kinney & Leaton, 1991).

A 1998 government study reported that alcoholism and alcohol-related problems cost our society $166 billion. Early in

1998, the United States had its 3 millionth highway fatality. By conservative estimate, half of those deaths were caused by drinking and driving, a number that closely approximates the total deaths in all of our country's wars (Ketcham & Asbury, 2000). And those who survive alcohol-related accidents often become our traumatic brain injury (TBI) patients.

Clinicians in many settings work with patients whose communication disorders are related, in some way, to chemical abuse. Mills (as cited in Trace, 1995) offers several examples of ways that substance abuse affects patients:

- Some clients are subject to mood swings, disorientation, depression, erratic behavior, or violence.
- People with fluency problems can experience periods of aggravated dysfluency, although some drink to calm nerves before speaking to groups.
- Some depressants slow cognitive processes and cause disorientation.
- Some depressants slow or alter the abilities to articulate or retrieve words efficiently.

There are, as Mills points out, many other ways that speech and language skills can be affected.

Families of clients with substance abuse problems are also affected. The abuse influences how family members view and interact with each other. The abuse may cause reluctance to support the person who is getting speech and language assistance. Or, family members may attribute everything that has happened to substance abuse. Many emotions are present in families when abuse occurs. Families may feel hostility, anger, disappointment, resentment, frustration, or other emotions in response to the addiction. These emotions need to be vented and controlled before family members can be truly supportive of the patient. The effects of the abuse may have numbed family members to the extent that the "family secret" is kept hidden from those outside the family and feelings are "stuffed inside." Denial and minimization are also very common.

The old myth of drunks and addicts living on Skid Row is incorrect. Only about 5% of active chemical abusers are "on the streets" (Kinney & Leaton, 1991). The large majority of individuals still function in society—going to school, holding jobs (or sometimes not holding them), paying mortgages, and attending speech and hearing clinics. A larger percentage of individuals on clinicians' caseloads is affected by chemical dependence than most professionals suspect. Clinicians should be aware of this, learn more about addiction and addictive behavior, and learn about resources to help clients (e.g., employee assistance programs, local treatment centers, Alcoholics Anonymous, Narcotics Anonymous, Cocaine Anonymous).

Grief

Individuals who are grieving generally have suffered a significant loss. They are in the process of trying to understand and adjust to the loss, and are dealing with how the loss will alter their lives. Grief can be associated with death, divorce, or physical or emotional separation. It can also occur with the loss of communication skills that result from laryngectomy, a stroke, the onset of a hearing impairment, or other disorders. Grief also can occur when diagnoses (e.g., mental impairment, dysarthria, aphasia) are made or when the hoped-for full recovery is not possible.

The works of Kübler-Ross (1969, 1986; Kübler-Ross & Kessler, 2000) dealing with grief and death, although sometimes controversial, have contributed considerably to our understanding of the grief process. Kübler-Ross feels that it is critical to help the grieving person realize that suicide is not the best option. Friends, family, and caring others can influence and stabilize the individual.

Different types of loss include real loss and symbolic loss (Tanner, 1980). Real losses include a death or separation. Symbolic losses include loss of self-esteem, stature, or an established role within a family. For example, a stroke victim may lose her position as head of the household, or a parent may lose his hope for having a college-educated child. Both types of loss (real and symbolic) are important to consider. Real or symbolic losses, or combinations of both, include the following:

- Loss of significant persons through death, divorce, or other separation (e.g., the adult child goes away to college or a child of divorce moves to the other parent's home).
- Loss of external objects through some event or disaster (theft, flood, fire, bankruptcy, divorce). Intangibles such as the loss of culture, religious beliefs, or attitudes also can occur.
- Loss of familiar daily possessions or routines. Individuals who are moved into a nursing home may grieve over the loss of seeing and being with treasured possessions or everyday items. Tanner (1980) suggests that a child with mental impairment who is institutionalized may grieve over not having familiar toys and possessions.
- Loss of previous physical or mental skills or capacities. Someone with a laryngectomy may grieve over the loss of being able to swim, or an adolescent with acquired deafness may grieve over the loss of listening to her CD player. One 45-year-old woman who had a stroke grieved over the loss of her $100,000-a-year government job.

- A developmental loss, which is usually gradual and typically related to different stages in life. Examples of such losses include a child's loss of parental presence when the child enters kindergarten, a parent's loss as the child enters school, "losing" a child to adulthood (college, the military, or matrimony), losing hearing or visual acuity with age, or gradual loss of memory or physical skills.
- Loss of security or usual reinforcements—leaving high school or college, insecurity following a heart attack, leaving a job and beginning a new one, relocating to a new city, or being taken out of class for speech therapy. (Adapted from Tanner, 1980, pp. 917–920)

The extent or severity of grief varies from that which is almost completely incapacitating to that which results in milder forms of short-term bewilderment, confusion, or depression.

There are several stages or components in the grief process. Kübler-Ross (1969, 1986) writes about five stages of the grief process: (a) *denial* ("I don't believe it." "This cannot be happening." "That's not true."); (b) *anger* ("Why me?" "It isn't fair!"); (c) *bargaining* ("If I work real hard, you'll help me overcome this." "God, if you will just _____, then I'll _____."); (d) *depression*; and (e) *acceptance*.

Other models have also been presented. For example, Matz (1991) writes about four phases:

- *"If I deny it, it can't be true."*
- *"I have the power to undo it."* There is a feeling of power or the ability to overcome the source of grief in this phase, but it is often unrealistic. The individual may experience hallucinations, delusions, or feelings like "If I can just see him, he would be okay" or "If she works real hard, she'll get her speech and language skills back."
- *"I can't do anything about it."* This is the point where an individual "hits bottom." Matz suggests that the individual hits bottom and, in the latter part of the phase, begins to rebound. Realism and tentative feelings of strength or potency begin to return.
- *"I am rebuilding, and every now and then I remember."* This individual has moved into acceptance. (Adapted from pp. 200–220)

It is important to remember that, irrespective of which model is used (there are others not addressed here), the stages or phases of grief are not clear-cut, distinct categories. Individuals do not necessarily move from one stage to another in discrete increments. Rather, it is common for clients to work at more than one phase simultaneously or to return periodically to elements of a previous stage. In this way, the grief process is cyclical; individuals do not necessarily move out of one phase into another and never return to a previous phase (Kübler-Ross & Kessler, 2000).

The amount of time it takes to move from denial to acceptance varies across individuals, varies in relation to the source of grief (e.g., death of a spouse or child vs. loss from theft), and differs according to the importance of the loss to the individual. Several factors, including the following, may interrupt the grieving process:

- Positively reinforcing denial.
- Punishing anger that is expressed (e.g., saying, "You shouldn't be so upset" or "There's no need to be this angry").
- Providing secondary gains (e.g., the individual gains special attention through grieving, which subsequently acts to perpetuate the utility of grief).
- Taking mood-altering drugs and alcohol, which act to "postpone the pain."
- Experiencing excessive distractions (e.g., immersing a patient in new activities). Patients need diversions and new activities, but not to the point that working through their feelings is ignored or postponed.
- Exhibiting anxiety about a griever's depression. Some depression is normal; excessive or extremely intense depression, however, does merit careful consideration.

The following factors also help facilitate normal grieving:

- Listen to the client. Do not feel that certain feelings have to be explained, defended, or even condoned.
- Permit the individual to have some control (e.g., which rooms to use, time of therapy, activities used in therapy).
- Provide perspective (e.g., conveying that the pain will end eventually and healing will occur).
- Acknowledge the reality of a loss. One clinician told a client that the deceased pet was "only a dog and there are plenty more." Clearly, this is inappropriate and fails to acknowledge the reality of that person's loss.

It is important to listen to clients, understand that they are hurting, acknowledge what they are saying, be supportive, and convey the ideas that the hurt will diminish and there will be better days. Clinicians frequently spend a lot of time with clients, so that they can understand their clients' communication abilities and needs. Speech–language pathologists and audiologists are not grief counselors, but they can facilitate (or impede) clients' grief processes.

Intense Grief

Normal grief, particularly with the death of a loved one, can include any number of reactions, such as the following (Brammer, 1993; Sue & Sue, 2003):

- Physical reactions—sleeplessness, sighing and shortness of breath, digestive problems, or loss of appetite
- Feelings of emptiness, tension, exhaustion, feeling cold, or awareness of distance from others
- Occasional preoccupation with the subject of a loss, for example, a deceased loved one
- Occasional feelings of guilt over failing to do something, an unkind comment made, or failing to say good-bye
- Changes in activities, restlessness, aimlessness, forgetfulness, searching for something to do, or going from one thing to another without any reason
- Starting to abuse a substance (e.g., older people beginning to abuse alcohol after a spouse dies)

Clients exhibiting excessively intense grief reactions in any of these areas or profound personality changes (unusual euphoria, strong hostility or irritability, or severe depression) should be seen by a mental health professional with expertise in grief work. Of note, some of these reactions may occur months or even years after the actual loss occurred. Do not be fooled into thinking that something in the past is necessarily unrelated to the types of presenting symptoms seen.

Brief Grief Help

Many of the disorders clinicians work with involve some form of loss; helping facilitate the grief process is important. Acceptance allows individuals to come to terms with reality and move constructively toward appropriate progress. This is not possible when someone denies a problem or is filled with anger. Some of the discussion in this section focuses on more intense and lengthy grieving. However, many patients move through the grief process quickly—sometimes in hours, days, or a week or two—particularly when clinicians are aware of what is happening and assist in expediting the process.

Points to Ponder #27

A couple comes to see you at the inpatient ward of the hospital. Ginny, the wife, is in despair because of her husband's situation. Chuck was the dean of a prestigious university. They had worked hard for many years, put their children through college, saved money, retired, and just started to travel to places they had only dreamed of when Chuck had a right hemisphere stroke. Now Chuck refuses to leave the house, is very depressed, drinks too much, is verbally abusive to Ginny, and has told her that she "might as well go find someone else. I'm no use to anyone anymore." Chuck also feels that when they go anywhere in public (a rare occurrence these days), everyone stares at him because he uses a cane. Describe how you might help this couple.

Crises

The term *crisis* is overused in everyday life. Many people use it when they are busy or there are lots of things going on. However, real crises do exist, and may be seen (or experienced) by audiologists and speech–language pathologists. A *crisis* is a state that exists when a person is thrown off balance emotionally by an unexpected and potentially harmful event, situation, or transition in life (Okun, 2002). The term usually refers to someone's reaction to a situation, not the situation itself (Brammer, 1993).

> **Crisis**
> *A person's reaction to an unexpected and potentially harmful event, situation, or transition in life.*

Okun (2002) outlines several basic types of crises that can occur:

- *Dispositional crisis,* which occurs when there is insufficient information to decide a proper course of action (e.g., which job to accept, what type of physician to see for a problem, what living arrangements to choose, whether to enroll for therapy).
- *Anticipated life transitions,* which involve certain events or stages that occur at different age levels (e.g., changing schools, divorce, or onset of a chronic or terminal illness).
- *Traumatic stress* (e.g., rape, assault, sudden death of a loved one, sudden loss of job, accident, war).

- *Maturational or developmental crisis,* which typically relates to such issues as emotional dependence, conflicts in values, sexual identity, responses to authority, capacity for emotional intimacy, as well as problems involving self-discipline (e.g., repeatedly losing jobs because of conflicts with authority, a midlife crisis, not being married or not having children by a certain age, intense homesickness or depression when away from home the first time).
- *Psychopathological crisis,* in which an emotional disturbance precedes and complicates a situation and, thereby, escalates it into a crisis.
- *Psychiatric emergency,* wherein overall abilities are so affected that the individual is unable to function in society without potential harm to self or others. This may be seen as a mental breakdown requiring hospitalization, or when someone is so violent that it is unsafe for that person to be in society. (Adapted from Okun, 2002, p. 245)

A crisis is very real and, when encountered, requires help and support.

Several fundamental properties of crises are that they are typically temporary, result in considerable distress and dysfunction to the individual, involve the loss of abilities to cope well, and can have long-lasting consequences, depending on what is done and the extent to which individuals and those who are around them react (or do not react) to the crisis (Brammer, 1993). Speech and hearing clinicians typically encounter certain types of crises more than others; for example, dispositional crises are seen more than psychiatric emergencies.

The major components of working with a crisis situation include the following:

- trying to help reduce tension in the other person
- accurately assessing the source and meaning of the stress that is occurring
- helping the client develop appropriate ways to respond to the situation
- providing emotional support, confronting denial or distorted perceptions, and helping develop appropriate cognitive perceptions (mindsets)
- helping develop appropriate coping mechanisms, including facilitating the use of other resources or support networks
- assisting by getting the person appropriate help, if needed (e.g., family or crisis intervention specialist) (Adapted from Okun, 2002, pp. 249–250)

Threat of Suicide

A threat of suicide may occur in some settings (e.g., rehabilitation centers or extended-care facilities) more than in others (e.g., elementary schools). However, the threat of suicide can occur in any setting where clinicians work, and it may be something clinicians see because they work closely with clients and have established relationships.

For example, a client with persistent tinnitus may tell an audiologist, "I can't live like this any more. I'm going to kill myself." One adolescent in the second author's school district said, "So many people (psychologist, social worker, speech–language pathologist) are worried about me and trying to help me that I'd just be better off dying."

Katon, Ludman, and Simon (2002) emphasize that an open discussion about suicidal thoughts and feelings of hopelessness often is the first step toward recovery. Effective treatment of the client's depression is the key to dealing with suicidal thoughts and feelings. But clinicians must take immediate action when suicide is mentioned. Meier and Davis (1993) discuss steps the clinician should take (besides listening) when a client discusses suicide.

Any mention of suicide or self-harm should be followed up on immediately. Do not be afraid to use the word *suicide,* thinking that you are giving the other person an idea by inquiring about something that was said. If the idea has occurred to the individual, the clinician should find out whether the person has a method in mind. Meier and Davis suggest that "the more specific and concrete the method, the greater the likelihood the client will attempt suicide" (p. 43). For example, there is a difference between someone saying, "I have a loaded gun in the car," when compared to, "I'm thinking about going out and buying a gun." Another question is whether the person has attempted suicide before. This may or may not indicate the likelihood that the person will follow through, but it does add potentially important insight into the possibility.

Take control of the situation. Someone in firm control can help restore order and predictability. This is not the time for indirect counseling approaches. Emphasize the positive. Sometimes expressing a positive comment becomes the "branch" that the person grabs for in deciding that suicide is not the best option.

Try to help strengthen the client's support system of family, friends, and participation in constructive activities (Katon et al., 2002). For example, arrange for a family member to take the person home and contact other appropriate professionals for assistance, if needed. Appropriate resources may include a help line or a mental health professional. Most areas have lists of resources that the clinician can utilize.

When a client is undergoing major grief, chemical dependence, suicidal thoughts, or any of the above-described situations, it is imperative that the clinician refer the client to qualified professionals such as substance abuse counselors and trained suicide support professionals. The authors strongly believe that ethically, clinicians must make use of these resources when a client experiences severe difficulties outside of the clinician's professional experience. The clinician must not be afraid to act quickly and decisively. Take control rather than ignoring the warning signs of a potential suicide. Appear firm, in control, caring, supportive, and take the time necessary to handle the situation.

➤ Concluding Comments

A number of difficult-to-deal-with client and behavior types have been described in this chapter. Because some of these have been described superficially, the reader is referred to several more detailed sources. In the fields of medicine, psychology, counseling, and communicative disorders, a number of resources offer information about difficult situations: Cormier and Hackney (1987), Enelow and Swisher (1986), Flasher and Fogle (2004), Lavorato and McFarlane (1988), Luterman (2001), McFarlane et al. (1984), Moursund (1993), and Okun (2002).

This chapter summarizes some of the difficult situations that professionals who treat communicative disorders may encounter during their careers and offers a number of suggestions for working with such situations. Clinicians may need to utilize the services of appropriate mental health professionals who are specifically trained to deal with crisis situations. There is no one perfect way of working with all of these circumstances, but, using the guidelines and suggestions outlined here, the student and the professional should have a good starting point.

TEN

Considerations in Working with Families of Children with Disabilities

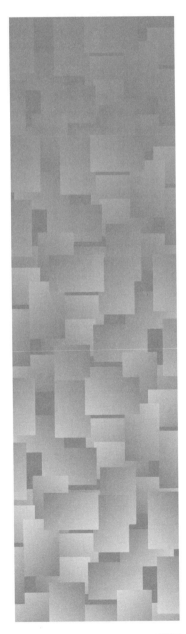

CHAPTER OUTLINE

Many experts document the need to involve whole families in the process of assessment, treatment, and counseling when serving children with communication disorders (Bernstein & Tiegerman-Farber, 2002; English, 2002; Fahey & Reid, 2000; Flasher & Fogle, 2004; Luterman, 2001; Shames, 2000). This has become even more necessary with federal legal mandates that in the public school setting, parents and families must be involved in planning for their children with disabilities (Polmanteer & Turbiville, 2000; Tiegerman-Farber, 2002). Speech–language pathologists and audiologists are increasingly serving on multidisciplinary teams in a variety of settings where families as well as clients are involved in assessment and treatment (Case, 2002; Giddan & Ross, 2001). Clinicians should view clients not just as individuals but as parts of a family system or unit comprised of (a) relationships between family members, (b) relationships between the family and school or the family and work, (c) the family's social support network (e.g., friends, other family members, church and other organizations), and (d) the legal system, social policy, and the public's attitudes that influence people with disabilities (Jones, 1993; Luterman, 2001). Family systems theory stresses that all parts are tied together and are thus interdependent.

The face of the American family is changing rapidly in composition and color. In 1950, 22% of all householders were unmarried; in 2000, 48% of all householders were unmarried. In 1970, 40% of householders had children; in 2000, 24% of householders had children. Between 1990 and 2000, the number of families headed by single mothers increased 25% to more than 7.5 million households (U.S. Bureau of the Census, 2000). In the year 2000, racial minorities and Hispanics comprised approximately one third of the U.S. population, having increased by more than 90% since 1980. In contrast, the non-Hispanic White population increased by 7.5% between 1980 and 2000.

In addition to these changes, there has been an increase in the numbers of children with communication disorders and other special needs. Many variables have contributed to this increase, including the increase in the number of medically fragile babies being saved (Moore-Brown & Montgomery, 2001; Rossetti, 2001) and the sharp increase in the number of children diagnosed with autism spectrum disorder (Heubner, 2000; Murray-Slutksy & Paris, 2000; Simpson & Zionts, 2000). Thus, it is likely that professionals who serve children with communication disorders and their families will see greater numbers of children with severe problems than in past decades.

Clinicians need to understand several key factors that are important in interviewing and counseling parents and other caretakers of children with communication disorders. These factors include the influence of poverty, strategies for dealing constructively with contentious or adversarial situations with parents, and understanding basic facts about how the presence of a child with a disability affects family dynamics. We hope that this chapter will alert readers to situations they may encounter and give readers a foundation for dealing effectively with situations that are becoming increasingly prevalent in the 21st century.

Poverty

The socioeconomic status (SES) of the client and the client's family has an impact on interviewing and counseling. When clinicians work with clients and their families from low-SES backgrounds, there are special considerations to keep in mind in order to remain sensitive and thus effective in providing the best services possible. To better understand and serve low-income children and their families, clinicians should know some basic statistics regarding this population.

According to Moore-Brown and Montgomery (2001), Payne (2003), and the U.S. Bureau of the Census (1999, 2000), the following statistics are relevant to understanding the current status of many U.S. residents:

- The child poverty rate in the United States is 2 to 3 times higher than that of most other major Western industrialized nations.
- Children in married-couple families are much less likely to be living in poverty than children in homes headed by single mothers. In 1997, 10% of children in married-couple families lived in poverty compared to 49% of children in female-householder families.
- At all levels of educational attainment, median female wages in the United States are 30% to 50% lower than male wages at the same level of educational attainment (U.S. Bureau of the Census, 1999).
- In 1999, 16.9% of the 12,109,000 U.S. children from all ethnic backgrounds lived in poverty.
- In 1999, 13.5% of White children, 33% of African American children, and 30.3% of Hispanic children lived in poverty.
- Native American reservations have a 31% poverty rate, the highest in the United States. In 2001, the current unemployment rate for Native Americans was 46% (Murphy, 2001).
- As discussed in Chapter 8, immigrants also experience much poverty. For most recent immigrants, median income is only 58% of that earned by U.S. natives. The

proportion of immigrant households that receive welfare benefits is 30% to 50% higher than that of native households (Camarota, 2001).

These statistics indicate that at the turn of the century in the United States, those most likely to live in poverty are children, immigrants, persons from some non-White ethnic groups, and children from households headed by single mothers.

As Payne (2003) notes, clinicians who work with children and their families should remember that students who bring the middle-class culture to school with them are decreasing in numbers, and students who bring the culture of poverty with them are increasing in numbers. Payne exhorts middle-class professionals to remember that schools and businesses operate from middle-class norms and follow the hidden rules of the middle class. Although most clinicians do not think about this variable, there may be actual cultural differences between middle-class clinicians and the low-income clients and families they interview and counsel in the process of providing assessment and treatment. When clinicians work with children and their families from low-income backgrounds, there are issues that present an extra challenge in providing effective services (Roseberry-McKibbin, 2000b). Six of these issues are described in this section.

First, single mothers who are from low-SES backgrounds and have children with communication disorders may need as much help themselves as their children do. The clinician who wants to counsel these mothers about bringing children to therapy, working with children in the home on assignments, and other tasks should remember that the mothers may be completely unable to do any of this without substantial support from an entire professional team. The second author has worked with families who lived in their cars; speech homework or obtaining hearing aids were not high priorities in these cases. Again, clinicians need to work with a team to provide support to the parents as well as the children who are in need of services (Paul, 2001). One thing teams can do to help low-SES children and their families is conduct training and maintain contact through video.

Videotapes are an invaluable resource, especially in poor communities where many people do not have reliable transportation and cannot come to meetings or inservices. Despite their poverty, many low-income families do own VCRs. Payne (2003) cites the story of the principal of a low-income school: 95% of the parents were on welfare, but the school was able to successfully reach them through providing information and instructions on 15-minute videotapes. Clinicians who feel frustrated at the lack of contact with clients and families might strongly consider using this practical method of reaching out to them.

Second, when working with low-SES clients and families, it is especially important for clinicians and other team members to have a comprehensive list of free or low-cost local services available to share with families. There is a direct link between SES and health-related problems. Many families with disabled children do not have health insurance that covers rehabilitation services. And even if these services are available, the families do not have transportation to the sites where they can be served. Families of children with substantial malocclusions that are negatively impacting their articulation skills usually are not able to afford orthodontia unless they obtain help from a free local clinic. Low-income children often have otitis media with effusion (Gravel & Wallace, 2000), but there is no insurance to cover the cost of doctor visits, medication, and pressure-equalizing tubes. In all of these situations and others like them, clinicians need to be prepared to share a list of affordable, related services and support systems so that clients and families can obtain the help that they need in many key areas of life, not just communication. Clinicians need to be empathic, caring, and persistent in helping these clients and families obtain the resources they need. When clients' and families' basic needs are met, they will be better able to work successfully on improving their communication skills.

A third issue is that clinicians, as members of a team, may find themselves facing clients and families with problems that are high priority but not related to the communication disorder (Weiss, 2002). This can require additional counseling and guidance on the clinician's part as well as referrals to other resources (e.g., social workers, Child Protective Services).

One problem that families in poverty often face is the threat of daily violence in their homes, neighborhoods, and schools. Haberman (1995) states,

> *Injuries, abuse, even death are facts of daily life among children in poverty ... [later], professionals frequently deal with students who are pregnant, on drugs, or in gangs, or who have dropped out and disappeared. All of these tragedies are deeply felt by professionals who have established close relationships with children and their families.* (p. 71)

The second author worked with Sevon, a 9-year-old boy whose single mother had taught him how to point a loaded gun just in case there was an attempted break-in at their apartment while she was at work. When clinicians work with clients and families who experience violence frequently, or are surrounded by the danger of it, the clinicians may encounter an attitude of "no hope" or "why bother?" (Haberman, 1995). Clinicians must not interpret this as resistance or lack of initiative. It is just that obtaining a hearing aid, working on fluency, carrying out a home program for a child with an articulation disorder, and other activities are extremely low priority for families who are concerned about staying alive and safe.

Fourth, it is important for clinicians to not be judgmental toward clients and families from low-income backgrounds. This is more easily said than done. The second author has worked with low-income mothers who had five or more children, all of whom had different fathers, and all of whom were born drug-addicted due to multiple drug use by the mother during the pregnancies. Needless to say, all the children were eligible for comprehensive special education services. One first-grade girl lived in a home with 13 children and a father, girlfriend, and two other women who were the biological mothers of the 13 children. One father from another home got his teenage daughter pregnant so the family could collect more welfare money after the baby was born. Clinicians must rise above their own feelings about situations such as these and remember that the families are doing the best they can in their individual circumstances. No matter how clinicians may feel about the choices families and clients make, the clients and families still deserve to be treated with respect, dignity, and a nonjudgmental attitude.

A fifth issue that clinicians should also remember is that grandparents may be raising the children because the parents are incapable of doing so. This raises the issue of sensitivity. Grandparents usually have not planned to raise a second family, and their resources may be limited both physically and financially. The second author worked with Dolores, the grandmother of Cody (who had a language disorder as well as a severe articulatory-phonological disorder). Cody's teenage mother was in jail (again) for drug use. Dolores, a widow, worked hard and long hours at a low-paying job and had very little energy for Cody when she got home. The school team was challenged by the fact that Cody's school attendance was irregular, he was malnourished, and there was virtually no homework follow-up, as well as little discipline or structure, for Cody at home. The team needed to provide a great deal of support for Cody at school because Dolores was unable to provide it for him at home.

A sixth issue that may arise as clinicians work with low-SES clients' families is that of value conflicts. Payne (2003) describes values of low-income families that may conflict with the values of the middle-class clinicians who serve them. When attempting to interview and counsel low-income clients and their families, clinicians should be alert for the following potential conflicts in values (adapted from Payne, 2003):

Clinician's Value	Client's or Family's Value
We should be planning for the future; decisions should be proactive.	The present is most important; decisions are made at this moment based on need for survival.
We all have choices, which exist on We can change our future a continuum. by making good choices now.	There is not much we can do to work against chance. This is our fate. Everything is polarized; it is one way or the other. "I can't do it" and "I quit" are common statements.
We need to plan ahead and set goals.	I want to survive today. The future is uncertain, and thus unimportant. I may not even live to experience it.
It is important to discuss abstract subjects and even introduce academic topics when necessary.	I do not value discussion of academic and abstract subjects. Discussions should center around people, relationships, and survival.
Authority is trustworthy, and we need to speak appropriately and respectfully to one another in our exchanges.	Authority figures represent the system, which is inherently dishonest and unfair. Thus, it is okay for me to argue loudly with you.

Clinicians who provide services to low-income clients and their families must be aware of these six issues, which often affect service delivery. Clinicians who work with large numbers of low-SES clients and families are encouraged to do additional reading and research about appropriate service provision to this population.

Points to Ponder #28

You just finished your master's degree, and have been offered a challenging job in a very low-income school district. You are a White, middle-class, 24-year-old female who has never worked with low-income children and their families before. What potential problems might you encounter in your job? How can you deal with these problems constructively so that the children can receive the best possible assessment and treatment?

Strategies for Dealing with Parents or Other Family Members in Contentious Situations

Many times, parents of children with disabilities are grateful for the clinician's and team's help and advice. Interviewing and counseling these parents is a joy because they are receptive, open, and thankful for the support they are given. However, this is not always the case. Parents can be angry, in denial, and even litigious. As one of our friends, a speech pathologist in the schools, told us, some parents call before even meeting her personally and say things like, "I'm prepared to fight!" It is important to reiterate and expand upon dealing with anger and denial as related to the case of contentious meetings in which feelings run high and parents may be planning to sue the clinician, the school district or clinic, or both. How can clinicians effectively meet, individually or in team settings, with parents who are "prepared to fight"? How can clinicians deal effectively with situations in which one or both parents appear determined to file a lawsuit? The following practical strategies from Dodge (2000), McClain and Romaine (2002), Moore-Brown and Montgomery (2001), and Paul (2001) can be helpful in defusing these types of situations and increasing the chances of a positive outcome for the child, parents, clinician, and other team members. (Note that these ideas can be applied in any setting, such as hospitals with neurologically involved adult patients and their caregivers.)

- *Always remember that for the majority of parents, nothing is more important than their child's happiness and success.* As Moore-Brown and Montgomery (2001) state, "Children are the most precious connection to a parent's being" (p. 256). Thus, it helps to emphasize continuously, throughout the meeting, that the ideas shared are in the child's best interests. The clinician can say things like, "We all want Daniel to be happy and successful. Let's discuss some ideas for helping that to come about" and "Daniel would be most successful if we…"
- *When meeting the parents, it is good to shake hands, even if the meeting is expected to be adversarial.*

- *Be interested in the parents as people.* We have found it helpful to ask parents what they do for a living and ask a few other questions about that topic. Parents, like all people, do not want to be seen as unidimensional beings who are "just parents." This is especially true for mothers who work full time inside the home caring for children. If possible, find out the parent's interest or hobby or a background fact. In one very difficult situation where the mother of a high school student was in the process of suing the school district, the second author made time to talk extensively with her about the fact that she was a widow, a special education teacher, and a music buff. Although this did take time, the mother and second author developed an excellent rapport and the mother was quite receptive to the second author's ideas about therapy for her son. The lawsuit was eventually dropped.

- *Begin the meeting on a positive note.* Discuss the child's strengths and favorable characteristics. The clinician can say something like, "I really enjoyed my time with Maria. She worked hard and has such a great spirit. She must bring you a lot of joy."

- Next, *try to find a point of agreement.* For example, one mother of a boy with autism came to a meeting with the clinician determined to take the district to court. After complimenting Joey's strengths, the clinician discussed the need to work on Joey's "social skills," which were a high priority for this mother. Instead of using the word "pragmatics," the clinician echoed the mother's exact concern and said things like, "We are prioritizing treatment activities that will increase Joey's social skills. For example…" and "Increasing Joey's vocabulary skills will enhance his social skills because…" The mother ended up very happy with Joey's IEP, and no lawsuit was filed.

- *Use the "foot in the door" technique to help get parents on your side.* When people agree with something minor (when they begin saying "yes"), they are more likely to agree with major ideas. When people have been agreeing and saying "yes," they are more likely to keep doing so. Thus, find a way to get parents saying "yes" at the very beginning of the meeting.

- At the beginning of the meeting, it is also good to *invite parents to jump in when they have something to say.* A clinician attended dozens of meetings where the parents were barely greeted and then each professional gave his or her testing results while the parents sat silently. This can be quite alienating for parents. The clinician can say something like, "As we are discussing our plans for Ganesha, please feel free to jump in any time with questions or ideas."

- *Watch the meeting seating arrangements and body language.* It is not helpful if the parents or family members are on one side of the table and the clinician or team is on the other. McClain and Romaine (2002) state that sitting across from someone with a table between the parties feels confrontational, which works well if one party is trying to appear authoritative or powerful. They recommend that unless the clinician is trying to project power, it is best to sit next to the other party. Make it a point to sit right beside the parent who is most unhappy and reflect that parent's body language (if appropriate). An occasional touch on the parent's arm may be helpful. The parent usually will feel that the clinician is, literally and metaphorically, on his or her side.

- At the risk of stating the obvious, it is ideal to *maintain good eye contact and use the parents' names throughout the meeting.* This makes the meeting more personal and makes parents feel less like they are just another item on the clinician's or team's checklist.

- *Provide parents with articles, books, or Web sites related to their child's needs.* In one highly charged meeting (where a lawsuit against the district was being considered), the clinician gave the father some information downloaded and printed from the Internet. She encouraged him to visit the Web site, which contained information related to his son Mikey's problems. Fortunately, this father was impressed and visibly relaxed when the clinician did this.

- *Validate parents' feelings and acknowledge their struggle.* We have discussed this elsewhere in the book, but it bears repeating. In Mikey's case, the clinician said to Mikey's father during the meeting, "It must be really challenging for you to be a single parent, work full time, and care for Mikey's extensive medical needs. That's a lot on your plate." It was moving to see this defensive, angry father visibly exhale and appear relieved that his truly challenging situation had been acknowledged. In another example, a clinician said to a mother, "It must be so hard for you to see Davis struggling with his hearing aids and his stuttering when his classmates hear normally and are fluent. That has to be really tough." As Dodge (2000) says, "When feelings are acknowledged and respected, parents tend to show relief that their concerns have been validated. Further, strange as it may seem, the parent's visible distress is lessened when genuine listening is used" (p. 87).

- *Ask parents how they feel they can help.* Write down their ideas and restate them later. We have found that it can be helpful to say things like, "Earlier in our meeting, you said that you thought Joey would be helped by reading daily with his home tutor. That was a great idea, and…"

- *Notice and mention something you like about the parents.* Parents appreciate hearing things like, "I so appreciate your taking time to come from work to this meeting. I know you are really busy" or "Johnny's kindergarten teacher tells me that your volunteer work in his classroom has been invaluable." We have found that *concerned* and *involved* are words that parents enjoy hearing, so we say things like, "It is clear that you are concerned and involved parents. I appreciate that."

- *Remember that when parents express anger, it is usually anger with the situation, not with the clinician.* It is quite helpful for the clinician to respond with reflective empathy. For example, a clinician said to some very angry parents, "I see that you feel really furious about the report I wrote for Krystal. You are quite upset about some of the things I said." During this 3-hour meeting (complete with lawyers and other professionals), the clinician repeatedly reflected the parents' (especially the father's) feelings of anger. Although the meeting was grueling, both parents were considerably calmer by the end.

• *Agree that parents are the experts on their child.* A friend of ours who has a son with autism has emphasized that she felt much better when clinicians said to her, "You are the expert on your child."

• *We have found that many parents like hearing the words "You're right."* Whenever possible, clinicians can say this to adversarial parents because it helps them to feel more in control at a time when they are feeling very much out of control.

• *If appropriate, use social validation.* Advertisers take advantage of this principle of human nature: People often make decisions based on what other people think and do. For example, we have found that sometimes parents are reluctant to have their children come to therapy because there may be a stigma attached. In these cases, it is useful to say things like, "We have had so many other parents share that same fear. But they have found, to their surprise, that the children feel that coming to therapy is 'cool,' especially because occasionally they receive toys and stickers."

• *In public school settings, remind parents that IEPs are temporary documents that can be rewritten.* This often helps parents feel less "boxed in."

• *Use a white board or flip chart to write down items and issues for discussion.* This helps the meeting stay in focus and lets parents know that their concerns are valid enough to be written down.

• *If parents and team members view a problem differently, write down the ideas of both parties.* For example, "School personnel note that Mark is entirely silent during class and at recess. Parents report that at home, he talks 'nonstop.'" We have found it helpful to use parents' exact wording when possible.

• *Remember, especially if attorneys or advocates are involved, that everyone wants to win.* Try to think of ways to help all parties feel that they have won.

• *If feelings are becoming unmanageable, take a 5-minute break for a drink, fresh air, or a quick change of scene.* Sometimes this can literally be "the pause that refreshes."

• *Attempt to remain calm and neutral at all times.* This can be quite difficult if parents verbally attack, but if the clinician starts to cry or gets angry or defensive, there is little hope for productivity. One clinician was in a meeting where the father scornfully waved at her and said, "We don't want this district employee" and indicated that he wanted someone with "better credentials." Remaining calm was challenging!

• *If someone in a meeting becomes angry and loses control, remove the audience.* Ask everyone else to leave or get the person alone in a different room. If someone loses control in front of a group, he or she often feels compelled to maintain or escalate the angry behaviors. The person feels a false sense of control or gain; he or she has everyone's attention! Removing the audience gives the angry person freedom to regain composure and back down without losing face (McClain & Romaine, 2002).

- *In those situations where a parent insists on being verbally abusive, terminate the meeting and indicate that a future meeting will be scheduled when the parent has calmed down.* These situations are rare, but they do occur. For example, a university supervisor met with a graduate clinician and the mother of a deaf girl. The mother was being verbally abusive despite several warnings. The supervisor stood up, closed her notebook, and said, "Mrs. N, this meeting is over. We will meet again when you are prepared to treat me and the student intern with respect and courtesy."

- *In situations where no mutual agreement can be reached, try to "leave the door open" so that parents can feel free to come back later.* We have been in situations where parents have rejected our initial diagnosis, sought other professionals' advice, and then came back because they realized that we were right in our judgment. Though the clinician may feel truly angry if no agreement can be reached, it is important not to give parents the feeling that they have "burned their bridges" and cannot return later (Paul, 2001).

Points to Ponder #29

You are working in a public school district that serves middle- and upper-income, highly educated families. It seems that many of these families have children with autism. You are preparing to meet in 30 minutes with the family of Abby, a fourth grader with autism, to discuss therapy goals and objectives. The principal stops by your room and says that Abby's father, a teacher, "hates hearing that there is anything remotely wrong with his little girl" and tends to yell at those who are trying to help. The father is bringing a tape recorder, and has mentioned that he has an excellent attorney who will also be attending the meeting to make sure that the meeting is carried out satisfactorily. Describe five strategies that you could try to implement to help this meeting go calmly and well.

Issues of Parents and Families of Children with Disabilities

Probably no other experience in life brings as much joy or excitement as the anticipation of a child. Parents dream of a normal, healthy child who will be a joy to raise and who will give them normal, healthy grandchildren. But what happens when this dream is shattered? What happens when that much-anticipated child is born with Down syndrome or is diagnosed with autism at the age of 3 years? What happens when that beautiful, smiling 9-month-old, who never seemed to turn her head when Mom entered the room, is diagnosed with a profound hearing loss? The phrase "death of a dream" is one that we have found to be the most succinct in summarizing the experience of parents who have a child with a disability. Clinicians may be the ones who make the initial announcement of the disability (e.g., the audiologist who diagnoses the profound hearing loss), or clinicians may be involved later in the child's experience as parents continue to struggle with the ongoing ramifications of the child's disability. Parents experience shock, grief, disappointment, anger, and many other powerful emotions when a child is not normal and healthy. It is helpful for clinicians in these situations to be aware of the following factors, and implement suggestions to support parents and other family members through difficult times. (Note that some of this information can also apply to a significant other or family member of an adult who has an acquired neurological impairment.)

• *Remember that more and more parents will experience living with a child who has moderate to severe disabilities.* In the early to middle 20th century, many medically fragile babies died. Today, with the technological advances that are available in the 21st century, extremely fragile infants are being saved, and these infants frequently have multiple and severe problems. Rossetti (2001; citing the March of Dimes, 1998) lists the following facts: Every 3½ minutes a baby is born with a birth defect; every 2 minutes a low-birth-weight baby is born; more than 3,700 babies are born weighing less than 1 pound at birth; every minute a baby is born to a teen mother; each day 415 babies are born to mothers who received late or no prenatal care; and the U.S. infant mortality rate is worse than that of 24 other nations.

• *Do not be shocked if parents express fears that they do not know how they will love their child because the child has made life so difficult* (Paul, 2001; Rossetti, 2001). Children with special needs often stretch their parents' financial, emotional, and physical resources to the breaking point. We worked with one single father who woke up five to six times a night to make sure his medically fragile son was still alive and that all medical devices were functioning properly and were in place.

- *Remember that with medically fragile infants, parents often feel very alienated and "cut off" because they cannot take the infants home and spend time with them early in life.* These fragile infants must spend their early days and even weeks in neonatal intensive care units. Feelings of estrangement are common (Owens, 2002). This can disrupt parents' later attachment to the child (Rossetti, 2001).

- *Parents may feel very overwhelmed and fearful.* We have worked with parents who felt so overwhelmed that their attitude toward us and the other team members was "We can't handle this. You do it!" The wish to be rescued is common, and clinicians have to gently help parents feel involved and empowered, even if the parents do not wish to be.

- *When meetings are held and information given, it is ideal if both parents can be there.* Luterman (2001) states that when a child has a communication disorder, it is often the case that the mother notices it and the father denies it. Thus, often the mothers come alone to meetings with professionals. When the mother tries to convey information to the child's father, she does not always remember it accurately and the father may not believe her. In many cultures, including U.S. culture, people often think of children's health care as "women's work," but it is important that both parents be involved when possible.

- *Deal with parents according to their preferred styles.* Luterman (2001) writes that fathers may feel more comfortable if they can be given facts, figures, and quantitative data. For example, when working with one couple whose child was born with severe and multiple problems, the clinician brought out a folder with information downloaded from the Internet, with specific Web site addresses where the parents could find more information about treatment of their son's condition. The father was visibly impressed and quite enthusiastic about this. The mother barely glanced at the papers, and said she did not use the computer. Again, clinicians must be flexible and willing to deal with parents' individual needs and preferred styles of exchanging information.

- *It is imperative that clinicians work as members of teams so that the parents have an array of professionals available to them.* For example, the parents of a child born with severe cerebral palsy will need to work with speech pathologists, physical and occupational therapists, physicians, social workers, and others.

- *Remember that siblings of children with severe disabilities may need counseling themselves.* Resentment can occur. Siblings often feel that they have "fallen by the wayside" as the child with special needs consumes much of the parents' time. This is especially true in single-parent homes. Sometimes clinicians can help a sibling feel important and involved by teaching him or her strategies for helping the child with special needs at home. We have sometimes taken siblings aside and asked them to be the "teachers," emphasizing that we need their help.

• *Remember that a child with a severe disability often causes profound lifestyle changes for parents.* Clinicians need to allow parents to express feelings. For example, one parent was a CEO for a major corporation and earned $80,000 a year. When her son was diagnosed with autism, she quit her job to stay home with him; today, the family struggles financially on one income. Life for this family is dramatically different, and the changes have not been positive. It is not uncommon for mothers who work outside the home to quit their jobs when a child is diagnosed with a severe disability, and the changes this engenders can be stressful for everyone.

• *When a child is diagnosed with a severe problem, parents may feel like failures and can experience great loss of self-esteem.* This is especially true in cultures where it is believed that a disabled child literally reflects the sins of the fathers and mothers (Roseberry-McKibbin, 2002).

• *Rossetti (2001) describes the "chronic sorrow" that parents feel when they have a severely disabled child.* If this chronic sorrow is not dealt with, other problems such as abuse and neglect can arise. A friend whose 17-year-old son has autism and mental retardation shared that she feels "fresh sorrow" on many occasions like birthdays and holidays.

• *Children with special needs are at risk for abuse and neglect.* Rossetti (2001) comments that an increased incidence of abuse is observed in children with a history of premature birth, low birthweight, and sickness during infancy. Children with disabilities put a great deal of stress on their caregivers, and without support, these caregivers may neglect or even abuse the children. Clinicians need to be alert for signs of this. Clinicians may also need to help facilitate "respite care," when the state or county provides a qualified helper to come and care for the child while the caregivers get a break. Some caregivers have shared that when the respite worker came to help, the caregivers checked into a hotel and slept!

• *Remember that parents may need to be referred for marriage counseling.* Readers with children know that even normal, healthy children can put stress on a marriage. If a child has a severe disability, the marriage may dissolve as the parents struggle to cope with their new roles and responsibilities. We are acquainted with several families that fathers have left because of the strain. One father deserted the child and his mother because he did not feel he could cope with his son's "imperfection" when his son was born deaf. Encourage parents to take time for themselves and to seek support from appropriate professionals, if necessary.

• *Remember that mothers, especially, may experience depression.* Fanning and McKay (2000) comment that men are generally not expected to be caregivers for family members who are sick or disabled. However, in most societies, including U.S. society, women are "expected to be caregivers as a natural extension of their nurturing role" (Fanning & McKay, 2000, p. 110). This can put extra burdens on mothers, who may experience depression as a result.

• *Recognize that many parents benefit from peer support.* We have witnessed parents talking with one another in our university clinic settings, seeming happy to even chat in the hallway with someone who is in similar circumstances. Parent support groups are often the self-described "lifeline" for parents of children with special needs, and clinicians can facilitate these parent groups.

Points to Ponder #30

You are working in a hospital that serves medically fragile infants and their families. Kayla, a 3-month-old girl, has been diagnosed with severe bilateral sensorineural hearing loss, velopharyngeal insufficiency, heart problems, and possible cerebral palsy. Her mother, a university professor, has taken a 6-month leave of absence to be in the neonatal intensive care unit with Kayla. Kayla's father, a computer technologist, rarely comes to visit Kayla. Kayla's mother breaks into tears one day and shares that she feels alone, overwhelmed, and fearful for her career and their family's happiness. She also confides that Kayla's father has begun to drink heavily, and that she's afraid he may be seeing another woman. What would you say to Kayla's mother? How would you handle this situation? What recommendations would you make?

▷ Concluding Comments

Today's clinicians deal with many challenges as they interview and counsel with families who have a child with a communication disorder. The influence of poverty, the circumstance of adversarial meetings, and the impact on the family of a child with a disability are three key areas that clinicians need to cope with effectively as they serve children with communication disorders and their families. If clinicians can interview and counsel effectively with whole families, and work within a family systems framework, the chances of the child's improvement are much greater.

ELEVEN

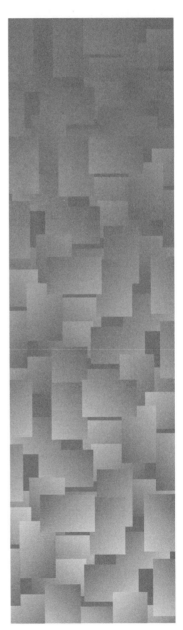

The Elderly

Larry Boles

CHAPTER OUTLINE

- Demographics of Aging
- Elder Culture
- Approaches to Counseling
- Concluding Comments

Counseling the elderly can be a rewarding endeavor for both the counselor and the elderly client. It is a rich opportunity for growth by both parties. It is not for the faint of heart, however. An informed counselor is a more effective counselor, and this chapter is intended to provide some of that information. The remainder of the information necessary for effective counseling of the elderly must come from further readings and from the elderly themselves.

This chapter will begin with a discussion of demographics of the elderly population (primarily in the United States)—essentially, "who they are." Following this is a discussion of the elderly in the context of their developmental stage. Issues that are (for the most part) unique to the elderly will be a part of this section—"how they are." Finally, some approaches to the counseling of the elderly will be discussed.

Demographics of Aging

In 2000, 35 million people in the United States were over the age of 65 (U.S. Bureau of the Census, 2000). Within that age group, the over-85 group showed the highest increase compared to the 1990 census. Women consistently outnumber men in the elderly population, and this gender discrepancy increases with age. There were 82 men for every 100 women in the 65- to 74-year range, 65 in the 75- to 84-year range, and only 41 in the 85-years-and-older bracket. The world's elderly population (ages 65 and older) is increasing by 795,000 every month. The United States is expected to have a 102% increase in the elderly population between the years 2000 and 2030. And then there are these startling statistics: Half of all the people on the planet who have ever lived to the age of 65 in human history are alive today, and there is one person over the age of 60 for every child below the age of 4 (Roszak, 2001).

Gender

The worldwide trend is that women outlive men. The bad news for women is that they also have a higher probability of living their older years in a severely disabled state. What are some of the consequences of the gender differences in the elderly? First, elderly men are more likely to be married, whereas elderly women are more likely to be widowed (Kinsella & Velkoff, 2001). Further, health is affected by marital status, and those who are married are more likely to be living in a healthier manner.

More than 30% of elderly women lived alone between 1990 and 1999, whereas only 15% of men did. This trend was even more pronounced in the old elderly (those over the age of 85). Although only about 6% of the elderly live in residential care facilities (Jacobzone, as cited in Kinsella & Velkoff, 2001), 75% of these residents are women (U.S. Centers for Disease Control, 1999).

Disease and Disability

Does increased life expectancy equate to increased health expectancy? It appears the answer to this is a resounding "no." The number of elderly people with chronic disabilities living in the United States has steadily increased in the last 2 decades, although the overall proportion of the elderly who are disabled is decreasing (Manton, Corder, & Stallard, 1997).

The elderly population is increasing in the United States and in most of the world. Women in this group outnumber men, and this discrepancy increases with increasing age. However, longer life is not the same as healthy life, and the elderly are susceptible to heart disease and stroke. Although a decreasing proportion of the elderly are living in residential care facilities, many of them are widowed or living alone.

Stroke

Cardiovascular disease is the primary cause of death in the elderly population, both in the United States and worldwide (Kinsella & Velkoff, 2001). This might surprise some readers, who may assume that cancer is the leading cause of death in the elderly. However, not only is cardiovascular disease the leading cause, but its leading role in death increases with advanced age, accounting for 49% of deaths to those 75 years and older, compared to 18% for cancers (Heikkinen, Jokela, & Jylha, 1996). The rate of disability is decreasing, however, at least in the United States (Spillman, 2004).

Aphasia is a frequent consequence of stroke, in addition to motor speech disorders and the communication deficits associated with right hemisphere brain damage. Comprehension and communication are impaired in individuals with aphasia. In treating people with aphasia and in leading numerous support groups for families and caregivers of those with aphasia, this author has noticed some patterns in the issues these individuals experience.

In the days immediately following a stroke, the client and the family[1] are most concerned with the client's survival. The concerns regarding communication (and even swallowing) are

---

[1]The term *family* here refers to those who are committed partners with the client. It is not meant to exclude those who are unrelated by birth or marriage to the client. *Client* in this context refers to the person who has sustained the stroke, although it could be argued that the entire family becomes the clinician's client.

secondary at this point. Family members are often under much stress. Some are flying in from other parts of the country or other countries; decisions regarding hospital visiting schedules for each family member are being discussed. The client is often contemplating his or her mortality at this stage. In the midst of this chaotic time, family members may be encouraged to help their loved one with feeding, dressing, grooming, walking, and communicating.

If admitted to a rehabilitation facility, the concerns may begin to turn toward "the long haul." Who will be with the client during the day? Who will be helping with therapies? Family members who flew in from far away may be concerned about returning home. What about insurance coverage for rehabilitation? Many families begin to be concerned about the loss of income (both immediate and long term) as a consequence of the client's stroke. The spouse or committed partner may be dealing with returning to work or, if previously unemployed, the difficulty in dealing with medical costs and the loss of income. The spouse or committed partner may also begin to be more acutely aware of the communicative consequences of aphasia, and of disability in general.

Certainly speech–language pathologists and audiologists are not the only health professionals to help the client and family cope with these issues. These professionals work as members of a team that also includes some combination of the following: client, family, social worker, psychologist, neuropsychologist, physician, nurse, dietician, physical therapist, occupational therapist, and recreational therapist. Others may also be a part of the team, depending on the circumstances. The above scenario is not intended to represent a universal pattern by any means, but it does illustrate a context within which the speech pathologist will be working.

Dementia

A chapter on counseling the elderly would be incomplete without a discussion of dementia. Estimates that 6% to 10% of adults in the United States have some form of dementia are consistent with findings in Canada as well (Lindsay, Sykes, McDowell, Vereault, & Laurin, 2004). Two thirds of these individuals have Alzheimer's disease and that number doubles if mild cases are included in the prevalence data. The risk for developing Alzheimer's disease doubles every 5 years after the age of 60.

Dementia does not just affect the elderly, of course. Caregivers of elderly adults are family members in 80% to 90% of cases (Rau, 1991). Memory impairment, catastrophic reactions, demanding and critical behavior, night waking, and hiding things are all problems commonly reported by families of individuals with dementia.

In addition to these problems in the elderly individual, family members have reported disorganization of household routines, difficulties with going away for holidays, restrictions on social life, and disturbances of sleep as prevalent (Thommessen et al., 2002). Further, these complaints were equally true in a group of family caregivers of individuals with Parkinson's disease and stroke. That is, the problems experienced by the elderly may be varied, but the effects these problems have on family caregivers are not necessarily specific to the condition.

"Wear and Tear" Aging

With cardiovascular disease, cancer, dementia, and other health issues associated with aging, it would be easy to conclude that aging brings with it inevitable decline. The story is not that simple, however. We have all noticed that some people "age well," whereas others seem to be "old before their time." Some research has given scientific credence to these perceptions. *Allostatic load* (Goymann & Wingfield, 2004) is a term referring to stresses in our lives that create a "biological burden." Examples are high blood pressure, obesity, and high cholesterol levels. When enough of these allostatic factors were present, Seeman, McEwen, Rowe, and Singer (2001) were able to predict a decline in physical functioning and an increase in anticipated mortality. This has also been called the "wear and tear" aging hypothesis (Vanitallie, 2002), in that certain stressors in life may contribute to a strain on the physiological system, increasing health risk and, ultimately, mortality.

In addition to the biological and physiological factors in the study by Seeman et al. (2001), sociological issues have been examined to determine their effect on allostatic load. Seeman, Singer, Ryff, Dienberg Love, and Levy-Storms (2002) discovered that men who were more "socially integrated" had lower allostasis, in a 58- to 59-year age group as well as a 70- to 79-year age group. The same pattern held for women, although not significantly so in the 70- to 79-year age group. Kubzansky, Kawachi, and Sparrow (1999) reported that high hostility and low education in men resulted in a higher allostatic load. Others have reported higher allostatic load associated with posttraumatic stress disorder (Vanitallie, 2002), sleep deprivation (Van Cauter & Spiegel, 1999), and "high-strain" jobs (Schnorpfeil et al., 2003; Steptoe, Cropley, & Joekes, 1999).

Interestingly, Schnorpfeil and colleagues (2003) found that the allostatic effects of high-demand jobs were strongly associated in older individuals. Lower allostatic load has been associated with being married, employed, and a parent (Steptoe, Lundwall, & Cropley, 2000), positive social experiences (Seeman et al., 2002), and low-strain jobs (Steptoe et al., 1999). Thus, individuals may be able to exercise some control over the quality of their lives, and possibly their longevity.

Points to Ponder #31

What factors contribute to the aging process? Describe four of these factors.

Psychological Aging

In addition to physiological aging, researchers have studied psychological aging. This research has been directed primarily toward adaptation. *Adaptation* in this context refers to the process of meeting one's biological, psychological, and social needs under changing circumstances. This occurs throughout life, of course, but the elderly, as a group, have much more frequent and recent experiences with death among family and friends, and sudden and frequent changes in health, employment, and living situations.

   Some researchers conceptualize adaptability in terms of stages of development (e.g., Birren, Sloane, & Cohen, 1992; Erikson, 1980), whereas others (Germain & Bloom, 1999) view aging from an ecological perspective. The ecological focus is on the ability to adapt to ever-changing circumstances in the environment.

   Germain and Bloom (1999) discuss four capacities they believe are important to adaptation (and relatively free of cultural bias). These are (a) human relatedness, or sustaining personal relationships and emotional support; (b) competence, or acting effectively in the environment; (c) self-esteem, or feeling capable, significant, effective, and worthy; and (d) self-direction, or taking responsibility, making decisions, and pursuing purposeful action. Consedine, Magai, and King (2004) found positive affect to be associated with more successful aging in the elderly.

Elder Culture

An excellent adjunct to this chapter is Chapter 8, "Working with Linguistically and Culturally Diverse Clients." We are not accustomed to thinking of age groups within our culture as having their own cultures, but this is quite the case, and the reader can learn much from this chapter.

Some of the demographic characteristics of elder culture have already been described in this chapter. Elderly men tend to live with their spouses, and elderly women are more likely to live alone. In Western culture, elderly individuals generally prefer to live apart from their children but also near them (Troll, 1997).

Although disease and decline are frequently included in accounts of aging, it is also true that the elderly have enormous political and economic influence in the United States. Further, never before have the elderly enjoyed so much education, travel, and physical and mental activity (Roszak, 2001).

Approaches to Counseling

There are two contexts in which a speech–language pathologist typically engages in counseling with the elderly: in support groups and in counseling. Support groups are often facilitated by speech–language pathologists and are often cofacilitated with a fellow health professional such as a social worker or psychologist. Counseling during the routine of communication therapy usually occurs with individuals or with couples. Certainly other contexts exist, and the reader is encouraged to generalize where appropriate.

An Approach to Leading Support Groups

The title of this section is worded deliberately. In an approach, there is more flexibility implied than in a "method" or even a "technique." A degree of vagueness is also inherent in an approach. Support groups can take many forms, depending on the leaders, the attendees, and the reason for the group's existence.

For example, some support groups are educationally oriented. People attend these to gain information. Guest speakers on particular topics are common in these groups. Other support groups are therapy oriented. People attend (and lead) these groups to help members process the emotional and psychological concerns inherent in the issues that brought the group together. Support groups offer different levels of support. At various times, and for various reasons, people are in more need of information or therapy.

It is possible, of course, for a therapy-oriented group to have information provided during a group meeting, just as an educationally oriented group may offer emotional support (whether planned or not). It is essential that the type of group being formed is known in advance, however. This may be decided prior to the first meeting, in announcements, or by the group during the first meeting.

Educationally Oriented Support Groups

In a time-limited educationally oriented support group, topics must be chosen early in the formation of the group. It is helpful to spend most of the first meeting processing the participants' needs regarding topics for discussion. The members of the group tend to dictate the level of intimacy with speakers, and that level may change from speaker to speaker. People may raise their hands, "asking permission" to ask a question when the speaker is a physician, but the same kind of professional courtesy does not seem to occur with peer advocates, speech pathologists, or other therapists.

It is very important that the members of the group have the greatest input into the choice of speakers and topics. Distribute a sheet of paper that has a column for the topic, a column for the name of a speaker (if the group member has a particular person in mind), and a contact number or e-mail address, if known. Although many participants do not have particular speakers in mind, everybody should write at least one topic, even if topics are duplicated on the page. This gives an idea of how many people would like information on each topic.

When a tentative list of topics and speakers has been generated, the logistics for the next steps may vary. For example, the clinician may make all the contacts with the speakers, or that task may be delegated to various members. The clinician may introduce each speaker, or delegate that to the person who requested the topic.

Consider providing refreshments at all meetings, even if only a beverage is provided (this task can also be delegated to members). It is simply a cultural decision to offer a small token of sharing, but it seems to make meetings more relaxed and friendly.

The last recommendation regarding educational groups is for a time-limited duration. A comfortable number of weeks (assuming weekly meetings) or months (assuming monthly meetings) is in the range of 6 to 10. This range means people will not grow weary of attending group sessions, yet is a reasonable time span so that one can look forward to the next meeting, knowing that they are few and precious.

Other logistical issues are more idiosyncratic or personal, depending on the facilitator, nature of the group, and size of the group. Issues to be aware of are how long each meeting lasts, how often meetings occur, how the room is set up (a speaker-and-audience arrangement is more conducive to a "lecture" format, whereas a circle is more conducive to a discussion), whether a break is helpful in the middle of each session, who the "master of ceremonies" is (and whether that rotates), and whether thank-you notes are written to speakers versus simply applauding at the end of the talk (or both). Ideally, many of these issues are considered in advance.

Therapy-Oriented Support Groups

Therapy-oriented groups and education-oriented groups have different purposes: Whereas educationally oriented groups provide valuable information on topics of concern, therapy-oriented groups offer emotional support to the elderly and their caregivers. Members of the latter type of groups may not know precisely what kind of group they want to form. Many people (and particularly the elderly) are uncomfortable calling a group a "therapy-oriented" or "emotional support" group, even if that is what they are seeking. It may be best to simply call a group a "support group" because support is what people want.

Points to Ponder #32

Describe the purpose of support groups. Why are they important for some clients and their families?

Group Dynamics

What will the group look like? Who will do the talking? Will people ask questions or tell their stories? How does the content of each session get decided? As these types of questions are answered, the group develops its style. A significant part of the style depends on the leader. I owe much of what I have learned to David Luterman, who helped me become comfortable in yielding control. This yielding helped me feel much better when I realized how much more satisfied I was with how my groups looked, with who did the talking, and with people feeling comfortable asking and answering questions, and telling their stories. (For an excellent discussion of these topics, see Luterman, 2001, particularly Chapter 7.)

The most important characteristic a group leader can bring to a session of any kind is mindfulness. Two key texts that discuss mindfulness are Kabat-Zinn's (1995) *Wherever You Go, There You Are,* and Kornfield's (1993) *A Path with Heart: A Guide Through the Perils and Promises of Spiritual Life.*

Mindfulness is that place we put ourselves when we are entirely, completely present. We are not concerned with our tasks after that moment, nor are we continuing to process the previous day or hour. Rather, our entire focus is on the moment.

Mindfulness

A state achieved when someone lets go of trying to figure out an issue and instead listens with full attention to the present.

This is different from "concentration." When we are concentrating, we may be analyzing what is being said or trying to "figure it out." *Mindfulness* is a letting-go of trying to figure it out, and, instead, listening with full attention to the present.

Some people find meditation the most effective way to accomplish mindfulness. Others are able to sit for a moment and "clear their heads" (although one could argue that this clearing is a form of meditation). When I feel satisfied with a session of therapy—either group or individual—I find that I have been mindful throughout the session. Conversely, when I have felt dissatisfied, I have often felt a lack of mindfulness. In our busy professional lives, taking those moments to focus on the present—on what is before our eyes—is often more valuable than trying to push through to the next appointment.

The leader would be wise to examine his or her goal first, before getting to the group goal. If you have your own agenda for what the group will "look like," I urge you to be open to letting the group form that agenda. If you spend a considerable amount of time talking throughout each session, the expectation will rapidly (I cannot overemphasize "rapidly") be that you will talk for much of all sessions. If you answer each question, that, too, will become an expectation.

Talk Show Hosts, Silence, and Experts. Establishing an "interaction norm" (Luterman, 2001) is important. A common pattern is to engage in what Elman (1999) calls a "talk show host" interaction norm. This occurs when a group member asks a question and the facilitator answers it. The natural pattern is for another group member to ask another question, which the facilitator again answers. This interaction norm is difficult to break once established. The danger is that a support group can become a lecture-style class, with the facilitator as the "expert" and the other group members becoming the "patients."

Many of us feel uncomfortable remaining silent when a question is asked, particularly when we feel we have "the answer." Two incorrect assumptions exist in this case. First, we wrongly assume that people are coming to the group for "answers." Although on a question-by-question basis it may be true that a question is asked in order for it to be answered, it is equally true that a higher level of support may be offered from actively listening. The second assumption is that we—the professionals—are the best ones to answer the question. True, we may have more current medical or rehabilitation information pertaining to a given question, but let us not be too presumptuous. Other group members may have equally valuable information worth sharing with other members.

Participative Listening. An alternative to the "talk show host" interaction norm is being a participative listener. This means we must do more than simply nod at the right times and reflect what has been said periodically, although those are good listening traits. A participative listener is simultaneously a member of the group, a participant in the dialog, and an empathic participant in the individual's sharing of a story. Here is an example from a support group for caregivers of people with aphasia:

SARA:	I have moments when I just don't want to do it anymore. I just want to be his wife again, not his *caregiver.*
FACILITATOR:	So your role in the household has changed quite a bit. That must be hard. Can you tell us more about your feelings about the role change?

Other responses would be equally effective, including silence, in that it may be appropriate to remain silent and let another group member respond. I have no formulaic methods for describing the ideal response in a given situation; the idea is to simultaneously be a facilitator, empathic listener, and group member.

Structure of Sessions

Open or Closed Group. In an open group, newcomers are free to join at any time. This often results in a core group of people who attend nearly all sessions, some who attend occasionally, and newcomers, who either become part of the new "core" or attend only occasionally.

In a closed group, newcomers are not welcome. Members of these groups tend to attend most sessions, as the "closing" of the closed group implies a commitment to the group. If a large enough waiting list develops, a new group can be formed.

A level of trust must be present for people to feel comfortable enough to share their emotions and stories. Revealing emotions and experiences can make one feel quite vulnerable. Thus, the closed group is often more conducive to therapy-oriented support groups because it may be difficult to discuss very personal issues with strangers.

Time. The number of meeting sessions may be open-ended or time-limited. A trade-off exists for either decision. On one hand, an open-ended number of sessions allows people to feel unhurried and relaxed regarding the revealing and discussing of issues important to them. ("If we don't get to it this week, there's always next week.") On the other hand, a finite number of sessions may keep participants more attentive and alert, knowing that a limited number of sessions exists in which to accomplish group and individual goals.

Time-limited groups may also send the message that the work people do during the group need not be confined to the group sessions. That is, in time-unlimited groups, a person or couple may wait until the group meeting before facing an issue, whereas with a time-limited group, the process of generalization may be facilitated more easily as people begin to think about what they will do when the group has ended.

Another important time issue is the duration for each session. It is usually best to keep the amount of time consistent, to begin on time, and for the leader to facilitate closure each session.

Group Goals

The leader would be wise to consider who "owns" the goals for group therapy. When the leader asks, "What would you like to accomplish during our time together?" some groups have members with immediate responses, whereas other groups have rather prolonged silences following the question. A strong leader will allow the silence. Sooner or later, people begin to speak. It rarely takes longer than 3 or 4 minutes before participants begin to express their goals.

As people express their goals, write them on a board so all can see. Sometimes this is enough to motivate people to continue the list. It is not necessary that everyone add to the list, but give enough time so that everyone has the opportunity to contribute.

Often a goal is stated that is specific to an individual case and not conducive to the group process. For example, a group member may state, "I just want my husband to talk like he used to," or "I want to make her understand how hard I work." I usually repeat what the person has said and ask for clarification.

FACILITATOR: So Claire, you want your husband to talk like he used to. We can't make that happen in here, but if he was talking more effectively, how would you feel?

CLAIRE: Well, I'd feel relieved. I wouldn't be so frustrated.

FACILITATOR: [*writes*] So, more relieved and decreased frustration. This is good.

Once goals are stated, it is helpful to maintain a focus on them. In time-limited groups, elicit almost as many goals as the number of sessions allotted, and then encourage people to think about one goal for the following week. The focus on goals begins with the start of each session, continues throughout the session, and concludes with summary or meditation on the goal for the session.

The Beginning of Sessions. The elderly are no different from anyone else regarding the busyness of their days. Focusing on the present and achieving mindfulness can be as difficult for the elderly as for the rest of us.

I find the most effective way to begin a session is to encourage people to sit comfortably in a position they can maintain for a few minutes. I then ask them to close their eyes and "clear" their minds. I tell them to focus only on breathing and relaxing, and when they find themselves thinking about something else, to simply return to focus on breathing. After 5 to 10 minutes, I sound a chime, and begin the session. This procedure is undoubtedly familiar to some readers as a method of meditation. Some people are uncomfortable with the idea of meditating. I do not announce that what they have just done is meditation (neither do I deny it, if asked). Some of my colleagues' students have resisted engaging in meditation on religious grounds. These colleagues have encouraged their students to consider this time as prayer, and the resistance has dissolved. I have not had as much resistance, but, on the other hand, I am with elderly clients more than these colleagues are.

The Session. After opening a session, I remind people of the goal they had in mind all week, and I wait for people to begin the group process. If this is a first-time, first-session group, a silence may ensue. A strong leader must accept that silence.

It may last several minutes, which is absolutely okay. I find that "tolerate" is no longer what I am doing during the silences because I have grown to appreciate these few minutes. During that silence, group members learn that their input is no less important than mine. They learn that this is their group, and they may use the time however they wish.

Sometimes a group member is somewhat more demanding of me during the initial silence. "What are we doing here, exactly?" is a phrase I've heard. My response is not sarcastic, nor is it intended to be glib: "We are addressing [I restate the goal]."

After people begin to feel more at ease with their roles as equal participants in the group, I begin to contribute. However, I find that I occasionally need to "back out" a little if the focus of the comments and questions begins to turn more to me than to other group members.

Session Closure. Sessions have beginnings and middles, and they also need to have effective endings. It is unwise to remain too rigid about the exact ending time for a session. On the other hand, participants (and leaders) often feel uncomfortable when session durations are too variable. What often makes sessions too short is a facilitators' discomfort with silence about two thirds to three quarters of the way through a session. Again, these silences are okay.

A session that goes over the allotted time is often caused by a group member's introduction of a new or emotion-filled topic late in a session. This situation is delicate. We do not want to discourage emotion or new topics. Neither do we want to minimize the importance of the topic introduced by the group member.

I find the best way to handle these "late-session bombs" is by attempting to relate the newly introduced topic to the following week's topic. If there is no good or realistic match to the following week's topic, I ask group members if they would prefer to postpone the following week's topic so we can explore this new issue. Assuming that is okay, closure can proceed. On rare occasions, I have asked the person who introduced the "late-session bomb" to stay after the session and talk with me about it.

The closure itself can take one of several forms. I will describe two. First, the group leader can summarize the session, acknowledge the participation by certain members, and thank all who came for their participation, whether that participation occurred verbally or in silence. The expression of this appreciation must occur with sincerity.

The second closure method is by again asking people to close their eyes and focus on breathing (i.e., meditation). Whatever method the facilitator chooses, a reminder of the following week's topic is helpful.

Points to Ponder #33

Describe what happens in a group session. What are the components of a group session?

Individual and Couples-Based Counseling

In our field, some of us believe that counseling individuals with communication disorders is synonymous with interviewing. Indeed, interviews are one context in counseling. As stated earlier in this chapter, providing information to people is a valuable use of our (and their) time. I submit an example from my clinical experience of counseling that went beyond the context and experience normally associated with interviewing.

A couple, Jim and Karen, were referred to me because Jim had had a stroke, and had mild to moderate aphasia. Jim was 78, and Karen was 73. He was able to converse, albeit with some difficulty. Karen understood him most of the time, but she was not sure how to help when he had word-finding difficulty. I worked with them to determine some effective strategies. When I started discussing how they could encourage other people to use these techniques, Jim suddenly began crying, and Karen soon became tearful as well. "We don't have any friends anymore," Jim said after a few moments. Jim and Karen had moved to a mobile home park just 2 years prior to the stroke, and their friends found it difficult to relate to Jim after the stroke. They told me that people seemed awkward and embarrassed when they spoke to Jim.

This emotionally laden session was very important to Jim and Karen (and, in fact, to me). They were concerned about their communication, without a doubt. They also were having difficulty coping with an issue that would not easily "go away." It would have been a disservice to them (and an unethical practice on my part) to say, "You want the Psychology Service, down the hall and to your left." On the other hand, I believed they were experiencing a struggle that was best handled by a social worker or psychologist with training in these issues.

My solution was to continue with the session, addressing the issue they presented, and at the end of the session, I referred them to a social worker to help them further with this issue. The continuance of the session is what I wish to address here. This couple felt comfortable enough with me to trust me with this devastating loss on their part. I felt compelled to honor their trust and proceed. The dialog went as follows:

JIM: We've lost our friends (*begins crying*).

KAREN: It's okay, dear. (*To me*) We moved to the Desert Homes Park 2 years ago. It's where all our friends were moving, so we decided to go too (*begins to cry*). So ... well, they don't come around anymore. They just can't look at Jim like this. I don't know what to do. I used to go over to their homes, but they just don't come over to ours.

JIM: (*Puts his hand on her shoulder*) It's okay.

KAREN: They just don't understand. I don't know. They don't understand how it hurts.

ME: That must be very sad.

KAREN: Yes.

JIM: Yes.

ME: Can you tell me more?

JIM: They used to visit, but now not. No more.

KAREN: Yes, they used to come over, but not anymore.

ME: Yes, that's what I mean. Say more about that.

KAREN: ...

I ended up referring Jim and Karen to a social worker. However, I was glad that, prior to this referral, I was able to help them process their emotions.

➤ Concluding Comments

I hope that this chapter has provided the reader with useful information and perhaps a broader context in which to conduct therapy. Helping the elderly requires the continual discovery of who they are as a group and who our clients are as individuals. Any particular approach to counseling is of little value without that discovery. Thus, the reader's job is not over at the end of this or any chapter. Because the discovery is often itself a therapeutic undertaking, I wish the readers a rich and rewarding journey along the way.

TWELVE

Ethical and Professional Matters

CHAPTER OUTLINE

The work of speech–language pathologists and audiologists is important, challenging, and fulfilling. These professionals are in the unique position of being able to help provide people with the gifts of improved communicative abilities and, therefore, an improved quality of life. For this very reason, there are important responsibilities that are an integral part of clinical practice. Throughout their careers, clinicians encounter a number of different patients, patients' families and other caregivers, and disorders. They also face a number of different ethical, professional, and procedural matters that affect the delivery of clinical services. Some of these matters have been addressed throughout this book. Several other items, particularly as they relate to interviewing and counseling activities, are discussed in the sections that follow.

Extensive reference is made in this chapter to the American Speech-Language-Hearing Association's (ASHA's) Code of Ethics (1995). The reader is encouraged to review the Code of Ethics for the matters discussed here, as well as for other ethical considerations and principles. Also, sources such as Resnick's (1993) *Professional Ethics for Audiologists and Speech–Language Pathologists* and Pannbacker, Middleton, and Vekovius's (1996) *Ethical Practices in Speech–Language Pathology and Audiology: Case Studies* contain extensive discussions about ethical matters related to clinical practice.

Key aspects of professionalism among helping professionals include having adequate knowledge of the academic discipline, developing the abilities to translate this professional knowledge into effective helping processes, being dedicated, putting the interests of the consumer ahead of personal interests, insisting on high standards of professional service to clients, and maintaining appropriate and consistent professional behavior. Professionalism involves having full qualification (i.e., knowledge and competence) and ethical integrity (Haynes & Pindzola, 1998).

Continuing Study

Knowledge and technology are changing constantly, and these are important factors in professional practice. The clinical worker will continue to be challenged by the need to acquire and incorporate new knowledge. No matter how much we know, it is only the basis for what we will or should learn.

ASHA's Code of Ethics, Principle IT-C, requires clinicians to "continue their professional development throughout their careers" (ASHA, 1995). Ongoing education is necessary for all clinicians in today's world, and at its heart is the desire to continue educating ourselves about the subject matter of our work. Education is vitally important as services are pro-

vided to an increasingly diverse society. To paraphrase Moursund (1993), clinicians who interview or counsel have clear
choices—either continue to learn or decay and either expand
knowledge or stagnate and regress.

Evaluation

Students and professionals are involved in demonstrating effectiveness of services delivered as part of service delivery ac-
countability (Hegde & Davis, 1995; Leith, 1993). In the field
of communicative disorders, there is a need to evaluate diagnostic and clinical treatment activities. There is also a need
to review interviewing and counseling efforts because these
are part of assessment and treatment activities. ASHA's (1995)
Code of Ethics, Principle I-G, addresses the area of evaluation
in stating, "Individuals shall evaluate the effectiveness of services rendered and of products dispensed and shall only provide services or dispense products when benefit can reasonably
be expected." Several other provisions of the Code of Ethics
also apply to many interviewing and counseling activities:

> Individuals shall provide all services competently.
> (Principle I-A)
> Individuals shall fully inform the persons they serve of
> the nature and possible effects of services rendered
> and products dispensed. (Principle J-D)
> Individuals shall not guarantee the results of any treat-
> ment or procedure, directly or by implication; how-
> ever, they may make a reasonable statement of
> prognosis. (Principle I-F)
> Individuals shall not misrepresent diagnostic information,
> services rendered, or products dispensed or engage
> in any scheme or artifice to defraud in connection
> with obtaining payment or reimbursement for such
> services or products. (Principle II-C)
> Individuals' statements to the public shall provide accurate
> information about the nature and management of
> communication disorders, about the professions, and
> about professional services. (Principle III-D)

At a minimum, the need to provide services competently will
apply to all sessions. Any or all of the preceding other provisions can apply to a given session, depending on the topics
addressed.

Clinicians need to be specific and objective in their self-
evaluations. This can be accomplished by thinking critically,
reviewing audiotapes or videotapes of sessions, and/or using
specific observational checklists or systems. The checklists in

Appendixes 7.A and 7.B are useful for this purpose. Other systems have been reported by Amidon (1965), Ivey (1994), P. A. McDonald and Haney (1988), Molyneaux and Lane (1982), and others. In the field of counseling, it has repeatedly been found that counselors who review videotapes of their counseling interactions gain increased confidence in their abilities and a greater awareness of the personal qualities they project during sessions. The same is true for clinicians in the fields of speech–language pathology and audiology.

Representation of Professional Credentials

The ASHA Code of Ethics, Principle ITI-A, states, "Individuals shall not misrepresent their credentials, competence, education, training, or experience." Another provision (Principle TI-B) states, "Individuals shall engage in only those aspects of the professions that are within the scope of their competence, considering their level of education, training, and experience" (ASHA, 1995). There are several implications of these provisions.

One concern is the possibility of patients' misconceptions about a clinician's academic degrees and areas of specialization. Writing about the practice of counseling, Edinburg, Zinberg, and Kelman (1975) note,

> *The counselor should not overlook misconceptions on the part of the client that have to do with his [or her] view of the counselor. If overlooked, these misconceptions, when discovered, give rise to a lack of trust in the counselor. For example, a client may address a single, female counselor with neither an M.D. nor a Ph.D. degree as "Mrs. Jones" or "Dr. Smith." It would be a mistake for the counselor to let the matter go on the assumption that the client might feel better being in treatment with someone who is married or who has a more professional status. Later, when the client learned the truth, he [or she] would be justified in feeling deceived by the counselor. A "slip" due to misinformation on the part of the client is easily corrected by the counselor simply stating the truth. (p. 55)*

In an unobtrusive but direct way, clinicians in such situations need to let patients know their correct status and professional title.

Infrequently, the principle of misrepresentation also applies to phony or so-called mail order degrees. For example, over the years, there have been outfits that supplied a medical degree (MD) diploma for the right price and "evidence of work or life experience." There are also some so-called universities that will assist aspirants in gaining a Doctor of Philosophy (PhD) or Doctor of Education (EdD) degree for the right price and minimal effort. Persons with such degrees who represent themselves to the public as "doctors" are guilty of misrepresentation and are engaging in misleading, self-serving behavior.

Confidentiality and Patient Records

At least two provisions of the Code of Ethics apply to patient records, appropriate access to such records, and confidentiality of these records:

> Individuals shall maintain adequate records of professional
> services rendered and products dispensed and shall
> allow access to these records when appropriately
> authorized. (Principle I-H)
> Individuals shall not reveal, without authorization, any
> professional or personal information about the per-
> son served professionally, unless required by law
> to do so, or unless doing so is necessary to protect
> the welfare of the person or the community.
> (Principle I-I)

Clinicians frequently interact with physicians, teachers, family members, and other speech–language pathologists or audiologists involved with a client. Professionals may seek information from others, or information may be requested from them. The sharing of information is appropriate and necessary, but only with the patient's knowledge and written permission. Virtually all settings have release of information forms to use for such permissions. The preservation of confidentiality is an important ethical matter. The maintenance of a patient's confidentiality involves protecting all written records or tape recordings and making sure that verbal discussions with or about clients are private and confidential. Talking about a client in any public place has the potential to cause big trouble.

Typically, it is useful to state the terms of confidentiality within the setting, including who will see any information and why. It is also helpful to discuss any forms patients are asked to sign. When asking someone to sign an exchange of information form, be aware that individuals from a linguistically or culturally diverse background with an oral tradition can be very intimidated by such a request. Their experience in signing documents may be limited to major life events such as weddings, deaths, immigration, or loans. Audio- or videotape recordings also should be collected or shared only with the written permission of clients. All written or recorded materials should be protected by the rules of patient confidentiality except for certain instances of neglect, abuse, or potential danger to the individual or others in the community that, by law, must be reported to appropriate authorities.

Human Subjects Involved in Research

Research is conducted in many settings, including hospitals, school districts, and public, university, and private clinics. The growth of research during the 20th century resulted in a dramatic increase in the number of studies involving people. Years ago, some subjects were exposed to various excessive and inappropriate risks, particularly in medical and psychological studies. Subjects were exposed, for example, to cancer, hepatitis, or syphilis; some were given untested drug treatments or placebo contraceptives; others were subjected to threats of electrical shock. In a number of these studies, the subjects were unaware that the research was being conducted, and they had no idea of the risks to which they were being subjected.

Today, federal and state regulations dictate a much closer review of research in most settings, particularly if patients are to be subjected to any form of physical, psychological, sociological, educational, or other risk. Common to research in all fields is a careful deliberation and approval process concerning possible risks to human subjects. Depending on the type of study and the setting, formal approval by a responsible institution, agency, committee, or individual may be needed before any research data are collected. In the formal approval process, potential risks to subjects are carefully weighed against potential benefits to them or society. It is of particular concern that potential subjects (or their parents or caregivers) be honestly informed about the risks and benefits of their participation; that it be made clear to them that they are free to choose whether they want to participate in the study; and that they are free to withdraw from the study at any time. The anonymity of subjects also is commonly protected in all reports that result from a study.

When interviews or counseling sessions are part of either teaching efforts or research, subjects need to agree to such participation. A signed informed consent to participate is necessary for most research projects. Sources such as Hegde (1994) and Silverman (1998) are good starting points for more information on procedures. Key administrators in various settings (hospitals, universities, school districts) can also help identify specific human subject policies and procedures applicable to those settings.

Points to Ponder #34

A local clinician in your area retires, and tells you that she would like you to take over her private practice. Flattered, you eagerly accept. Unfortunately, you find that there were some questionable practices going on that you need to address. Describe three types of unethical actions that might have been going on in a private practice.

Note Taking and Tape Recording

Adequate records of any assessment and treatment activities are necessary in clinical practice (see ASHA, 1994; Paul-Brown, 1994), including interviewing and counseling activities. At a minimum, notes should reflect who was in attendance, primary points discussed or information shared by either party, areas of agreement or disagreement, and future activities or courses of action. Such notes should be sufficiently readable and detailed to adequately depict the session, even if needed years later. There are several potential problems with taking notes during sessions: It can create tension, be distracting, break the flow of conversation, and even lead to biased responses as interviewees take cues and adjust responses based on what is being recorded (Donaghy, 1990). Thus, although necessary in many situations, record keeping should not be the main focus during interviews and counseling sessions (Garrett, 1982). Rather, the emphasis should be on putting clients at ease, encouraging them to talk freely, guiding the conversation into areas and directions deemed appropriate, and interpreting the clues given by clients' words and behavior.

Taking notes should not distract from or interfere with the flow of an interview (Benjamin, 1981; Okun, 2002). Notes should be taken openly, not in a hidden or secretive manner. In some cases, taking notes can convey to clients that the clinician is concerned about what is being said and is genuinely interested in the topics discussed. However, note taking should not be—and should not appear to be—used as a crutch or as an escape from interacting with interviewees.

Clinicians should also take interviewees' cultural backgrounds into account. For example, some Native Americans and Native Alaskans may view note taking as a disrespectful indication that the clinician is not truly listening (Hays, 2001).

Notes are probably beneficial for most interviewers. It is a good idea to write more detailed case notes immediately following an interview or counseling session. Recalling the facts immediately after an interview is a constructive alternative to disrupting the session by writing extensive notes. Laptop computers can be used to record some notes in certain settings; however, prior approval for use of one is a good idea. It is important to make sure clients are comfortable with the use of this technology. The clinician who uses a laptop computer also needs to take special care to prevent the appearance of "taking a deposition" rather than conducting an interactive interview.

With the availability of audio- and videotaping equipment, a detailed and accurate record of an interview is possible in most clinical and educational settings. Both of these ways of recording client sessions are permissible, but only with prior approval. Taping another individual without his or her knowledge and consent, for whatever reason, is inappropriate.

Discussing Fees

The need to discuss fees and payments for services does not occur in some settings; Head Start programs, schools, and other publicly or privately supported settings, for example, do not charge fees. The subject of fees does come up in most other settings such as hospitals, private and community-based clinics, and most university speech and hearing clinics.

Some clinicians feel uncomfortable discussing fees with clients, so this discussion is often relegated to a clinic secretary, the business office, or a university supervisor. Discussing fees with clients, however, is important whether they are paying the entire fee for the services or they are being partially or fully reimbursed by a third party (e.g., private or public insurance, a relative, or an employer).

Clinicians should provide clients with complete price and fee information prior to rendering actual services. People need to know what they will be charged for the services to be provided. When appropriate, it is the professional's responsibility to discuss fees in an honest, forthright, and knowledgeable manner. For students, discussing fees with clients may or may not be appropriate, depending on the policies of the university clinic or the site of the internship. A supervisor, clinic secretary, or clinic director should be consulted before a student discusses fees with clients.

Making Referrals

The clinician who makes a referral transfers the client to another professional who is more able, through specialization or experience, to provide the specific service needed by the client (Shertzer & Stone, 1980). By referring a client elsewhere, the clinician attempts to serve the client's best interests. Examples of a referral might be for a medical consultation, special education evaluation, psychological or psychiatric evaluation, or services from another communicative disorders professional who has greater expertise in or resources for assisting with the problem at hand. The Code of Ethics (ASHA, 1995) states, "Individuals shall use every resource available, including referral when appropriate, to ensure that high quality service is provided" (Principle I-B).

The sincere, secure professional is aware of the need for, and is comfortable making, appropriate referrals to other specialists (English, 2002). Such an individual is not afraid to make a recommendation when it is in the best interests of a client. Clients are more likely to accept and act on referrals when clinicians give clear and straightforward, but tactful, reasons for their referrals. The following are useful guidelines for referrals that have been adapted from MacLean and Gould (1988) and Sweeney (1971):

1. If possible, be personally acquainted and familiar with the professionals or agencies you are suggesting. Become familiar with services within your community.
2. Discuss the reasons for suggesting the referral with clients.
3. Describe for clients the types of information and areas of concern that they should share with the professional or agency to whom individuals are being referred.
4. Everyone involved should have a clear understanding about any information that will be shared between clinicians and other professionals or agencies, and how this sharing will be accomplished (e.g., by mailed report or by telephone call).

Referrals to other speech and hearing professionals who are out of the local area can be made through the use of ASHA's *Guide to Professional Services in Speech–Language Pathology and Audiology,* the *ASHA Directory,* or various state association directories. All of these resources are updated periodically.

Lavorato and McFarlane (1988) note that some clients balk at seeing another type of specialist, particularly a psychologist, psychiatrist, or other mental health professional. Resistance may occur because of the stigma attached; anticipated cost; or simply frustration, anger, or confusion about being referred elsewhere. These authors suggest four ways to make such a referral. One way is to calmly but directly recommend that the client "consult with" or "talk with" another specialist. Terms such as *consider psychotherapy* or *be evaluated by* should not be used; the words *talk with* are more casual and nonthreatening. A second method is to use the terms *counseling* or *counselor* rather than *psychotherapist* or *psychologist*. Lavorato and McFarlane's third suggestion is to use descriptive phrases such as "see a specialist who can help with problems you are experiencing." Their fourth suggestion is to use the client's own statements as a springboard for the form of the recommendation. Lavorato and McFarlane (1988, pp. 252–253) provide the following examples:

CLIENT: Seeing you is like getting psychotherapy.
CLINICIAN: I'm glad our sessions are helping you. Have you considered seeing a specialist in psychotherapy?

CLIENT: I'm so upset I don't know how I'll handle this problem.
CLINICIAN: I'm sensing that the problem preoccupies you. That burden could be relieved by seeing a counselor. I'd like to suggest that _____.

Many needs for referral are relatively obvious, particularly when they are related to medical issues. However, the situation is sometimes a little less clear-cut when there is a need for psychological forms of counseling. The information in Chapter 6 should be helpful in determining the need for a referral. Other sources of information include Clark (1994b), Luterman (2001), and Rollin (2000).

Referrals for some individuals from linguistically or culturally different cultures may require special consideration. What a clinician may interpret as interpersonal resistance may actually have its base in cultural values (Sue & Sue, 2003). Or, there may be logistic problems some clinicians fail to consider. For example, as Zuniga (1998) writes,

> *Does the family have transportation for following through with a referral you make? They may gladly agree with all your plans but be embarrassed to inform you that they have no means of transportation or they may not know*

how to traverse freeways that you assume everyone can negotiate. (p. 214)

With certain patients, particularly newer immigrants, it may be necessary to accompany them to model the use of elevators, to help with office protocol, to help interpret, or for comforting purposes.

Reliability and Validity

Reliability and validity are important concepts in the scientific method, and they also apply to various clinical activities. In interviewing and counseling, *reliability* is yielding the same or consistent results at different times. *Validity* is the degree to which information appears to be true. It is important for clinicians to consider the reliability and validity of information obtained in interviews. A positive relationship between the information obtained on a written case history, behavior observed, and information collected during interviewing and counseling sessions should be apparent if clinicians are to accept the data as being reliable. Thus, a comparison of the information gathered across these three situations is a good check on the consistency and the accuracy of the information.

Reliability
In interviewing and counseling, when information or results remain consistent at different times.

Validity
In interviewing and counseling, the degree to which information appears to be true.

The deliberate distorting, withholding, or fabricating of information is not usually a concern in most settings because clients have sought help and are motivated to be honest and cooperative. The primary exceptions here are certain malingerers, insurance reimbursement frauds, or defensive reactions (including defense mechanisms). However, in the absence of these problems, remember that a clinical or educational environment may be uncomfortable or unfamiliar to some interviewees and certain areas of discussion may be very sensitive. Thus, a client's written and verbal accounts and the behavior a clinician observes may not be fully consistent.

There are a number of ways to check the validity of an oral report. Clinicians can ask themselves the following questions before accepting information at face value:

1. Can the information be verified or reproduced?
2. Is there adequate and reliable information available?
3. Does the information come from several different sources?
4. Does the information gathered from records, from testing, and from background information correspond with the results of an interview?

5. Does the information correspond with our professional judgment and with the opinions of others?
6. Does the client provide information freely, quickly, and without obvious reluctance or hesitation? Of course, such a free and speedy provision of information is based on having adequate skills in the language used during an interaction.

When clinicians rely primarily or exclusively on closed-ended questions, it is particularly difficult to determine the validity or truthfulness of the client's responses (Enelow & Swisher, 1986; Shipley & Wood, 1996). When using closed questions, clinicians should consider the level of information that is requested in each question, the social acceptability of the information asked for, and the response choices the questions allow. For example, if a clinician were to ask parents about their methods of discipline at home, some parents might be reluctant to share this information out of fear that the interviewer would find their approaches unacceptable.

Parents might be justifiably concerned that if they admit to corporal punishment, the professional might contact Child Protective Services. Clinicians need to be especially sensitive to families who emigrate from countries where child discipline laws differ from those of the United States. In many Haitian families, for example, discipline is enforced through corporal punishment that child welfare authorities in the United States might view as abusive (McEachern & Kenny, 2002). In the Philippines, teachers may hit children with sticks if they are noncompliant in the classroom. Thus, clinicians may need to help parents recognize U.S. laws regarding the difference between child abuse and discipline so that parents do not unknowingly commit crimes. The second author worked with a Chinese family in which the mother, according to the fourth-grade son George, would hit him and his brother with implements until the implements broke. George added that the bruises usually faded in a few days. The second author and school vice principal held a meeting with the parents to inform them about U.S. laws regarding child abuse. The parents had no idea they were breaking any laws.

There is another way to look at clients' responses. That is, any response a clinician receives—whether accurate or inaccurate—is valid if clinicians consider that the client is honest and trustworthy with them at that point in time. In other words, there may be an important reason why an interviewee is not completely honest. In such cases, the clinician should note the level of concern or anxiety in an interviewee and, at some point, consider exploring the subject openly.

When discrepancies occur in an interview, they should not be ignored (Darley, 1978). The information or behavior in question should be verified unobtrusively at a later point, either during the same interview or on another occasion. Except when confrontation techniques are needed for some reason, blunt challenges to the veracity of information provided by the interviewee are typically avoided whenever possible.

Finally, as noted in Chapter 4, clinicians should remember that agreement does not necessarily mean information is accurate or valid. An entire family or group may agree on something, but that does not mean their perceptions are necessarily accurate. Remember, at one time in history, almost everyone "knew" the world was flat; the sources of this information were reliable (i.e., consistent) but the information simply was not valid.

Being Culturally Aware

The United States is changing demographically at a very fast rate. The population is growing older, living longer, and becoming more ethnically and culturally diverse (see Chapter 8). About 50% of ASHA members provide services to individuals who do not speak English as their native language (ASHA, 1993). In many cities, English is not the most prevalent language and a large number of languages and dialects are spoken.

The importance of culture was described in Chapter 3 and again in Chapter 8. To work effectively with a diverse population, clinicians need to learn about cultures and their values and traditions. Clinicians have a responsibility to learn about the backgrounds of their clients so that they are more aware of and sensitive to the differences among people from different cultures. Effective cross-cultural practice is enhanced when clinicians are able to identify and accept, in a nonjudgmental way, alternative ways of viewing the world (Sue & Sue, 2003).

Culturally effective clinicians avoid imposing their own values and expectations on clients from different cultural backgrounds, avoid stereotyping and applying overall group generalities onto specific clients, and appropriately modify their activities with individual clients and families (Weiss, 2002). To learn more about working effectively across cultures, the following sources are highly recommended: Battle (2002), Coleman (2000), Paniagua (1998), Pederson and Ivey (1993), Roseberry-McKibbin (2002), and Sue and Sue (2003).

Avoiding Discrimination

ASHA's Code of Ethics, Ethical Proscription I-C, states, "Individuals shall not discriminate in the delivery of professional services on the basis of race or ethnicity, gender, age, religion, national origin, sexual orientation, or disability" (ASHA, 1995). Discrimination based on any of these characteristics is obviously unethical, inappropriate, and in many cases, illegal.

One form of discrimination that some clinicians may be unaware of relates to Section 504 of the Rehabilitation Act of 1973. This law was passed to end many types of discrimination against persons with disabilities. The law prohibits discrimination against individuals with disabling conditions by mandating that "any program or activity of a recipient of federal financial assistance cannot discriminate against handicapped [sic] people." Thousands of hospitals, public elementary and high schools, colleges and universities, and other facilities receive federal assistance of some form and, therefore, fall under Section 504's provisions.

For example, hospitals must provide services equitably to clients with and without hearing impairments. To ensure that equal service and levels of patient knowledge are provided, the hospital may be required to provide a telecommunication device for the deaf (TDD), a qualified interpreter, or other services. Appropriate adaptations are also needed in many other educational and clinical settings to ensure equal treatment for individuals who are deaf, hard-of-hearing, or blind, or who have cerebral palsy, mental impairment, or other types of physical or mental disabilities. Further information and guidelines are available from the U.S. Department of Health and Human Services or the appropriate departments dealing with civil rights in the states. The National Center for Law and the Deaf, a public service of Gallaudet College in Washington, D.C., also prepares excellent explanations of this and other laws as they pertain to deafness and hearing impairment.

Points to Ponder #35

A university has started a speech pathology and audiology clinic, and you have been hired as the director. Describe four important factors you will keep in mind as you set up the clinic.

Criticism of Other Professionals

It is not unusual for the clinician to encounter clients, or the family members and caregivers of clients, who have sought the advice of several different professionals. Consequently, these clients may have received varied and conflicting information. When asked about the logic or accuracy of another professional's opinion, clinicians need to be very careful not to criticize or second guess others. Typically, it is best for clinicians to limit discussion to their own direct observations and the information they have collected. Some awkward situations can be handled by pointing out differences in the times or dates of previous testing (such as testing done several years ago versus today) or differences resulting from the test environments or procedures used. Clinicians may also need to inform clients that differing opinions exist about disorders. Within the field, there can be several schools of thought about disorders and treatments, each of which can lead to positive clinical results.

Sometimes it can work well to say something like, "Jill [the other professional] and I graduated from different universities. Each university curriculum is slightly different, and our professional practices reflect those differences."

Even when clinicians do not approve of or agree with another opinion, they should still be careful not to criticize another professional. Rather, a positive approach is typically much more effective. Clinicians can present the rationale for their conclusions and recommendations and be willing to suggest or discuss alternative courses. If the logic of a clinician's thinking is followed by the client on a step-by-step basis, there is usually no need to defend any recommendations made or to criticize others. Although it is sometimes tempting to criticize the work of another person, particularly when inadequate services were provided, such criticisms rarely do anything positive except make the criticizer feel superior for a couple of moments. The wise clinician is well aware that criticism of someone else rarely accomplishes anything positive and often has long-lasting negative consequences. As the adage goes, "What goes around comes around."

Inappropriate Personal Relationships

Clinicians are warned, as are practitioners in other helping professions, against involvement in inappropriate personal relationships. It is not unusual for a clinician to be attracted to a client or to a family member or caregiver of a client. Such attraction is human nature—it is normal and certainly nothing for a clinician to feel guilty about (Enelow & Swisher, 1986). However, for a clinician to take action on such an interest or desire is usually inappropriate and it can have very negative, long-term consequences for all parties. The incidence and problems associated with inappropriate personal relationships are discussed more frequently in fields such as medicine, psychiatry, psychology, and counseling (Biggs & Blocher, 1987; Corey, 2001; Enelow & Swisher, 1986; Kennedy & Charles, 2001; Moursund, 1993). The issue of sexual involvement emanating from the workplace has surfaced more in these fields than in the field of communicative disorders. However, although neither well publicized nor typically mentioned in literature, these situations do occur in this field, and they are more likely to occur in long-term treatment relationships. Professionals have lost their jobs and even their careers over such indiscretions, and some have ended up in court over difficulties resulting from inappropriate personal relationships. After years of education and practice, careers have been destroyed because of inappropriate relationships, and this does not even begin to address the effects on a client or on a client's significant other, children, other family members, and friends. It is certainly wise for clinicians to consider the long-range consequences and implications before engaging in such relationships. Friendships and social relationships with clients or their caregivers, no matter how platonic, are seldom wise (Orr & Adams, 1987).

In one situation in the second author's school district, a special education teacher and her husband befriended the family of Casey, a student in the teacher's special education classroom. Things went well; there were picnics, parties, outings … until Casey accused the teacher's husband of molesting her. The result was an ugly and vicious court battle, with the husband's teaching career and reputation in tatters, and thousands of dollars in legal bills for the school district.

There is a trite but relevant expression about boundaries with clients and families: "When in doubt, don't."

Terminating Clinical Services

Providing closure means wrapping things up appropriately. Clinicians use the word *terminating*, but as soon as the word is used, readers may have some form of a negative reaction similar to the reaction caused by these terms: *statistics, test, masters comps,* or *Internal Revenue Service.* Moursund (1993) writes eloquently about the concept of termination in our culture:

> *It is a hallmark of our culture that we are reluctant to talk openly about ending relationships or cutting off contact. We say "see you later" instead of "goodbye" and disguise*

the finality of long-term partings (graduations, moving away) with promises to keep in touch. Even death, that most final of endings, is referred to as passing on, and Western religion is replete with reassurances that important relationships need not end—that, in the words of the old hymn, "we shall meet in the sweet bye-and-bye." Ending a meaningful relationship is unpleasant if not downright painful; none of us likes to give up something we care about. It is easier to pretend that it will not happen, that it is not happening, that it did not happen, and then deal with the reality later, when we have found new friends and new interests and the pain of parting has had time to subside. It is a great temptation to clients and therapists (being, after all, people like everyone else) to treat their endings in the same way: To ignore the fact that termination is coming, to disguise its reality with pseudo-plans to meet again in one way or another, or to slide through the last sessions without knowing that they will, in fact be the last. (p. 91)

Termination, particularly from ongoing treatment, can be difficult for both clinicians and clients unless clinicians have planned for it, and prepared their clients and themselves for this ending. Remember that in a helping profession, it is the clinician's obligation to provide the quickest and most efficient clinical services possible (MacLean & Gould, 1988). The termination of an ongoing relationship should be discussed, at least periodically, throughout the course of the therapeutic relationship (Hackney & Cormier, 1994; Moursund, 1993). With regard to counseling, it has been said that the stage for termination begins to be set during an initial interview as the working agreement for meeting treatment goals is established (Edinburg et al., 1975). Although this does not always happen, clinicians do need to prepare their clients (and themselves) throughout the course of service delivery for the day when clinical services will no longer be needed. When the day does come, the client should understand why—for example, because the goals have been met or because no additional progress appears possible.

When a relationship terminates, the actual parting is sometimes sad and emotionally trying. Some clients and clinicians may even go through a form of grieving because, in essence, a loss is occurring. The other party will no longer be seen on an ongoing basis. It is like the sadness many parents experience when their sons or daughters leave home. At parting, one or both of the parties may experience a variety of emotions—anger, fear, guilt, or a sense of loss (Moursund, 1993). These are natural reactions that need to be acknowledged. However, Moursund (1993) also notes that clinicians can and should feel good about the progress made and accomplishments gained. In effect, clinicians can feel good that they "put themselves out of a job" because of a job well done.

There are some specific considerations clinicians should keep in mind when terminating a clinical relationship. The termination should be timed wisely and appropriately. Any loose ends should be tied up. The clinician should consider whether any referrals are appropriate for follow-up care or for treatment of any other problems. In terminating a relationship, clinicians should attempt to "keep the door open" so their client feels free to contact them with future questions or concerns (McDonald & Haney, 1988). It is also a good idea for clinicians to follow up on their clients after termination. Most clients truly appreciate a call sometime later just to make sure they are doing well. Clinicians also feel good knowing that their patients are maintaining progress, when this is the case.

Risk Management Strategies

There is a certain element of risk in all human service activities, including speech–language pathology and audiology. These fields are not considered to have "catastrophic exposure" (ASHA, 1994), but legal action is brought against practitioners from time to time. A majority of these actions involve questions about improper assessment or treatment, hearing aid dispensing, employment conflicts, physical injuries, and improper diagnosis. Less frequent legal actions have involved sexual harassment, property damage, failure to provide sufficient information to clients, and false guarantees of results (ASHA, 1994). Many areas of litigation involve discussions with others in areas of assessment and treatment, which often involve interviewing and counseling interactions.

ASHA (1994) has identified six general areas—awareness and education of the practitioner, effective communication, documentation, confidentiality, informed consent, and client safety—of exposure to risks of conduct (see Appendix 12.A). Problems in these areas can result in legal and ethical difficulties. In reviewing ASHA's risk areas, notice that many of these items have been addressed in the context of interviewing and counseling in this chapter or throughout the book.

Dealing with Failures

Sir James M. Barrie reportedly said, "We are all failures—at least the best of us are" (MacLean & Gould, 1988, p. 43). As hard as it may be to admit, there are some people a clinician simply cannot help. Some clients may not mesh well with a clinician's personality or may not be willing to enter into a helper–helpee relationship. Being honest about this possibility is a sign of wisdom and clinical maturity.

No one should expect to succeed all the time. As Kennedy and Charles (2001) comment, interviewers and counselors who cannot accept their own limitations and at least occasional defeats are probably in the wrong line of work. No clinician is immune to the experience of failure. In a professional field, clinicians expect to succeed and be able to help, but this is not always possible. In their book, *The Imperfect Therapist,* Kottler and Blau (1989) point out that professionals in the helping professions can be their own worst enemies if they do not acknowledge self-doubts, or if they fail to realize when they are in trouble. Kottler and Blau also remind us that failures can be useful in that, if properly understood, they help clinicians improve their future performance. A clinician's growth is related to finding out what works well, recognizing what does not work well, and trying to discover why.

> Concluding Comments

This chapter discusses a number of topics dealing with ethical and professional matters. There are undoubtedly many additional areas that are unique to settings and cases. In some settings, procedure and policy manuals are available to specify how certain matters should be handled. In other cases, the reader may want to review sources such as ASHA's Code of Ethics (ASHA, 1995), the "Scope of Practice" article (ASHA, 1990), or "Preferred Practice Patterns" (ASHA, 1993); consult with peers or supervisors; and use good sense. Always, though, the clinician should consider what is best for the client and what is the professional thing to do.

APPENDIX 12.A
Six Areas of Exposure to Risks of Conduct and Methods of Reducing These Risks

1. Awareness and Education of Practitioner

- Identify potential risks.
- Eliminate or reduce risks by providing an accepted standard of care.
- Practice within the scope of your professional competence, licensure, and certification.
- Use only licensed or registered titles.
- Stay current with developments in your profession.
- Keep abreast of evolving standards of practice.
- Maintain professional competence through continuing education.
- Know state licensing laws.
- Know applicable codes of ethics.
- Know relevant scopes of practice.
- Know and use current preferred practice patterns, guidelines, and position statements.
- Use only equipment and test materials with which you are trained or knowledgeable.
- Refer when you do not possess the knowledge, expertise, and credentials to provide a needed service.
- Be certain of licensure, certification, and other qualifications of all persons to whom referrals are made, as well as those of employers or employees.
- Know and use the policies and procedures of the hospital or organizations at which you are employed.

2. Effective Communication

- Establish a positive relationship with clients.
- Be a good listener.
- Explain test results, treatment goals, treatment plans, and procedures, as well as realistic outcomes.
- Take time to explain answers in lay terms.
- Avoid making statements that mislead clients into unreasonable expectations.
- Address both benefits and limitations of products or treatment.
- Encourage observation of procedures by caregivers.

- Make full disclosure of fees, billing schedules, and arrangements for missed sessions before treatment begins or equipment is dispensed.
- Provide written warranties and disclaimers of guarantees.
- Secure signature of client, caregiver, or significant other to acknowledge transfer and indicate understanding of written warnings, warranties, and disclaimer of guarantees.

3. Documentation—Record Keeping and Reporting

- Be aware that the care with which documents are kept will reflect the quality of care clients receive, and that these documents may be subpoenaed.
- Make all entries accurate, thorough, and legible.
- When corrections are necessary
  —never "white out" or obliterate;
  —draw a line through incorrect information;
  —initial and date the correction; and
  —note why the correction was necessary.
- Document all personal and telephone contacts with client and family.
- Keep copies of all correspondence with or about the client.
- Document all contacts with other professionals regarding the client.
- Document failure to show, cancellation, or rescheduling of appointments.
- Document noncompliant behavior by describing behavior that leads to that opinion, rather than making judgmental or opinionated statements.
- Document limitations of treatment progress.
- Document recommendations.
- If team recommendations differ from your own, document your own recommendations and state rationale and conclusions.
- Keep records of all dispensed products.
- Keep records of equipment maintenance and calibration.
- Document warnings or dangers of products.
- Document informed consent for evaluation and treatment procedures.
- Document consent for dispensing or receiving client information.
- Document when and where all client information was sent.

4. Confidentiality

- Release to a specific entity only information that was requested in writing.
- Obtain a signed and witnessed release.

- Know who is authorized to view or receive records by awareness of
  —state regulations,
  —policies and procedures of hospitals or organizations with which you are affiliated,
  —the client's rights of access to records, and
  —provider's right of reasonable restrictions on access.
- Document does not have to be provided at any time or any place requested by the client, but must be provided at a mutually agreed-on time and place.
- Provider may need information to be available to explain or interpret information.
- Provider can charge reasonable fees for copies.
- Use fax or other forms of electronic mail cautiously to prevent disclosure to unauthorized individuals.

5. Informed Consent

- Obtain informed consent for evaluation and treatment procedures.
- Inform the client of the following elements to obtain a valid informed consent:
  —nature of ailment, proposed treatment, risk, consequences of treatment
  —probability of success
  —treatment alternatives
  —prognosis
- Determine who has the authority to sign an informed consent by securing knowledge of
  —state laws for determining minor status,
  —state and local laws for determining legal guardian for minors in the absence of a parent, and
  —policies and procedures of the hospital or organization with which you are affiliated.
- Treat minors only when accompanied by a parent or guardian or when written permission has been obtained to treat in their absence.

6. Client Safety

- Make sure physical environment is free of hazards.
- Structure activities to reduce client injury.
- Follow universal infection control procedures.
- Ensure the availability of emergency services based on evaluation and treatment risks.

THIRTEEN

A Few Final Thoughts

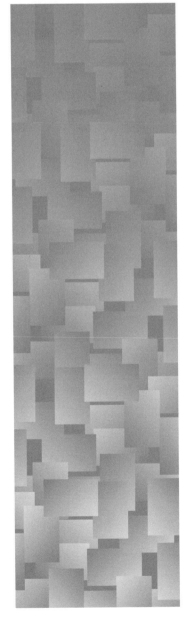

Interviewing and counseling with individuals, families, and other caregivers is an important and rewarding aspect of practice. It provides wonderful opportunities to get to know people better, and to serve the needs of those impacted by a communicative disorder. When clinicians interview and counsel well, they provide substantial help to others and find these activities very fulfilling.

Learning to interview and counsel—or improving skills and abilities in these areas—involves acquiring basic knowledge and skills, observation, practice, and experience. Formal instruction in interviewing and counseling, such as through a class, is certainly highly advantageous. Unfortunately, as noted several times in this book, undergraduate and graduate-level coursework in interviewing and counseling with communicative disorders is often inadequate.

In 1994, Culpepper, Mendel, and McCarthy surveyed all American Speech-Language-Hearing Association–accredited university programs and reported that, at a majority of universities, less than 25% of graduates had taken a course in counseling. Only 17% of the respondents at these universities felt that graduates were adequately prepared to meet the counseling needs of clients with communicative disorders. This parallels Gregory's (1995) statement that many students and professional clinicians comment on never having had a course in counseling, or do not recognize when counseling was covered in a course. So, students who are attending a school that offers counseling coursework should take advantage of it. The knowledge will be important in professional practice.

Students in programs that do not have interviewing and counseling coursework and practica available, or professionals who have completed their preprofessional education without such exposure, should consider taking at least a foundational course in this area. Often coursework in interviewing and counseling is available in disciplines such as counseling, psychology, regular or special education, social work, or other education- or health-related disciplines.

Other helpful sources of information include attending workshops or seminars and reading materials about interviewing and counseling, either in communicative disorders or more general works in these areas. These forms of instruction provide the basic principles of interviewing and counseling. The following are readable and useful resources about interviewing and counseling in general:

Corey, G. (2001). *Theory and practice of counseling and psychotherapy* (6th ed.). Belmont, CA: Wadsworth.

Donaghy, W. C. (1990). *The interview: Skills and applications.* Salem, WI: Sheffield.

Garrett, A. (1982). *Interviewing: Its principles and methods* (3rd ed.). New York: Family Service Association of America.

Ivey, A. E. (1994). *Intentional interviewing and counseling: Facilitating client development in a multicultural society* (3rd ed.). Pacific Grove, CA: Brooks/Cole.

Kennedy, E., & Charles, S. C. (2001). *On becoming a counselor: A basic guide for nonprofessional counselors and other helpers* (3rd ed.). New York: Crossroad.

Meier, S. T., & Davis, S. R. (1993). *The elements of counseling* (2nd ed.). Pacific Grove, CA: Brooks/Cole.

Okun, B. F. (2002). *Effective helping: Interviewing and counseling techniques* (6th ed.). Pacific Grove, CA: Brooks/Cole.

Pederson, P. B., & Ivey, A. E. (1993). *Culture-centered counseling and interviewing skills: A practical guide.* Westport, CT: Praeger.

Shipley, K. G., & Wood, J. M. (1996). *The elements of interviewing.* San Diego, CA: Singular.

Stewart, C. J., & Cash, W. B. (2003). *Interviewing principles and practices* (10th ed.). Dubuque, IA: William C. Brown.

Sue, D. W., & Sue, D. (2003). *Counseling the culturally diverse: Theory and practice* (4th ed.). New York: Wiley.

Useful resources for interviewing and counseling related specifically to the field of communication disorders include the following:

Andrews, J. R., & Andrews, M. A. (1990). *Family based treatment in communicative disorders: A systemic approach.* Sandwich, IL: Janelle.

Bloom, C. M., & Cooperman, D. K. (1992). *The clinical interview: A guide for speech–language pathologists and audiologists* (2nd ed.). Rockville, MD: National Student Speech-Language-Hearing Association.

Clark, J. G., & Martin, F. N. (Eds.). (1994). *Effective counseling in audiology: Perspectives and practice.* Englewood Cliffs, NJ: Prentice Hall.

English, K. M. (2002). *Counseling children with hearing impairment and their families.* Boston: Allyn & Bacon.

Flasher, L. V., & Fogle, P. T. (2004). *Counseling skills for speech–language pathologists and audiologists.* New York: Thomson/Delmar Learning.

Luterman, D. M. (2001). *Counseling the communicatively disordered and their families* (3rd ed.). Austin, TX: PRO-ED.

Rollin, W. J. (2000). *Counseling individuals with communication disorders: Psychodynamic and family aspects* (2nd ed.). Woburn, MA: Butterworth-Heinemann.

Schum, R. L. (1986). *Counseling in speech and hearing practice.* Rockville, MD: National Student Speech-Language-Hearing Association.

Shames, G. H. (2000). *Counseling the communicatively disabled and their families: A manual for clinicians.* Boston: Allyn & Bacon.

Sweetow, R. (1999). *Counseling for hearing aid fittings.* San Diego, CA: Singular/Thomson.

Webster, E. J., & Ward, L. M. (1993). *Working with parents of young children with disabilities.* San Diego, CA: Singular.

As mentioned in previous chapters, valuable resources for learning more about culture and working with different cultural groups include Battle (2002), Brice (2002), Corey (2001), Goldstein (2000), Lynch and Hanson (1998), Paniagua (1998), Pederson and Ivey (1993), Roseberry-McKibbin (2002), and Sue and Sue (2003). Other useful works are listed in References at the end of this book.

Observing interviewing and counseling situations bolsters an understanding of the principles described in this book, in coursework, or in workshops or seminars. Observing interviewing and counseling sessions can be particularly useful when the session is being conducted by an experienced, skilled practitioner. It is less helpful to observe individuals who are just learning or are less effective interviewers or counselors. By observing others in clinical settings, students and professionals can improve their understanding of the various techniques available and the many situations and reactions that can occur. Clinicians in communicative disorders also can benefit by observing skilled practitioners in other disciplines.

Observation can be done in person (either in the room or through observation windows) or by videotape. Audiotapes of particular situations are beneficial in some circumstances, but many nonverbal behaviors and interchanges cannot be observed this way. Using some type of checklist or observational system when observing is recommended. This helps provide structure and purpose to what is being observed because observers focus on specific techniques or factors in the interchange.

Academic preparation and observation provide a base of knowledge and understanding, but practice and "online" interviewing and counseling experience are also necessary. In the field of communicative disorders, everyone who has progressed from early academic coursework to the clinical practicum is aware that taking coursework or reading about something is different from actual clinical service. Exposure to information is the basis of knowledge, but applying this information to patients and caregivers often is a different story. Clinicians learn to effectively assess and treat different communicative disorders through a combination of academic knowledge and direct experience. Similarly, effective interviewers and counselors learn by doing. Practice allows clinicians to solidify their basic knowledge and understanding, directly experience the effects of using different approaches and techniques, determine the most effective techniques for different situations, and refine the myriad of skills and abilities needed to interview and counsel competently and confidently.

As noted previously, clinicians need to continue developing and refining abilities and skills throughout their careers. Clinicians will continue to learn more about interviewing and counseling and different communicative disorders from new experiences with clients, from the study of new research articles and books, from participation in professional conferences, and so forth.

Finally, enjoy the process of interviewing and counseling and the opportunities to interact with others. Interviewing and counseling activities are richly rewarding, enjoyable, and highly beneficial aspects of professional service.

References

American Speech-Language-Hearing Association. (1990). Scope of practice: Speech–language pathology and audiology. *Asha, 32*(Suppl. 2), 1–2.

American Speech-Language-Hearing Association. (1992, May). Our multicultural agenda: We're serious. *Asha, 34,* 38–39.

American Speech-Language-Hearing Association. (1993, March). Preferred practice patterns for the professions of speech–language pathology and audiology. *Asha, 35*(Supp. 11), 1–102.

American Speech-Language-Hearing Association. (1994, March). Professional liability and risk management for the audiology and speech–language pathology professions. *Asha 36*(Suppl. 12), 25–38.

American Speech-Language-Hearing Association. (1995, March). Code of Ethics—1995. *Asha, 37,* 74–75.

Amidon, E. (1965). A technique for analyzing counselor–counselee interaction. In J. F. Adams (Ed.), *Counseling and guidance: A summary view* (pp. 50–56). New York: Macmillan.

Anderson, P. P., & Fenichel, E. S. (1989). *Serving culturally diverse families of infants and toddlers with disabilities.* Washington, DC: National Center for Clinical Infant Programs.

Arambula, G. (1992). Acquired neurological disabilities in Hispanic adults. In H. Langdon (with L. L. Cheng) (Ed.), *Hispanic children and adults with communication disorders: Assessment and intervention* (pp. 373–407). Gaithersburg, MD: Aspen.

Atkins, D. V. (1994). Counseling children with hearing loss and their families. In J. G. Clark & F. N. Martin (Eds.), *Effective counseling in audiology: Perspectives and practice* (pp. 116–146). Englewood Cliffs, NJ: Prentice Hall.

Banks, J. (1999). Multicultural education in the new century. *School Administrator, 56,* 4–7.

Barbara, D. A. (1958). *The art of listening.* Springfield, IL: Thomas.

Battle, D. E. (Ed.). (2002). *Communication disorders in multicultural populations* (3rd ed.). Woburn, MA: Butterworth-Heinemann.

Bebout, L., & Arthur, B. (1992). Cross-cultural attitudes about speech disorders. *Journal of Speech and Hearing Research, 35,* 45–52.

Benjamin, A. (1981). *The helping interview* (3rd ed.). Boston: Houghton Mifflin.

Bernstein, D. K., & Tiegerman-Farber, E. (2002). *Language and communication disorders in children* (5th ed.). Boston: Allyn & Bacon.

Biggs, D., & Blocher, D. (1987). *Foundations of ethical counseling.* New York: Springer.

Bingham, W., Moore, D., & Gustad, J. (1959). *How to interview* (2nd ed.). New York: Harper.

Birren, J., Sloane, R. B., & Cohen, G. (1992). *Handbook of mental health and aging.* San Diego, CA: Academic Press.

Bliss, L. S. (2002). *Discourse impairments: Assessment and intervention applications.* Boston: Allyn & Bacon.

Bondurant-Utz, J. A. (1994). Cultural diversity. In J. A. Bondurant-Utz & L. B. Luciano (Eds.), *A practical guide to infant and preschool assessment in special education* (pp. 73–98). Boston: Allyn & Bacon.

Boone, D. R., & Prescott, T. (1972). Content and sequence analysis of speech and hearing therapy. *Asha, 14,* 58–62.

Brammer, L. M. (1993). *The helping relationship: Processes and skills* (5th ed.). Boston: Allyn & Bacon.

Brammer, L. M., Abrego, P. J., & Shostrom, E. L. (1993). *Therapeutic counseling and psychotherapy* (6th ed.). Englewood Cliffs, NJ: Prentice Hall.

Brice, A. E. (2002). *The Hispanic child: Speech, language, culture and education.* Boston: Allyn & Bacon.

Bridges, N. A. (2001). Therapists' self-disclosure: Expanding the comfort zone. *Psychotherapy: Theory/Research/Practice/Training, 38*(1), 21–30.

Brown, D., & Brown, S. (1975). Procedures for behavioral consultation. *Elementary School Guidance and Counseling, 10,* 95–102.

Buell, L. H. (1985). *Understanding the immigrant Iraqi.* San Diego, CA: Los Amigos Research Associates.

Burgoon, J. K. (1994). Nonverbal signals. In M. L. Knapp & G. K. Miller (Eds.), *Handbook of interpersonal communication* (2nd ed., pp. 229–285). Thousand Oaks, CA: Sage.

Burns, D. (1999). *Feeling good: The new mood therapy* (Rev. ed.). New York: Avon.

Camarota, S. (2001). Immigrants in the United States—2000: A snapshot of America's foreign-born population. Retrieved from Center for Immigration Studies, http://www.cis.org/articles/2001/back101.html

Campbell, M. (1993, June–July). Teams and teamwork: Parental perspectives. *Asha, 36,* 32–33.

Cappannelli, G., & Cappannelli, S. (2002). *Say yes to chance.* Cincinnati, OH: Walking Stick Press.

Carmen, B., & Uram, S. (2002). Hearing loss and anxiety in adults. *The Hearing Journal, 55*(4), 48–55.

Case, J. (2002). *Clinical management of voice disorders* (4th ed.). Austin, TX: PRO-ED.

Chan, S. (1998a). Families with Asian roots. In E. W. Lynch & M. J. Hanson (Eds.), *Developing cross-cultural competence: A guide to working with young children and their families* (pp. 251–354). Baltimore: Brookes.

Chan, S. (1998b). Families with Filipino roots. In E. W. Lynch & M. J. Hanson (Eds.), *Developing cross-cultural competence: A guide to working with young children and their families* (pp. 355–408). Baltimore: Brookes.

Cheng, L. L. (1989). Service delivery to Asian/Pacific LEP children: A cross-cultural framework. In K. G. Butler (Ed.), *Cross-cultural perspectives in language assessment and intervention* (pp. 181–194). Gaithersburg, MD: Aspen.

Cheng, L. L. (1991). *Assessing Asian language performance* (2nd ed.). Oceanside, CA: Academic Communication Associates.

Cheng, L. L. (2002). Asian and Pacific American cultures. In D. E. Battle (Ed.), *Communication disorders in multicultural populations* (3rd ed., pp. 71–112). Woburn, MA: Butterworth-Heinemann.

Cheng L. L., & Butler, K. (1993, March). *Difficult discourse: Designing connection to deflect language impairment.* Paper presented at the Annual Convention of the California Speech-Language-Hearing Association, Palm Springs, CA.

Cheng, L. L., & Hammer, C. S. (1992). *Cultural perspectives of disabilities.* San Diego, CA: Los Amigos Research Associates.

Cheng, L. L., & Ima, K. (1989). *Understanding the immigrant Pacific Islander.* San Diego, CA: Los Amigos Research Associates.

Ciaramicoli, A. P., & Ketcham, K. (2000). *The power of empathy.* New York: Penguin Putnam.

Clark, J. G. (1994a). Audiologists' counseling purview. In J. G. Clark & F. N. Martin (Eds.), *Effective counseling in audiology: Perspectives and practice* (pp. 1–17). Englewood Cliffs, NJ: Prentice Hall.

Clark, J. G. (1994b). Understanding, building, and maintaining relationships with patients. In J. G. Clark & F. N. Martin (Eds.), *Effective counseling in audiology: Perspectives and practice* (pp. 18–37). Englewood Cliffs, NJ: Prentice Hall.

Clarke, P. A. (1968). *Child–adolescent psychology.* Columbus, OH: Merrill.

Clemes, S., & D'Andrea, V. (1965). Patients' anxiety as a function of expectation and degree of initial interview ambiguity. *Journal of Consulting Psychology, 29,* 397–404.

Cohen, D., & Speken, R. H. (1985). Interviewing older adults. In A. Tolor (Ed.), *Effective interviewing* (pp. 118–135). Springfield, IL: Thomas.

Coleman, T. J. (2000). *Clinical management of communication disorders in culturally diverse children.* Boston: Allyn & Bacon.

Consedine, N., Magai, C., & King, A. (2004). Deconstructing positive affect in later life: A differential functionalist analysis of joy and interest. *International Journal of Aging and Human Development, 58,* 49–68.

Corey, G. (2001). *Theory and practice of counseling and psychotherapy* (6th ed.). Belmont, CA: Wadsworth/Thomson Learning.

Cormier, L. S., & Hackney, H. (1987). *The professional counselor: A process guide to helping.* Englewood Cliffs, NJ: Prentice Hall.

Cozad, R. L. (1974). *The speech clinician and the hearing impaired child.* Springfield, IL: Thomas.

Culpepper, B., Mendel, L. L., & McCarthy, P. A. (1994, June/July). Counseling experience and training offered by ESB-accredited programs. *Asha, 36,* 55–58.

Cunningham, C., & Davis, H. (1985). *Working with parents.* Philadelphia: Open University Press.

Dainow, S., & Bailey, C. (1988). *Developing skills with people: Training for person-to-person client contact.* New York: Wiley.

Dana, R. H. (1993). *Multicultural assessment perspectives for professional psychology.* Boston: Allyn & Bacon.

Darley, F. L. (1978). The case history. In F. L. Darley & D. C. Spriestersbach (Eds.), *Diagnostic methods in speech pathology* (2nd ed., pp. 37–96). New York: Harper & Row.

DeBlassie, R. R. (1976). *Counseling with Mexican American youth: Preconceptions and processes.* Austin, TX: Learning Concepts.

Dillard, J. M., & Reilly, R. R. (1988a). Communicative skills approach to interviewing. In J. M. Dillard & R. R. Reilly (Eds.), *Systematic interviewing: Communication skills for professional effectiveness* (pp. 36–65). Columbus, OH: Merrill.

Dillard, J. M., & Reilly, R. R. (1988b). Introduction: A perspective on interviewing. In J. M. Dillard & R. R. Reilly (Eds.), *Systematic interviewing: Communication skills for professional effectiveness* (pp. 2–13). Columbus, OH: Merrill.

Dillard, J. M., & Reilly, R. R. (1988c). The professional: An introspection of self. In J. M. Dillard & R. R. Reilly (Eds.), *Systematic interviewing:*

Communication skills for professional effectiveness (pp. 14–35). Columbus, OH: Merrill.

Dodge, E. P. (2000). Communication and collaboration. In E. P. Dodge (Ed.), *The survival guide for school-based speech–language pathologists* (pp. 57–96). San Diego, CA: Singular.

Domyancic, L. (2000). *Service delivery to Russian immigrants: An ethnographic survey.* Unpublished master's thesis, California State University, Sacramento.

Donaghy, W. C. (1990). *The interview: Skills and applications.* Salem, WI: Sheffield.

Doster, J. (1972). Effects of instructions, modeling, and role rehearsal on interviewer behavior. *Journal of Consulting Psychology, 39,* 202–209.

Dwairy, M. A. (1998). *Cross-cultural counseling: The Arab–Palestinian case.* New York: Haworth Press.

Edinburg, G. M., Zinberg, N. E., & Kelman, W. (1975). *Clinical interviewing and counseling: Principles and techniques.* New York: Appleton-Century-Crofts.

Ellis, A. (2001). *Overcoming destructive beliefs, feelings, and behaviors: New directions for rational emotive behavior therapy.* New York: Prometheus Books.

Elman, R. (1999). *Group treatment of neurogenic communication disorders: The expert clinician's approach.* Boston: Butterworth-Heinemann.

Emerick, L. (1969). *The parent interview.* Danville, IL: Interstate.

Emerick, L. L., & Hatten, J. T. (1979). *Diagnosis and evaluation in speech pathology* (2nd ed.). Englewood Cliffs, NJ: Prentice Hall.

Enelow, A. J., & Swisher, S. N. (1986). *Interviewing and patient care* (3rd ed.). New York: Oxford University Press.

English, K. M. (2002). *Counseling children with hearing impairment and their families.* Boston: Allyn & Bacon.

Erickson, C. E. (1950). *The counseling interview.* New York: Prentice Hall.

Erikson, E. (1980). *Identity and the life cycle.* New York: Norton.

Fahey, K. R., & Reid, D. K. (2000). *Language development differences and disorders: A perspective for general and special education teachers and classroom-based speech–language pathologists.* Austin, TX: PRO-ED.

Fanning, P., & McKay, M. (Eds.). (2000). *Family guide to emotional wellness.* Oakland, CA: New Harbinger.

Fast, J. (2002). *Body language.* New York: Evans.

Fitzgerald, M. H., & Barker, J. C. (1993). Rehabilitation services for the Pacific. *The Western Journal of Medicine, 59,* 50–55.

Flasher, L. V., & Fogle, P. T. (2004). *Counseling skills for speech–language pathologists and audiologists.* New York: Thomson/Delmar Learning.

Fogle, P. (1998). Demystifying counseling. *ADVANCE for Speech–Language Pathologists and Audiologists, 8*(44), 24–26.

Fretz, B. (1966). Postural movement in a counseling dyad. *Journal of Counseling Psychology, 13,* 335–343.

Freud, A. (1967). *The ego and the mechanisms of defense* (Rev. ed.). New York: International Universities Press.

Fung, F., & Roseberry-McKibbin, C. (1999). Service delivery considerations in working with clients from Cantonese-speaking backgrounds. *American Journal of Speech–Language Pathology, 8*(4), 309–318.

Garrett, A. (1982). *Interviewing: Its principles and methods* (3rd ed.). New York: Family Service Association of America.

Gelso, C. J., & Karl, N. J. (1974). Perceptions of "counselors" and other help givers: What's in a label? *Journal of Counseling Psychology, 21,* 243–247.

Germain, C., & Bloom, M. (1999). *Human behavior in the social environment: An ecological view* (2nd ed.). New York: Columbia University Press.

Giddan, J. J., & Ross, G. J. (2001). *Childhood communication disorders in mental health settings.* Austin, TX: PRO-ED.

Giles, H., & Street, R. L., Jr. (1994). Communicator characteristics and behavior. In M. L. Knapp & G. R Miller (Eds.), *Handbook of interpersonal communication* (2nd ed., pp. 103–161). Thousand Oaks, CA: Sage.

Gilliland, H. (1992). *Teaching the Native American* (2nd ed.). Dubuque, IA: Kendall/Hunt.

Glass, L. (2002). *I know what you're thinking: Using the four codes of reading people to improve your life.* New York: Wiley.

Goldberg, S. A. (1993). *Clinical intervention: A philosophy and methodology for clinical practice.* New York: Merrill.

Goldstein, B. (2000). *Cultural and linguistic diversity resource guide for speech–language pathologists.* San Diego, CA: Singular/Thomson Learning.

Goymann, W., & Wingfield, J. (2004). Allostatic load, social status and stress hormones: The costs of social status matter. *Animal Behavior, 67,* 591–602.

Gravel, J. S., & Wallace, I. F. (2000). Effects of otitis media with effusion on hearing in the first 3 years of life. *Journal of Speech, Language, and Hearing Research, 43,* 631–644.

Greenberg, L. S., Watson, J. C., Elliott, R., & Bohart, A. C. (2001). Empathy. *Psychotherapy: Theory/Research/Practice/Training, 38*(4), 380–384.

Gregory, H. H. (1995). Analysis and commentary. *Language, Speech, and Hearing Services in Schools, 26*(2), 196–200.

Gutierrez-Clellen, V. F. (1999). Language choice in intervention with bilingual children. *American Journal of Speech–Language Pathology, 8*(4), 291–302.

Haberman, M. (1995). *STAR teachers of children in poverty.* West Lafayette, IN: Kappa Delta Pi Publications.

Hackney, H., & Cormier, L. S. (1979). *Counseling strategies and interventions* (2nd ed.). Englewood Cliffs, NJ: Prentice Hall.

Hackney, H., & Cormier, L. S. (1994). *Counseling strategies and interventions* (4th ed.). Boston: Allyn & Bacon.

Hammer, C. S. (1994). Working with families of Chamorro and Carolinian cultures. *American Journal of Speech–Language Pathology, 3*(3), 5–12.

Hansen, V. (2001). The platinum rule, protocol and process. *The Hearing Review, 8*(4), 28–84.

Hanson, M. J. (1998). Ethnic, cultural, and language diversity in intervention settings. In E. W. Lynch & M. J. Hanson (Eds.), *Developing cross-cultural competence: A guide for working with young children and their families* (pp. 3–22). Baltimore: Brookes.

Harris, G. (1993). American Indian cultures: A lesson in diversity. In D. Battle (Ed.), *Communication disorders in multicultural populations* (pp. 78–113). Stoneham, MA: Andover Medical Publishers.

Hartbauer, R. E. (1978). Counseling the uninformed and misinformed. In R. E. Hartbauer (Ed.), *Counseling in communicative disorders* (pp. 107–122). Springfield, IL: Thomas.

Hayes-Bautista, D. E., Hurtado, A., Valdez, R. B., & Hernandez, A. C. R. (1992). *No longer a minority: Latinos and social policy in California.* Los Angeles: Chicano Studies Research Center, University of California.

Haynes, W. O., & Pindzola, R. H. (1998). *Diagnosis and evaluation in speech pathology* (5th ed.). Boston: Allyn & Bacon.

Haynes, W. O., & Pindzola, R. H. (2004). *Diagnosis and evaluation in speech pathology* (6th ed.). Boston: Allyn & Bacon.

Hays, P.A. (2001). *Addressing cultural complexities in practice: A framework for clinicians and counselors.* Washington, DC: American Psychological Association.

Hegde, M. N. (1993). *Treatment procedures in communicative disorders* (2nd ed.). Austin, TX: PRO-ED.

Hegde, M. N. (1994). *Clinical research in communicative disorders: Principles and strategies* (2nd ed.). Austin, TX: PRO-ED.

Hegde, M. N., & Davis, D. (1995). *Clinical methods and practicum in speech–language pathology* (2nd ed.). San Diego, CA: Singular.

Heikkinen, E., Jokela, J., & Jylha, M. (1996). Disability and functional status among elderly people: Cross-national comparisons. In G. Caselli & A. Lopez (Eds.), *Health and mortality among elderly populations* (pp. 202–220). Oxford, England: Oxford University Press.

Hershorn, M. (2002). *60 second anger management.* Far Hills, NJ: New Horizon Press.

Heubner, R. A. (2000). *Autism: A sensorimotor approach to management.* Austin, TX: PRO-ED.

Hodgkinson, H. (1998). Demographics of diversity for the 21st century. *Education Digest, 64,* 4–7.

Holliday, P. A. C. (2001). Demand may exceed supply in future job market. *The ASI Leader, 6*(8), 18.

Hulit, L. M., & Howard, M. R. (2002). *Born to talk: An introduction to speech and language development* (3rd ed.). Boston: Allyn & Bacon.

Hutchinson, B. B. (1979). Dialogues: Client-centered communication. In B. B. Hutchinson, M. L. Hanson, & M. J. Mecham (Eds.), *Diagnostic handbook of speech pathology* (pp. 1–29). Baltimore: Williams & Wilkins.

Ima, K., & Cheng, L. L. (1989). *Understanding the refugee Hmong.* San Diego, CA: Los Amigos Research Associates.

Isaac, K. M. (2001). What about linguistic diversity? A different look at multicultural health care. *Communication Disorders Quarterly, 22*(2), 110–113.

Ivey, A. E. (1994). *Intentional interviewing and counseling: Facilitating client development in a multicultural society* (3rd ed.). Pacific Grove, CA: Brooks/Cole.

Ivey, A., Pedersen, P., & Ivey, M. (2001). *Intentional group counseling: A microskills approach.* Pacific Grove, CA: Brooks/Cole.

Joe, J. R., & Malach, R. S. (1998). Families with Native American roots. In E. W. Lynch & M. J. Hanson (Eds.), *Developing cross-cultural competence: A guide to working with young children and their families* (pp. 127–164). Baltimore: Brookes.

John-Roger, S., & McWilliams, P. (1992). *The portable Life 101.* Los Angeles: Prelude Press.

Johns, G. (1975). Effects of informational order and frequency of applicant evaluation upon linear information processing competence of interviewers. *Journal of Applied Psychology, 60,* 427–433.

Johnson, C. D. (1994). Educational consultation: Talking with parents and school personnel. In J. G. Clark & F. N. Martin (Eds.), *Effective counseling in audiology: Perspectives and practice* (pp. 184–209). Englewood Cliffs, NJ: Prentice Hall.

Jones, S. D. (1993). Communicating with parents and teachers. In R. L. Lowe (Ed.), *Speech–language pathology and related professions in the schools* (pp. 241–260). Boston: Allyn & Bacon.

Kabat-Zinn, J. (1995). *Wherever you go, there you are: Mindfulness meditation in everyday life.* New York: Hyperion.

Kanfer, F., Phillips, J., Matarazzo, J., & Saslow, G. (1960). Experimental modification of interviewer content in standardized interviews. *Journal of Consulting Psychology, 24,* 528–536.

Katon, W., Ludman, E., & Simon, G. (2002). *The depression helpbook.* Boulder, CO: Bull Publishing.

Keefe, S. E. (1988). *Appalachian mental health.* Lexington: University Press of Kentucky.

Kennedy, E., & Charles, S. C. (2001). *On becoming a counselor: A basic guide for nonprofessional counselors and the helping professions* (3rd ed.). New York: Crossroad.

Ketcham, K., & Asbury, W. F. (2000). *Beyond the influence: Understanding and defeating alcoholism.* New York: Bantam.

Kinney, J., & Leaton, G. (1991). *Loosening the grip: A handbook of alcohol information* (4th ed.). St. Louis, MO: Mosby-Year Book.

Kinsella, K., & Velkoff, V. (2001). *An aging world.* U.S. Census Bureau, Series P95/01-1. Washington, DC: U.S. Government Printing Office.

Kleinke, C. L. (1986). *Meeting and understanding people.* New York: W. H. Freeman.

Knapp, M. L. (1972). *Nonverbal communication in human interaction.* New York: Holt, Rinehart & Winston.

Knapp, M. L., & Hall, J. A. (1992). *Nonverbal communication in human interaction* (3rd ed.). New York: Holt, Rinehart & Winston.

Kornfield, J. (1993). *A path with heart: A guide through the perils and promises of spiritual life.* New York: Bantam.

Kottler, J. A., & Blau, D. S. (1989). *The imperfect therapist: Learning from failure in therapeutic practice.* San Francisco: Jossey-Bass.

Kozloff, M. A. (1994). *Improving educational outcomes for children with disabilities.* Baltimore: Brookes.

Kroth, R. L. (1985). *Communicating with parents of exceptional children: Improving parent–teacher relationships* (2nd ed.). Denver, CO: Love.

Krumboltz, J. D., & Thoresen, C. E. (1969). The effect of behavioral counseling in group and individual settings on information-seeking behavior. *Journal of Counseling Psychology, 11,* 324–333.

Kubzansky, L., Kawachi, I., & Sparrow, D. (1999). Socioeconomic status, hostility, and risk factor clustering in the Normative Aging Study: Any help from the concept of allostatic load? *Annals of Behavioral Medicine, 21,* 330–338.

Kübler-Ross, E. (1969). *On death and dying.* Englewood Cliffs, NJ: Prentice Hall.

Kübler-Ross, E. (1986). *Death, the final stage of growth.* New York: Touchstone.

Kübler-Ross, E., & Kessler, D. (2000). *Life lessons.* New York: Touchstone.

Lang, G., van der Molen, H., Trower, P., & Look, R. (1990). *Personal conversations: Roles and skills for counsellors.* London: Routledge.

Langdon, H. W., & Cheng, L. L. (2002). *Collaborating with interpreters and translators: A guide for communication disorders professionals.* Eau Claire, WI: Thinking Publications.

Lavorato, A. S., & McFarlane, S. C. (1988). Counseling clients with voice disorders. *Seminars in Speech and Language, 9,* 237–255.

Leith, W. R. (1993). *Clinical methods in communication disorders* (2nd ed.). Austin, TX: PRO-ED.

Leslie, L. A. (1992). The role of informal support networks in the adjustment of Central American immigrant families. *Journal of Community Psychology, 20*(3), 243–256.

Lian, C. H. T., & Abdullah, S. (2001). The education and practice of speech–language pathologists in Malaysia. *American Journal of Speech–Language Pathology, 10*(1), 3–9.

Lin, Y-N. (2002). The application of cognitive-behavioral therapy to counseling Chinese. *American Journal of Psychotherapy, 56*(1), 46–58.

Lindeman, B. (2001). Reaching out to immigrant parents. *Educational Leadership, 58*(6), 62–67.

Lindsay, J., Sykes, E., McDowell, I., Vereault, R., & Laurin, D. (2004). More than the epidemiology of Alzheimer's disease: Contributions of the Canadian study of health and aging. *Canadian Journal of Psychiatry, 49,* 83–92.

Luterman, D. M. (2001). *Counseling persons with communication disorders and their families* (4th ed.). Austin, TX: PRO-ED.

Lynch, E. W., & Hanson, M. J. (Eds.). (1998). *Developing cross-cultural competence: A guide for working with young children and their families* (2nd ed.). Baltimore: Brookes.

MacLean, D., & Gould, S. (1988). *The helping process: An introduction.* New York: Croom Helm.

Madding, C. C. (2002). Socialization practices of Latinos. In A. E. Brice (Ed.), *Hispanic child: Speech, language, culture and education* (pp. 68–84). Boston: Allyn & Bacon.

Manton, K., Corder, L., & Stallard, E. (1997). Chronic disability trends in elderly United States populations: 1982 to 1994. *Proceedings of the National Academy of Sciences of the United States of America, 94,* 2593–2598.

Martin, F. N. (1994). Conveying diagnostic information. In J. G. Clark & F. N. Martin (Eds.), *Effective counseling in audiology: Perspectives and practice* (pp. 38–69). Englewood Cliffs, NJ: Prentice Hall.

Mathers-Schmidt, B. A. (2001). Paradoxical vocal fold motion: A tutorial on a complex disorder and the speech–language pathologist's role. *American Journal of Speech–Language Pathology, 10*(2), 111–125.

Matsuda, M. (1989). Working with Asian parents: Some communication strategies. *Topics in Language Disorders, 9,* 45–53.

Mattes, L., & Omark, D. (1991). *Speech and language assessment for the bilingual handicapped* (2nd ed.). Oceanside, CA: Academic Communication Associates.

Matz, M. (1991). Helping families cope with grief. In S. Eisenberg & L. E. Patterson (Eds.), *Helping clients with special concerns* (pp. 213–238). Prospect Heights, IL: Waveland Press.

McClain, G., & Romaine, D. S. (2002). *The everything managing people book.* Avon, MA: Adams Media.

McCroskey, J. C., Richmond, V. P., & Stewart, R. A. (1986). *One on one: The foundations of interpersonal communication.* Englewood Cliffs, NJ: Prentice Hall.

McDonald, P. A., & Haney, M. (1988). *Counseling the older adult: A training manual in clinical gerontology* (2nd ed.). Lexington, MA: Lexington Books.

McDonald, R. T. (1962). *Understand those feelings.* Pittsburgh, PA: Stanwix House.

McEachern, A. G., & Kenny, M. C. (2002). A comparison of family environment characteristics among White (non-Hispanic), Hispanic, and African Caribbean groups. *Journal of Multicultural Counseling and Development, 30*(1), 40–58.

McFarlane, S. C., Fujiki, M., & Brinton, B. (1984). *Coping with communicative handicaps: Resources for the practicing clinician.* San Diego, CA: College-Hill Press.

McMullin, R. E. (2000). *The new handbook of cognitive therapy techniques.* New York: Norton.

Mehrabian, A. (1972). *Nonverbal communication.* Chicago: Aldine Atherton.

Meier, S. T. (1989). *The elements of counseling.* Pacific Grove, CA: Brooks/Cole.

Meier, S. T., & Davis, S. R. (1993). *The elements of counseling* (2nd ed.). Pacific Grove, CA: Brooks/Cole.

Merriam-Webster Collegiate Dictionary (10th ed.). (1993). Springfield, MA: Merriam-Webster.

Mokuau, N., & Tauili'ili, P. (1998). Families with Native Hawaiian and Pacific Island roots. In E. W. Lynch & M. J. Hanson (Eds.), *Developing cross-cultural competence: A guide for working with young children and their families* (pp. 409–440). Baltimore: Brookes.

Molyneaux, D., & Lane, V. W. (1982). *Effective interviewing: Techniques and analysis.* Boston: Allyn & Bacon.

Moore-Brown, B. J., & Montgomery, J. K. (2001). *Making a difference for America's children: Speech–language pathologists in the public schools.* Eau Claire, WI: Thinking Publications.

Morrison, J., & Anders, T. F. (2001). *Interviewing children and adolescents: Skills and strategies for effective DSM–IV diagnosis.* New York: Guilford Press.

Moses, K. L. (1985). Dynamic intervention with families. In E. Cherow (Ed.), *Hearing-impaired children and youth with developmental disabilities* (pp. 82–98). Washington, DC: Gallaudet College Press.

Moursund, J. (1985). *The process of counseling and therapy.* Englewood Cliffs, NJ: Prentice Hall.

Moursund, J. (1993). *The process of counseling and therapy* (3rd ed.). Englewood Cliffs, NJ: Prentice Hall.

Mowrer, D. E. (1988). *Methods of modifying speech behaviors: Learning theory in speech pathology* (2nd ed.). Prospect Heights, IL: Waveland Press.

Murphy, J. (2001). The Native American situation. Retrieved July 2001, from http://nativeamculture.about.com/culture/nativeamculture/library/weekly/aa052301a.htm

Murray-Slutsky, C., & Paris, B. (2000). *Exploring the spectrum of autism and pervasive developmental disorders: Intervention strategies.* Austin, TX: PRO-ED.

Nation, J. E., & Aram, D. M. (1991). *Diagnosis of speech and language disorders* (2nd ed.). San Diego, CA: Singular.

National Coalition of Hispanic Health and Human Services Organization. (1988). *Delivering preventive health care to Hispanics: A manual for providers.* Washington, DC: Author.

Nellum-Davis, P., Gentry, B., & Hubbard-Wiley, P. (2002). Clinical practice issues. In D. Battle (Ed.), *Communication disorders in multicultural populations* (3rd ed., pp. 461–482). Stoneham, MA: Butterworth-Heinemann.

Nicolosi, L., Harryman, E., & Kresheck, J. (2004). *Terminology of communication disorders* (5th ed.). Baltimore: Lippincott.

Obler, L. (2001). The language of peer and social groups. In J. B. Gleason (Ed.), *The development of language* (5th ed., pp. 455–488). Boston: Allyn & Bacon.

Okun, B. F. (2002). *Effective helping: Interviewing and counseling techniques* (6th ed.). Pacific Grove, CA: Brooks/Cole.

Orr, D. W., & Adams, N. O. (1987). *Life cycle counseling: Guidelines for helping people.* Springfield, IL: Thomas.

Owens, R. E. (2001). *Language development: An introduction* (5th ed.). Boston: Allyn & Bacon.

Owens, R. E. (2002). Mental retardation: Difference or delay. In D. K. Bernstein & E. Tiegerman-Farber (Eds.), *Language and communication disorders in children* (5th ed., pp. 436–509). Boston: Allyn & Bacon.

Pachter, B., & McGee, S. (2000). *The power of positive confrontation.* New York: Marlowe.

Paniagua, F. A. (1998). *Assessing and treating culturally diverse clients* (2nd ed.). Thousand Oaks, CA: Sage.

Pannbacker, M., Middleton, G. F., & Vekovius, G. T. (1996). *Ethical practices in speech–language pathology and audiology: Case studies.* San Diego, CA: Singular.

Paul, R. (2001). *Language disorders from infancy through adolescence: Assessment and intervention* (2nd ed.). St. Louis, MO: Mosby.

Paul-Brown, D. (1994, May). Clinical record keeping in audiology and speech–language pathology. *Asha, 36,* 40–42.

Payne, R. K. (2001). *A framework for understanding poverty.* Highlands, TX: aha! Process.

Payne, R. K. (2003). *A framework for understanding poverty* (Rev. ed.). Highlands, TX: aha! Process.

Pederson, P. B., & Ivey, A. (1993). *Culture-centered counseling and interviewing skills: A practical guide.* Westport, CT: Praeger.

Peña-Brooks, A., & Hegde, M. N. (2000). *Assessment and treatment of articulation and phonological disorders in children.* Austin, TX: PRO-ED.

Peterson, H. A., & Marquardt, T. P. (1994). *Appraisal and diagnosis of speech and language disorders* (3rd ed.). Englewood Cliffs, NJ: Prentice Hall.

Phillips, J., Matarazzo, R., Matarazzo, J., Saslow, G., & Kanfer, F. (1961). Relationships between descriptive content and interaction behavior in interviews. *Journal of Consulting Psychology, 25,* 260–266.

Pol, L. G., Adidam, P. T., & Pol, J. T. (2002). Health insurance status of the adult, non-elderly foreign-born population. *Journal of Immigrant Health, 4*(2), 103–110.

Polmanteer, K., & Turbiville, V. (2000). Family-responsive individualized family service plans. *Language, Speech, and Hearing Services in Schools, 31*(1), 4–14.

Powell, W. W., Jr. (1968). Differential effectiveness of interviewer interventions in an experimental interview. *Journal of Consulting and Clinical Psychology, 32,* 210–215.

Prescott, T., & Tesauro, P. (1974). A method for quantification and description of clinical interactions with aurally handicapped children. *Journal of Speech and Hearing Disorders 39,* 234–243.

Purkey, W. W., & Schmidt, J. J. (1987). *The inviting relationship: An expanded perspective for professional counseling.* Englewood Cliffs, NJ: Prentice Hall.

Rache, L., Bernstein, L., & Veenhuis, R. (1974). Evaluation of a systematic approach to teaching interviewing. *Journal of Medical Education, 49,* 589–595.

Randall-David, R. (1989). *Strategies for working with culturally diverse communities and clients.* Washington, DC: Association for the Care of Children.

Rau, M. (1991). Impact on families. In R. Lubinski (Ed.), *Dementia and communication* (pp. 152–167). Philadelphia: B. C. Decker.

Resnick, D. M. (1993). *Professional ethics for audiologists and speech–language pathologists.* San Diego, CA: Singular.

Reyes, B. (1994). Management of adult neurogenic patients: A multicultural perspective. In H. Kayser (Ed.), *Seminars in speech and language: Communicative impairments and bilingualism* (pp. 165–173). New York: Thieme.

Richardson, S., Dohrenwend, B., & Klein, D. (1965). *Interviewing: Its form and function*. New York: Basic Books.

Riley, F. T. (1972). The effects of seating arrangement in the dyadic interaction interview upon the perceptual evaluation of the counseling relationship among secondary students. *Dissertation Abstracts International, 33*(4–A), 1447–1448.

Rogers, C. (1951). *Client-centered therapy*. Boston: Houghton Mifflin.

Rogers, C. (1986). In I. Kutash & A. Wold (Eds.), *Psychotherapist's casebook: Theory and technique in practice* (pp. 197–208). San Francisco: Jossey-Bass.

Rollin, W. J. (2000). *Counseling individuals with communication disorders: Psychodynamic and family aspects* (2nd ed.). Woburn, MA: Butterworth-Heinemann.

Roseberry-McKibbin, C. (1997). Understanding Filipino families: A foundation for effective service delivery. *American Journal of Speech–Language Pathology, 6*(3), 5–14.

Roseberry-McKibbin, C. (2000a). Mirror, mirror on the wall: Reflections of a third culture American. *Communication Disorders Quarterly, 22*(1), 56–60.

Roseberry-McKibbin, C. (2000b). Multicultural matters: Implications of living in poverty. *Communication Disorders Quarterly, 21*(4), 242–245.

Roseberry-McKibbin, C. (2001). *The source for bilingual students with language disorders*. East Moline, IL: LinguiSystems.

Roseberry-McKibbin, C. (2002). *Multicultural students with special language needs: Practical strategies for assessment and intervention* (2nd ed.). Oceanside, CA: Academic Communication Associates.

Roseberry-McKibbin, C., Brice, A. E., & O'Hanlon, L. (2005). Serving English language learners in public school settings: A national survey. *Language, Speech, and Hearing Services in Schools, 36*(1), 48–61.

Roseberry-McKibbin, C., & Domyancic, L. (2002). Families from Russian backgrounds. In C. Roseberry-McKibbin (Ed.), *Multicultural students with special language needs: Practical strategies for assessment and intervention* (2nd ed., pp. 167–188). Oceanside, CA: Academic Communication Associates.

Roseberry-McKibbin, C., & Hegde, M. N. (2006). *An advanced review of speech–language pathology: Preparation for PRAXIS and comprehensive examination* (2nd ed.). Austin, TX: PRO-ED.

Rosenfeld, H. (1967). Nonverbal reciprocation of approval: An experimental analysis. *Journal of Experimental and Social Psychology, 3*, 102–111.

Rossetti, L. M. (2001). *Communication intervention: Birth to three* (2nd ed.). San Diego, CA: Singular/Thomson Learning.

Roszak, T. (2001). *Longevity revolution: As boomers become elders*. Berkeley, CA: Berkeley Hills.

Saenz, T. I., Huer, M. B., Doan, J. H. D., Heise, M., & Fulford, L. (2001). Delivering clinical services to Vietnamese Americans: Implications for speech–language pathologists. *Communication Disorders Quarterly, 22*(4), 207–216.

Salas-Provance, M. B., Erickson, J. G., & Reed, J. (2002). Disabilities as viewed by four generations of one Hispanic family. *American Journal of Speech–Language Pathology, 11*(2), 151–162.

Scheuerle, J. (1992). *Counseling in speech–language pathology and audiology*. New York: Merrill.

Schnorpfeil, P., Noll, A., Schulze, R., Ehlert, U., Frey, K., & Fischer, J. (2003). Allostatic load and work conditions. *Social Science and Medicine, 57,* 647–656.

Schum, R. L. (1986). *Counseling in speech and hearing practice*. Rockville, MD: National Student Speech-Language-Hearing Association.

Schuyler, V., & Rushmer, N. (1987). *Parent–infant habilitation: A comprehensive approach to working with hearing-impaired infants and toddlers and families*. Portland, OR: IHR [Infant Hearing Resource] Publications.

Seeman, T., McEwen, B., Rowe, J., & Singer, B. (2001). Allostatic load as a marker of cumulative biological risk: MacArthur studies of successful aging. *Proceedings of the National Academy of Sciences of the United States of America, 98,* 4770–4775.

Seeman, T., Singer, B., Ryff, C., Dienberg Love, G., & Levy-Storms, L. (2002). Social relationships, gender, and allostatic load across two age cohorts. *Psychosomatic Medicine, 64,* 395–406.

Shafir, R. Z. (2000). *The Zen of listening: Mindful communication in an age of distraction*. Wheaton, IL: The Theosophical Publishing House.

Shames, G. H. (2000). *Counseling the communicatively disabled and their families: A manual for clinicians*. Boston: Allyn & Bacon.

Sharifzadeh, V. S. (1998). Families with Middle Eastern roots. In E. W. Lynch & M. J. Hanson (Eds.), *Developing cross-cultural competence: A guide for working with children and their families* (2nd ed., pp. 441–482). Baltimore: Brookes.

Shertzer, B., & Stone, S. C. (1980). *Fundamentals of counseling* (3rd ed.). Boston: Houghton Mifflin.

Shinn, R. E., Goldberg, D. M., Kimelman, M. D. Z., & Messick, C. M. (2001). *2000–2001 demographic survey of undergraduate and graduate programs in communication sciences and disorders*. Minneapolis, MN: Council of Academic Programs in Communication Sciences and Disorders.

Shipley, K. G., & McAfee, J. G. (1998). *Assessment in speech–language pathology: A resource manual* (2nd ed.). San Diego, CA: Singular.

Shipley, K. G., & McAfee, J. G. (2004). *Assessment in speech–language pathology: A resource manual* (3rd ed.). Clifton Park, NY: Delmar Learning.

Shipley, K. G., & Wood, J. M. (1996). *The elements of interviewing*. San Diego, CA: Singular.

Silverman, F. H. (1998). *Research design and evaluation in speech–language pathology* (4th ed.). Englewood Cliffs, NJ: Prentice Hall.

Simpson, R. L., & Zionts, P. (2000). *Autism: Information and resources for professionals* (2nd ed.). Austin, TX: PRO-ED.

Spillman, B. (2004). Change in elderly disability rates and the implications for health care utilization and cost. *Milbank Quarterly, 82,* 157–194.

Steptoe, A., Cropley, M., & Joekes, K. (1999). Job strain, blood pressure and response to uncontrollable stress. *Journal of Hypertension, 17,* 193–200.

Steptoe, A., Lundwall, K., & Cropley, M. (2000). Gender, family structure and cardiovascular activity during the working day and evening. *Social Science Medicine, 50,* 531–539.

Stewart, C. J., & Cash, W. B. (1978). *Interviewing: Principles and practices* (2nd ed.). Dubuque, IA: William C. Brown.

Stewart, C. J., & Cash, W. B. (2003). *Interviewing: Principles and practices* (10th ed.). Dubuque, IA: William C. Brown.

Stone, J. R., & Olswang, L. B. (1989, June–July). The hidden challenge in counseling. *Asha, 31,* 27–31.

Sue, D. W., & Sue, D. (2003). *Counseling the culturally diverse: Theory and practice* (4th ed.). New York: Wiley.

Sweeney, T. J. (1971). *Rural poor students and guidance.* Boston: Houghton Mifflin.

Sweetow, R. (1999). *Counseling for hearing aid fittings.* San Diego, CA: Singular/Thomson Learning.

Tannen, D. (1994). *Talking from 9 to 5.* New York: Morrow.

Tanner, D. C. (1980). Loss and grief: Implications for the speech–language pathologist. *Asha, 22,* 916–928.

Taylor, J. S. (1992). *Speech–language pathology services in the schools.* Boston: Allyn & Bacon.

Taylor, O. L., & Clarke, M. G. (1994). Culture and communication disorders: A theoretical framework. In H. Kayser (Ed.), *Seminars in speech and language: Communicative impairments and bilingualism* (pp. 103–114). New York: Thieme Medical Publishers.

Terrell, S. L., & Jackson, R. R. (2002). African Americans in the Americas. In D. E. Battle (Ed.), *Communication disorders in multicultural populations* (3rd ed., pp. 33–70). Woburn, MA: Butterworth-Heinemann.

Thommessen, B., Aarsland, D., Braekhus, A., Oksengaard, A., Engedal, K., & Laake, K. (2002). The psychosocial burden on spouses of the elderly with stroke, dementia and Parkinson's disease. *International Journal of Geriatric Psychiatry, 17,* 78–84.

Thornton, C. (1994, April 4). Empowering families of children with disabilities. *ADVANCE for Speech–Language Pathologists & Audiologists, 4*(7), 8–9.

Tiegerman-Farber, E. (2002). Interactive teaming: The changing role of the speech–language pathologist. In D. K. Bernstein & E. Tiegerman-Farber (Eds.), *Language and communication disorders in children* (5th ed., pp. 96–125). Boston: Allyn & Bacon.

Timmerman, L. M. (2002). Comparing the production of power in language on the basis of gender. In M. Allen, R. W. Preiss, B. M. Gayle, & N. A. Burrell (Eds.), *Interpersonal communication research: Advances through meta-analysis* (pp. 73–88). Mahwah, NJ: Erlbaum.

Trace, R. (1995, July 10). Treating the patient with a substance abuse problem. *ADVANCE for Speech–Language Pathologists & Audiologists, 5*(27), 9.

Troll, L. (1997). Growing old in families. In I. Deitch & C. Howell (Eds.), *Counseling the aging and their families* (pp. 3–16). Alexandria, VA: American Counseling Association.

U.S. Bureau of the Census. (1999). *Statistical abstract of the United States, 1999* (119th ed.). Washington, DC: U.S. Government Printing Office.

U.S. Bureau of the Census. (2000). *Statistical abstract of the United States. 2000* (120th ed.). Washington, DC: U.S. Department of Commerce.

U.S. Centers for Disease Control. (1999). *Health United States 1999 with Health and Aging Chartbook,* www.edc.gov/nchs/releases/99news/hus99.htm.

Van Cauter, E., & Spiegel, K. (1999). Sleep as a mediator of the relationship between socioeconomic status and health: A hypothesis. *Annals of the New York Academy of Sciences, 896,* 254–261.

Vanitallie, T. (2002). Stress: A risk factor for serious illness. *Metabolism, 51,* 40–45.

Van Riper, C. (1979). *A career in speech pathology.* Englewood Cliffs, NJ: Prentice Hall.

Van Vliet, D. (2002). Counseling the boomers. *The Hearing Journal,* 55(3), 84.

Wallace, G. I. (1993). Adult neurogenic disorders. In D. Battle (Ed.), *Communication disorders in multicultural populations* (pp. 239–255). Stoneham, MA: Andover Medical Publishers.

Walton, P. (1995). Whose "culture" are we talking about anyway? *National Association for Multicultural Education,* 2(4), 1.

Webster, E. J., & Ward, L. M. (1993). *Working with parents of young children with disabilities.* San Diego, CA: Singular.

Weindling, F-H. (2000). Speech–language pathology: A home care viewpoint. *American Journal of Speech–Language Pathology,* 9(2), 99–106.

Weiss, A. L. (2002). Planning language intervention for young children. In D. K. Bernstein & E. Tiegerman-Farber (Eds.), *Language and communication disorders in children* (5th ed., pp. 256–314). Boston: Allyn & Bacon.

Westby, C., & Vining, C. B. (2002). Living in harmony: Providing services to Native American children and families. In D. E. Battle (Ed.), *Communication disorders in multicultural populations* (3rd ed., pp. 135–178). Woburn, MA: Butterworth-Heinemann.

Willis, W. (1998). Families with African American roots. In E. W. Lynch & M. J. Hanson (Eds.), *Developing cross-cultural competence: A guide for working with children and their families* (2nd ed., pp. 483–488). Baltimore: Brookes.

Zebrowski, P. M., & Schum, R. L. (1993). Counseling parents of children who stutter. *American Journal of Speech–Language Pathology,* 2(2), 65–73.

Zuniga, M. E. (1998). Families with Latino roots. In E. W. Lynch & M. J. Hanson (Eds.), *Developing cross-cultural competence: A guide to working with young children and their families* (pp. 209–250). Baltimore: Brookes.

Index

About the Authors

Dr. Kenneth Shipley is currently associate provost at California State University, Fresno. He formerly served as associate dean of the College of Health and Human Services. He continues to serve as a professor of speech–language pathology and was formerly chair of the Department of Communicative Disorders and Deaf Studies. Dr. Shipley has authored numerous publications, including books, journal articles, and assessment tools. He has served as a speech–language pathologist in public schools and has consulted for and provided services in hospital, rehabilitation, and private practice settings.

Dr. Celeste Roseberry-McKibbin is currently a professor in the Department of Speech Pathology and Audiology at California State University, Sacramento. She also serves as an itinerant speech–language pathologist in south Sacramento public schools, providing direct services to students with communication disorders. She has numerous publications, including books and journal articles, and has made over 150 presentations at the local, state, and national levels. Dr. Roseberry-McKibbin received her college's Outstanding Teacher Award in Spring, 2005.